Tending *the* Holy

Spiritual Direction
Across Traditions

EDITED BY

NORVENE VEST

MOREHOUSE PUBLISHING
A Continuum imprint
HARRISBURG • LONDON • NEW YORK

Morehouse Publishing
P.O. Box 1321
Harrisburg, PA 17105

Morehouse Publishing is a Continuum imprint.

Cartoons in "CHAPTER ELEVEN: The Care and Feeding of the Gen-X Soul" by N. Graham Standish.

Cover design by Trude Brummer

Library of Congress Cataloging-in-Publication Data

Tending the holy : spiritual direction across traditions / edited by Norvene Vest.
    p. cm. — (Spiritual directors international series)
Includes bibliographical references.
  ISBN 0-8192-1918-5
1. Spiritual direction. I. Vest, Norvene. II. Series.
  BV5053.T45 2003
  261.6'1—dc21

                                                          2003002705

Printed in the United States of America

03 04 05 06 07 08   6 5 4 3 2 1

Tending *the* Holy

Contents

II. CHRISTIAN SPIRITUAL TRADITIONS

III. SPECIAL SPIRITUAL PERSPECTIVES

Introduction

The framework for this book was stimulated in large part by the evocative language used by Spiritual Directors International in their mission statement: "Throughout human history, individuals have been called to accompany others seeking the Mystery we name God. In this time, Spiritual Directors International responds to this call by tending the holy around the world and across traditions."

God is indeed Mystery, and every form of religion is an effort to respond faithfully to the mystery of the sacred by whatever name. The sacred breaks through into human experience in many ways, and humans respond variously to the awesome experience of the holy. In this book we present a range of perspectives from which the holy is tended, multiple ways in which people accompany others whose lives reveal the presence of the sacred. Our authors represent five religious traditions as well as contrasting points of view within the broad lens of Christian tradition and ongoing practice.

Those who seek the Mystery and those who accompany them are united in the conviction that the sacred is somehow present within creation, and that humans are invited to be engaged with the mysterious presence here and now. That common ground—seeking the Mystery, tending the holy—is by no means widely shared in the twenty-first century. More and more people live as if the sacred were absent or unimportant, as if seeking the holy within daily experience were merely a luxury for those who do not have more pressing responsibilities. For example, we need look no further than the increasingly narrow legal interpretations of the U.S. constitutional requirement for "separation of church and state." Intended originally to protect the practice of all religious expression, it is now used to prevent public acknowledgment of the divine presence. Consciousness of ultimate Mystery has been edged aside for many who find themselves defined by too many things, too little time, and a desperate desire for order and control in a world that seems chaotic. In such a time, it becomes ever more important for those of us who do share a sense of the necessity of human engagement with ultimate reality to listen to one another with our hearts, even and perhaps especially when our approaches and our ways of speaking differ.

While the holy may increasingly be seen as absent from ordinary "public" experience, the longing for some form of spirituality seems to be increasing. We know that demand is rising for books on spirituality and for classes in spiritual direction, even as there is corresponding confusion about what those terms mean. The purpose of this book is by no means to move toward a defining consensus, but even as we explore multiple perspectives about tending the holy, we find common ground.

The first ingredient for the soil of this common ground is found in the sense of being "drenched" in God, or surrounded by the hints of the sacred. Those who tend the holy or spiritual directors, whatever they call themselves, are people who seem almost unable to turn away from the Mystery. We find life to be empty without an ongoing relationship with "the more." Something beyond ourselves and somehow bigger than we are keeps calling us forth. Thus, we find human life itself to be more than a mere container for discrete individuality; human mastery is of less interest to us than exploring the possibilities involved in surrender to the unknown. Indeed, we might almost say that one of the primary reasons for seeking spiritual direction is the longing for a place to speak about and to the holy. All the authors here, whatever their perspective, write from the conviction that Mystery exists as a haunting presence for us and that engagement with Mystery brings fullness of life.

Mystery, of course, is mysterious—not a puzzle finally to be solved, but a wonder at which to marvel. The divine nature is intrinsically intangible, elusive, never subject to confinement by thought or word or by any of the five senses. On the other hand, Mystery is somehow always present in the midst of sensory reality. Holiness is not only a quality of God; it is shared by all creation and often found in places once thought to be "secular"—in matter as well as in spirit, in body as well as in mind, in working life as well as in the church, temple, or mosque. Our contributors show us some ways to attend to the signs of the holy from a number of standpoints.

The second ingredient of this common soil is the importance of perspective. Spiritual directors in general, and our contributors in particular, know that life with Mystery is not primarily about a single experience, however ecstatic that moment, but is rather about meaning that emerges from ongoing experience and reflection. As we accompany others and seek companions ourselves, we see helpful, important patterns that unfold only as more and more of the tapestry is woven. In particular, we begin to notice that our momentary thoughts and our overflowing emotions may not be very sound guides to what is truly important. With such companions we learn to recognize forms of blindness that are characteristic of our particular temperaments so we can be released from dependence on involuntary but habitual reactions and their limitations. Each of our authors has a special way of describing encounters with limitation and the movement toward genuine inner freedom, but all share the goal of helping the seeker to a wider perspective.

The third and final ingredient common to all our authors is that the seeker's experience with Mystery is expected to have some consequences in his or her life. If it is authentic, the growing relationship with the sacred that emerges from the companionship of spiritual direction will influence the seeker's way of being in the world. In a certain sense, spiritual direction or tending the holy is always an applied art; it is directed toward a transformed life. For that reason, many of our chapters offer specific though anonymous examples of individual and institutional change made in the small increments of ongoing companionship in the Spirit. I am particularly grateful to those of our authors who have shared parts of their own unfolding life experience as guides to what is possible.

The chapters that follow give examples of how different faith traditions tend the holy, accompanying others in seeking and perhaps naming or engaging Mystery. As you read each chapter, you might want to ask yourself: How is the holy envisioned or approached from this perspective? What form does spiritual direction take? What are seekers encouraged to attend to and look for? How is deepening maturity gauged? Other questions and perhaps answers may occur to you as you read that will help in your own search and in being a companion to others.

Part One of the book addresses worldwide faith traditions, including chapters from Buddhist, Islamic, Hindu, and Jewish perspectives. Part Two explores a few of the streams of Christian spirituality, especially that of the Ignatian or Jesuit perspective, as well as Evangelical, Carmelite, and Benedictine viewpoints. While a Franciscan point of view is not included in Part Two, St. Francis's vision of life with the holy is central to Chapter Nine. That chapter integrates a number of perspectives, building on St. Francis's spirituality to look at the way our ongoing spiritual lives interface with ethical concerns such as the environment, social justice, and peace-making. For us spiritual directors especially, the chapter may raise questions about how much of our focus is responsive—centered primarily in issues spontaneously raised by directees—and how much is proactive—initiating conversations with our directees about the relationship of their spiritual lives to broader economic, social, and political concerns. In general, Part Three endeavors to widen the perspective even further, initiating a conversation with other, expanded views of the sacred, including spiritual direction with institutions, younger adults, and feminists.

In reading these chapters, you may find your heart touched and your mind challenged. You may feel at home with some points and others may seem alien. Carefully noticing when you disagree is often fruitful, because whenever we experience ourselves as strange yet still acceptable, there is opportunity for growth. I hope this book will support a conversation that will expand and continue in your own life, as you are strengthened in your work of tending the holy wherever you are.

Peace, in all the languages that touch your heart,
Norvene Vest

PART ONE

Worldwide
Faith
Traditions

CHAPTER ONE

Making a Cup of Tea

*Some Aspects of Spiritual Direction within
a Living Buddhist Tradition*

Tejadhammo Bhikku

The young monk approached the elder seeking permission to go to another monastery in order to spend some time in intensive meditation practice. The elder refused his request. A week or two later he again approached the elder with the same request, but this time added some points he hoped would entice the elder to grant permission for the journey. Again, the elder replied that he must remain where he was. Some weeks later, refusing to let go of his plan, he approached the elder with what he thought was a fool-proof scheme. The young monk would go to the other monastery for practice but on the way would visit the elder's relatives who were ill and take some small gifts to them on his behalf. The elder's response was direct and simple: "Tell me why you want to do this." The young monk hesitated and then replied, "In order to deepen and improve my meditation practice." The old monk looked directly at him and said quietly, "Wonderful! Come back here this evening at nine o'clock." With that, the elder walked back into his hut. The younger monk thought that he was going to make the arrangements for him to travel, although it did cross his mind that nine o'clock at night was a strange time to be setting out on such a journey.

Feeling a little uncertain, he stood at the door of the elder's hut just before nine o'clock. Without a word, the thera emerged and, taking the young monk by the hand, led him across the sandy courtyard of the monastery toward the main chapel or shrine hall. Silently he unlocked the outer gates and, after they entered, locked them again. Likewise, he opened the heavy wooden inner doors and, as soon as they stepped into the darkness within, he locked the doors behind them. Standing in the dark the young monk wondered what was going to happen. The thera quietly moved toward the darkened altar and then lit a single candle, which radiated a small pool of light into the dark hall. There was light enough so that they could see each other's faces and the face of the Buddha image resting above the altar table. The thera then knelt, bowed three times, and sat down in the posture of meditation. The student followed his example and sat beside him. He thought that the old man was going to teach him some kind of meditation. "Soon he will start his instruction," thought the student.

After many minutes there was still nothing but silence. The student realized that he could see a little more by the light of the candle flame. While the teacher sat still and silent, he looked around the hall and into its darker recesses. This soon became boring and he began to examine the lines on the teacher's face, watching the way the golden light played over its ancient landscape. Still there was only silence and the almost imperceptible sound of the old man breathing gently. The student thought that he may as well do some meditation himself, since there was clearly to be no teaching tonight. He fixed his posture and began his meditation, but his mind was like a waterfall or a river in flood sweeping away all before it. Now this thought, now that. This memory swept up and away by plans and schemes. Thoughts and feelings, images and ideas, in a ceaseless cascade that was exhausting. He lost all sense of time very quickly, but the pain and discomfort he felt told him that they must have been sitting for an age. He opened his eyes and looked at the old man, who sat as silent as stone, the rise and fall of his breathing so light it was almost impossible to detect. He could have been carved of stone or wood except for the strange vividness of his stillness. The elder opened his eyes, turned toward him, and said, "Good." He bowed again and the student followed. Extinguishing the candle, they moved toward the door. When the elder unlocked the doors, the clanking sound of the keys seemed to echo loudly throughout the dark shrine. They emerged into the moonlit night and the doors were locked again. The outer gates were opened and then locked behind them. They stepped back into the sandy courtyard, now flooded with a soft white light from the almost full moon high above them.

"Thank goodness that's finished. We must have been there for hours," thought the student, already anticipating his bed and sleep. Reaching his hut the elder turned toward his student and said, "Tomorrow evening at the same time." The student was alarmed and a little disconcerted at this. He didn't mind doing meditation, but when was the teaching going to begin?

Back in his own *kuti* (hut), he looked at the clock only to discover that they had been in the shrine room for a little over an hour. His heart sank.

The scenario was repeated for many, many nights. Each evening the pair crossed the courtyard and entered the shrine, and each evening they sat together in complete silence. The time they sat together grew longer and longer. After many nights and many long hours of sitting in the gentle darkness with his teacher, the young monk finally followed him into the silence and stillness. The river of the mind gathered into still pools and the roar of the waterfall fell away. The light of the single candle became as nothing in the presence of the elder. One morning they emerged from their practice just before sunrise and prepared to go on alms round into the village together. As they stepped out of the monastery gate, it occurred to the student that the old man had not said his by now customary, "Tomorrow evening at the same time." As the sun slowly rose and they walked quietly together toward the edge of the village, he knew that he didn't want to go anywhere, that just this walking was enough.

In this small story we glimpse the way in which the elder, "thera" in the Buddhist tradition, gives direction and helps to open the eyes of the student. The thera says very little and gives no explicit or wordy instructions. There is no long discussion of the student's problems and no criticism of his thoughts, words, or deeds. There is no analysis of the student and certainly no questions except the simple and direct, "Tell me why you want to do this," which is immediately followed by a very encouraging, "Wonderful . . . ," and then the concrete instruction to come to the teacher's kuti or hut that evening. No explanation is offered as to what will take place and none is sought, though there may be much questioning within the heart and mind of the student. The student knows and trusts that the teacher seeks only his well-being and happiness and therefore follows his instruction. The teaching or direction given that night and over the many nights that follow is also wordless. After many hours and nights of painful struggle in the presence of the thera, the student finally emerges into a new kind of freedom. The new freedom of heart and mind is not an end in itself but is an opening that simply allows for further growth and movement toward the goal of all practice in the Buddhist tradition: *cetovimutti,* or the complete liberation of heart and mind. Boundlessness. Limitlessness. *Nibbana.* At the end of the story, the thera again makes no comment and his silence is understood and accepted as authenticating what has taken place. This small event and its positive outcome are not the end of the relationship but a further deepening of it.

This story outlines or provides a taste of what you might encounter on the path of spiritual direction within the Buddhist tradition as found in Theravadin Buddhist practice and, more specifically, within a monastic context or setting. At the heart of all Buddhist practice is the experience of *bhavana* or meditation—the cultivation of complete liberation of heart and mind or the destruction of greed, hatred, delusion, and fear. Much that may be thought of as spiritual direction is bound up with the experience and practice of meditation.

There is no single word, term, or set of terms within Buddhist teaching that describes spiritual direction as it is broadly understood in the Western European tradition. There is, however, an interesting correspondence between the Christian Orthodox traditions and Buddhist practice in the area of spiritual direction. The importance of finding a suitable elder (*thera* in Pali, *geron* in Greek) who can act as a guide and mirror for the practitioner is one link at the level of practice. The emphasis on the elder's Wisdom and Compassion or love rather than any kind of formal learning is another interesting convergence. The many stories describing spiritual direction in the various lives of the Desert Fathers, the *Vita Antonii of Athanasius*, the *Apophthegmata Patrum*, the *Philokalia*, and other early Christian texts have their counterparts in the Buddhist tradition.

Watching, observing, interacting, and being with the student are seen as essential elements in giving real direction. The director or thera is one who can look into the heart and mind of the student in order to encourage him to see for himself. The Buddha teaches the importance of opening the eye of *Dhamma* (*Dhammacakku*), allowing one to see things just as they are. This is realizing within oneself the unsatisfactoriness and suffering (*dukkha*), the transience/impermanence (*anicca*), and the self-lessness/not-self (*anatta*) of our existence and experience. This is what the spiritual director seeks to help the student to do—to be open to the real or truth (*sacca*).

The director employs a wide range of skilful means to assist the student to realize this experience of opening of the eyes of the heart and mind. Frequently the director becomes a mirror for the student, allowing the student to see him or herself clearly with honesty and integrity in the director and within their interaction. Sometimes the director mirrors the student's emotions or moods and sometimes deflects them via their opposite—what the Buddha calls "the antidote."

The relationship between director and directed is unequal in terms of power and authority, yet students are always encouraged to find their own real authority and power. Direction is not about gaining knowledge from one who knows but rather about being in a living relationship with one who is knowing, which makes possible the ending of all dukkha (suffering and unsatisfactoriness) and fosters the experience of real liberation of heart and mind.

The experience of direction is very much embedded within a story or living narrative that is relational, frequently nondirective, nontheoretical, and very immediate. It deals with what is arising here and now rather than with theoretical constructs about past events or projections into an unknown and un-arisen future. This immediacy also allows for a great deal of genuine humor in the encounter between student and director, a humor that arises out of and is deeply rooted in genuine, non-pious humility. However, it is important to add that students may not always see what directors have placed before them until a short time afterward.

This chapter will attempt to outline these and other aspects of Buddhist spiritual direction through the recounting of stories and narratives of direction in the hope that story might convey what theory never can.

Nissaya or Dependence: The Beginning of the Relationship

In a monastic setting, the relationship between the thera or director and the student begins with the taking of *nissaya* or dependence during the ceremony of ordination. Nissaya or requesting dependence is an important part of the ordination ceremony and an essential part of establishing the relationship between teacher and student or master and disciple. "Aham Bhante nissayam yacami" (Venerable Sir, I beg or plead for dependence) is repeated three times and followed by, "Upajjhayo me Bhante hohi" (May you be my preceptor, Venerable Sir). The Upajjhaya responds with a simple "Sadhu" (It is well) or with "Pasadikena Sampadehi" (Make an effort in this with friendliness). The young student replies, "Sadhu Bhante" (Yes, Venerable Sir), and then says three times, "Ajjataggedani Thero mayham bharo ahampi Therassa bharo" (From this day forward the thera's burden will be mine, I shall be the burden of the thera).

This small part of the ordination is literally its center and comes just before the candidate is questioned by the two *acariyas* (formal teachers). During the questioning the candidate is asked for the name of his *upajjhaya* (preceptor/director). Having a preceptor is essential because it guarantees that new monks will have someone on whom they can depend and rely for real guidance and instruction, someone with whom they have a relationship of growing trust and confidence. In this nissaya or dependence, both individuals have very specific duties and responsibilities. The relationship between the newly ordained monk and his preceptor is an interactive kind of dependence in which the teacher/master also takes very seriously his duty and obligation to the young monk. While the new monk is now in a relationship of dependence on the thera (rather like the geron in the Orthodox tradition), the elder also enters the relationship with a serious level of personal commitment. The seriousness with which this is regarded can be seen in the reluctance shown by some theras in taking many new disciples.

The Young Monk

Having entered into this nissaya, the young monk cannot choose to do many simple things that may have previously been possible. Permission is required from the thera even to go outside the monastery gates for a short walk. In a traditional setting, then, the newly ordained has become in a very real sense apprenticed to the older, more experienced, and hopefully wiser thera. There is a traditional period of dependence of five years; less is considered inadequate to have properly begun the formation of the new monk. During this period of time, the student must remain with the elder. The student is expected to take care of the elder, making sure that his hut is kept clean and that his robes are washed and that any other areas in which he might genuinely care for the elder are looked after. It is in these interactions—which appear to be so mundane, so simple, so ordinary— that the real and most powerful direction takes place. The student's responsibilities may be found set out clearly in the *Visudhimagga* (Part II, Chapter 3, vv. 66–73). Either the student or the teacher may end the dependence/ nissaya relationship within the five-year limit, usually by mutual consent. Normally this would arise if the student wishes to take dependence with another teacher, if the student disrobes, or if his present teacher has passed away. Otherwise, their relationship or heart connection will continue to grow and develop long after five years has passed.

The student must be willing to reveal his thoughts and feelings, the inner movements of heart and mind to the director, so that the director may guide and assist him toward the goal of liberation of heart and mind (cetovimutti). This requires great trust, faith, and confidence (saddha), which will grow as the student witnesses for himself the day-to-day care, kindness, and wisdom of the thera. Each observes the other mindfully and with *metta* or loving-kindness. The student is expected to rouse up the energy (*viriya*) for practice and show diligence in carrying out the instructions of the thera. Great honesty and fearlessness are also essential in this relationship. The student requires great perseverance and patience because, although he recognizes that this is a relationship of inequality in terms of power and position, he is always encouraged and helped to find his own power and to see for himself.

The Elder or Thera

The elder ("thera") in turn has a very serious responsibility to the young monk. He cares for his physical well-being in terms of food, clothing, and lodgings, and this is taken very seriously by most elders. He is responsible for his student's spiritual training and development and must act as model and guide or, in short, as director. Elder and student are expected to grow in friendliness (metta). The thera endeavors to help open the eyes of the younger monk so that he might see clearly.

The thera is expected to have qualities such as wisdom and compassion as well as being responsible for the training of his student. The *Digha Nikaya* of the Pali Canon (*Sigalaka Sutta*) lists some of the qualities the thera should possess. He is expected to provide the student with experience to augment what he has studied. He should nurture in him all that is good and wholesome and help him to let go of all that is harmful and unwholesome. He is expected to provide for his safety in every quarter. This short passage ends with the idea of the thera's creating a place of peace, free from all fear, in which the student might dwell. He should lead the student toward complete freedom of heart and mind. Naturally it is expected that the thera will have had years of personal experience and have cultivated his own meditation practice as well as possessing qualities such as patience (*khanti*) and great loving-kindness (metta). The thera has power and authority within the community that might under other circumstances make him a figure of fear, yet in this relationship he is rather like a very kind and loving elder brother or father whose only concern is for the well-being and happiness of the student. For the relationship to truly grow and be fruitful and for the director to be able to bring the student to truly see or eventually to open the eyes of Dhamma (Dhammacakkhu), a quality of openness is needed. By living with the student and interacting with him at many different levels and in many different ways each day, the thera can see even more clearly into the heart and mind. He will watch the simplest of actions such as how the student sweeps, walks, dresses, and eats in order to see more clearly what the temperament of the student might be. Based on this and on his own wisdom, he then decides what meditation practices may be most suitable at any given time. This is outlined in the *Visudhimagga* (Part II, Chapter 3, vv. 74–122).

Some Formal Structures

Etiquette

The monastic rule and tradition require quite formal, ritualized modes of behavior and interaction between the thera and the student, which would also apply between a layperson and the thera. The behaviors appear to focus on the recognition of the relationship's inequality and involve ritual bowing, prescribed gestures for asking questions and receiving answers and making requests of the thera, as well as specific ways of making offerings (formal and informal) to the thera. At first these ritual behaviors may be seen as ways to cultivate genuine humility, respect, and mindfulness, but as the relationship develops and deepens, they easily become signs of love and gratitude on the part of the student and are clearly received as such by the thera. The thera may appear to cultivate a kind of indifference to these gestures, especially in the early period of their relationship. However, no sloppiness or forgetfulness of these acts of mindfulness is allowed to slip by without comment or correction. It is important to mention that the thera will not express any sense of personal affront or hurt in the midst of these corrections. The behavior of the thera and student are governed by these rules especially when in a public forum or while conducting official monastic business or meetings. Outside of such situations, the two often develop a real ease and comfort with each other. When errors or mistakes are made on the part of the student (or the thera), ritualized forms of confession may be used.

Confession

There are two forms of confession: one is required prior to the recitation of the monastic rule twice per month; the second is more occasional, intimate, and personal. The first may be made to the thera or to another monk. The second is usually reserved only for the thera.

Here is the formula for the formal request for forgiveness before recitation of the Patimokkha. "Aham Bhante sambahula nanavatthukayo thullaccayayo apattiyo apanno ta patidesemi" (I, Venerable Sir, having fallen many times into grave offences with different bases, those do I confess). The elder then responds by asking, "Passasi avuso?" (Do you see, venerable friend?), to which the younger replies, "Ama Bhante passami" (Yes, Venerable Sir, I see). The thera then says, "Ayatim avuso samvareyyasi" (In future, friend, you should be more restrained or mindful). "Sadhu sutthu Bhante samvarissami" (It is well indeed, Venerable Sir, I shall be restrained), replies the younger monk. This last sentence is repeated three times.

A more general and in some sense more personal form of confession or reconciliation is found in use between the thera and student. Having made traditional offerings of candles, incense, and flowers to the thera, the student then says, "Ayasmante ramadena dvarattayena katam sabbam aparadham khamatha me Bhante" (Forgive me, Venerable Sir, for any wrongdoings done carelessly to the Revered One by way of the three doors of body, speech, and mind). The thera then responds with, "Aham khammami, tayapi me khamitabbam" (I forgive you; you should now forgive me). The younger then says, "Khamami Bhante" (I do forgive you, kind Sir). The thera may then confess in a similar manner to the student.

The way this formula for confession of faults is constructed is very instructive about the nature of the relationship between the student and the director or elder. Each respects the other; each recognizes the possibility of offending the other—in the case of the younger, either deliberately or inadvertently. In the thera's case, presumably inadvertently. Each seeks to be reconciled regularly with the other and each is nonjudgmental and noncritical with the other. Tellingly, the thera simply asks, "Do you see?" rather than launch into a long diatribe on the particular fault in question. This is an example of one of the formal structures or markers in the relationship between director and directed.

Meditation Interviews

Another structure may be found in the formal interviews that take place within the context of meditation retreats. Here the student would be expected to present himself to the thera not unusually once a day, even if the retreat goes on for many months. The thera may ask a series of simple questions or perhaps even only one question in order to determine where the student's efforts at meditation are leading him. The student's answer or response may be followed by further questions, by silence, or by repeating the original question a number of times. Rarely are these interviews very long in duration, since they are primarily meant to offer some direct and simple guidance that is immediately relevant. The thera may have in mind a particular point at which he wishes the student to arrive during a period of practice. These interviews are not times for long-winded discussions or philosophical speculations. The thera may even appear to be quite brusque or rude in these situations, simply wishing to deal with the bare facts of the practice as it is being experienced by the disciple. The thera is thought to be reading the heart/mind of the younger monk during this meeting and, while he listens very carefully, he is trying to help the student to listen to his own words and heart. Hence the sometimes disconcerting practice of asking the student to repeat an answer several times. The thera will often give very specific instructions that he expects the student to carry out when he resumes his formal practice.

Outside the context of a formal retreat, the thera may also wish to discuss the student's meditation practice as well as his efforts to live the monastic rule. In my own experience, the more wisdom possessed by the thera, the more informal these meetings will be and the more he will simply live with the student and provide powerful and positive guidance in an apparently indirect way. The spiritually advanced director is able to draw out the heart and mind of the student in the context of the most ordinary situations and things. He will not rely on setting up situations but will be continually responding to whatever is arising within the immediate moment. Just this, just now.

The heat in the room was stifling as the teacher announced the imminent arrival of the visitor and the young monk began to squirm at the prospect of being stuck all afternoon in the heat in the presence of the important visitor. The visitor was a senior monk from a nearby monastery the younger monk had met before while attending a ceremony some days earlier. The teacher had said it was important that the young monk remain for the afternoon and that, although he could not speak with the visitor because of his poor language skills, he might nonetheless find the meeting interesting and useful. He gazed out the window and looked longingly and sleepily (after all, they had just finished lunch) at the banana palms moving in the breeze and at the mountaintop off in the hazy distance with its gathering cloud canopy. Maybe it would rain after all and then it might cool down. Maybe. He certainly hoped so. The voice of the teacher brought him back into the room and its sticky heat. The visitor would arrive at one o'clock. So there would not be enough time to go back to his little hut halfway up the mountainside. He would have to remain here for the next forty-five minutes and wait. Wait for the waiting to begin. He suggested to the teacher that perhaps he could go to his hut and return later, and even as the words left his lips, he knew that he was lying. Once he reached the safety of his hut there would be no return for the afternoon visitor. Still, the answer was no. He must stay where he was and wait. The young monk was truly disappointed and irritated to hear that, no matter what, he had to remain while the visit took place and the two older monks chatted away in a language that he could not understand and about monastic business that was of no concern or interest to him. He was only too well aware of how long and boring these formal monastic visits could be. There would be the usual exchange of courtesies and politeness and then long, rambling discussions about all manner of monastic politics and business. He felt annoyed, too, at this intrusion into his valuable practice time by a visitor that he hardly knew and that he cared little about. In fact, when he had met the visitor previously he had taken an instant dislike to him because of his very apparent and overt venality. He was the private secretary to the abbot of an important monastery and he knew it. The "secretary-monk," as he had come to think of him, was a man who was full of himself and most un-monk-like in his behavior. Added to this undesirable characteristic, he spat and sprayed spittle when he spoke and gave off an unpleasant smell. In fact, he stank. Even other monks had commented on his repulsive body odor, his dirty, unwashed, but expensive robes, and his habit of spraying spittle as he spoke. He had an unfortunate squint that caused him to look at you with one eye while the other was turned up at an angle of more than forty-five degrees toward the sky. He looked sly and untrustworthy. One monk had even hinted that he might be dishonest (there was a long and rambling story of some funds having gone missing from a temple fair some years earlier). In the mind of the young monk, here was a completely unpleasant, unworthy, and unwelcome intrusion into his day of study and meditation.

Again the faint rattling noise of the waving banana palms drew his attention out of the room. The clouds were thickening over the mountain. He thought about the animals that would be seeking shelter now from the oncoming storm. The breeze picked up and the banana palms rattled rapidly, but inside the room, the temperature continued to climb. He began to imagine the sound of rain on the banana palms, which always began at first as a gentle plop-plop and then soon became a thunderous rushing sound like pebbles poured across galvanized iron roofs. For a brief moment he felt coolness course through his body, only to be too quickly replaced by the unpleasant humidity and heat of the small room in which he sat. His teacher was busy moving some cushions and arranging a small table near the cushions that now faced each other. In a small and almost empty room, he had managed to create a clearly defined yet open meeting space that, while it appeared formal, looked welcoming.

The student roused himself and began to look for a broom with which to sweep the room before the arrival of the now, in his mind, dreaded and dreadful visitor. As he swept he still mumbled to himself inwardly about the nuisance that this visitor was and, although the teacher moved about the room busily moving books and a small tray of tea-making equipment, he felt that he was being watched.

Small patches of dust at the edges of the mat were overlooked as he thought about the way his afternoon routine was being disturbed and destroyed. Both the temperature and humidity continued to rise and he felt as though the whole world inside the room had become a hot and sweaty mess. How, he wondered, did the tiny figure of his teacher manage to remain cool in this climate? At this time of the year, when the world seemed ready to melt, he was always cool and comfortable, the surface of his skin showing only the finest and lightest sheen of sweat in the most ferocious part of the hot season. The young monk could smell the odor of his own sweat and feel it running down his back and legs. If only he could be allowed to go to his hut. He knew it was not possible. Monastic etiquette and the relationship of dependence on his teacher meant that he must remain and be at the very least courteous, polite, and try to be attentive.

Coughing and appropriate throat clearing from downstairs announced that the guest had arrived and would soon be escorted up the stairs and into the teacher's room by one of the temple boys. The sound of bare feet padding on the creaking stairs, some wheezing, and then there was that face, those eyes, one looking ahead and the other gazing up at the ceiling, and then the body rising up out of the floor as he ascended the staircase and entered the room as if by magic. The teacher smiled and welcomed him, inviting him to take the seat already prepared. Before sitting down, he bowed his respect three times (rather sloppily, thought the student, a clear sign of his arrogance. The teacher would no doubt be aware of this arrogance and lack of sincerity). The secretary wheezed again, sounding like a child's rubber toy being squeezed of all its air. The rank smell he carried with him rose with the dust at the edges of the mat as he sat down and folded himself onto the cushion. Now was the time for the young monk to pay his respects to the visiting senior, who was well aware of his importance in relation to this young foreigner. The student bowed low and very carefully, perhaps too carefully, he thought. Now here was a real double bind: having to show respect to this monk and show it very mindfully in front of the master and yet not be too respectful to the secretary-monk who sat with a look of such self-satisfaction on his face, while receiving each bow. The teacher motioned him to stop and be seated to one side. The master and the visitor began their conversation, and so began a long and agonizing period of waiting for the student.

At first he tried listening to their conversation, but his rudimentary knowledge of their language made this quite impossible and it soon became very frustrating. He then watched the motes of dust moving in a beam of sunlight, trying to detect any pattern of movement that might be present. Nothing but dust and sunlight presented itself. From where he sat, the window was at an awkward angle and he could not look out of it, so instead he tried to listen for the sound of the banana palms rattling in the breeze. The monk's voices were just loud enough to prevent him from hearing the palms. He tried to imagine their sound instead. His legs began to ache. He shifted uncomfortably on his small cushion, feeling the wetness at the back of his knees and under his arms as he moved around, trying to find an easier position. No comfort, no coolness, and still the older monks droned on. Occasionally his teacher would laugh a little and smile broadly, although the secretary seemed to find nothing amusing or even remotely funny in what was being said. Instead, he sat as if transfixed, with one eye firmly focused on the master and the other apparently looking at the tiny geckos that scuttled across the ceiling, seemingly unaware that they were upside-down. Both eyes were humorless and seemed to be endlessly looking for something just out of reach. The student looked at the ceiling, trying to imagine how this man saw the world with his eyes pointing in different directions, but this too became boring. Soon he fell into a hazy mindlessness, sinking into the heat and sweltering humidity. Suddenly his reverie was broken by the sound of his teacher's voice speaking in English, "We will have tea. Please make tea for our guest."

He swayed a little on his cushion as if waking up from a long sleep, a sleep that he was unable to remember having had. The guest politely declined the offer of tea but the master insisted it be made and offered. The young monk rose very slowly and carefully from his seat, not wishing to let either of the monks see that his legs had gone to sleep as they talked on. Picking up the small tray that held two tiny clay cups and a very tiny teapot, he made his way outside to make the unwanted tea. He lit the kindling in the small fireplace and then placed some larger pieces of wood on the fire and watched with a sleepy fascination as the fire caught and the bright yellow and orange flames arose. Placing the kettle of well water over the flames, he sat and waited. If he listened carefully, he could just hear the voices of the monks in the room behind him. The small verandah on which the fireplace was located was hot and its wooden boards dry as dust. It wouldn't take much for it to burn down, he thought idly. He was getting annoyed. So much time being wasted and still the water hadn't boiled. Making tea that nobody wanted. Making tea for a very odorous visitor. Wasting his precious study time, his precious time for meditation practice. The water suddenly boiled and he tossed some dry tea leaves into the tiny pot and poured in the water, which splashed everywhere, lightly scalding his fingers and wetting the edge of his robe. Quickly he lifted the tray and went back into the room of his master. Placing the tray on the floor, he politely bowed to the master and then offered the tray of tea in the very formal way that monastic etiquette dictated. The teacher took the tray, placed it to one side, and continued his conversation.

Much time passed. Steam rose and vanished from the tiny teapot and, as their conversation continued, the tea grew cold, un-drunk and then undrinkable. Perhaps another hour passed, perhaps less, but it felt like days to the student. The teacher again called for tea to be made. The visitor politely declined the kind offer, yet again the teacher insisted. Once again, the young monk found himself outside on the verandah relighting the now cold fire all over again and waiting once more for the water to boil. He tossed the unused and by now bitter liquid into a nearby potted plant; some of the wet tea leaves fell onto the dry wooden verandah boards. Wet and slippery, they were hard to pick up, and he flicked them roughly from his fingers into the base of the small potted tree. Now he was really annoyed. Making tea that was unwanted and unnecessary. Spending all of this time sitting in pain and considerable discomfort being forced to listen to a conversation that he couldn't understand, did not concern him, and was of no interest to him. This whole business was really quite silly and an inordinate waste of his time. How could the teacher not see this—after all, he was a serious student? He wanted to get back to his study and meditation, not sit around listening to nonsense and making cups of tea. He was becoming more annoyed, more irritated, even a little angry at this imposition. The water boiled, lifting the lid of the kettle noisily, and again he quickly made the tea and reentered the room. The polite formalities of bowing and offering ended with not a word from the master. He once again resumed his uncomfortable seat.

The tea remained untouched. The conversation continued, now animated, now almost lapsing into silence as if they were finally running out of things to talk about. He feared that the near silence may just be a drawing of breath. His body ached and his mind now ached with it. The boredom he felt was truly was intolerable. "We will have some tea."

The words floated across his mind like some strange cloud formations in a blank sky and he knew that he had heard correctly. The teacher wanted more tea made. "Surely he can't be serious," he thought. "What nonsense. What a waste of time. What a waste of tea. What?" He bowed and picking up the tea tray, left the room, and stormed onto the verandah. The sun had shifted in the sky and the verandah was now in shade, but he couldn't feel it, didn't notice the shadows lengthening. The fire had of course long gone out, so a new one had to be lit all over again. Roughly, he tore at the kindling and broke half a dozen matches trying to light it. He tossed larger pieces of wood onto the tiny fire, almost putting it out, but it rose up, wrapped itself around them, and began to blaze. Quickly he filled the kettle with water from a large stone jar by the steps and placed it on the fire with a great clanking sound. The lid was bent slightly and hard to fit, so he tossed it to one side. He stood staring into the water and then squatted down to await its boiling. More waiting and more boredom as he stared into the kettle watching for the first sign of steam or a tiny bubble to form on its pock-marked base. Noticing the lengthening shadows creeping across the dusty courtyard, he felt real anger now at the way in which his whole afternoon had been wasted. Making useless cups of tea, serving two monks who paid him no attention and who said no thanks for his tea making and his polite attentiveness. The heat was still intense and perspiration flowed steadily down his arms and legs. The robe at his waist was wet and clung to his body unpleasantly. He cast the old tea and its leaves off the verandah into the dust below, almost hitting one of the sore-covered temple dogs as it ambled by looking for food, which it would almost certainly not find until after dawn the next day when the monks returned from their alms rounds. As the dog looked up and ran off quickly, he felt a tiny moment of regret that he had missed. After all, cold tea and a few tea leaves would not have really hurt the dog.

Waiting, his impatience and anger grew steadily. It became almost without an object, just irritation, just annoyance, just anger. His mind and heart were ablaze with anger. He was seething with anger and resentment. He was on fire. Looking back into the kettle, he saw the water boiling furiously. He had missed the first tiny bubbles and now before him the kettle rocked and rattled unsteadily as its contents convulsed and threw boiling water out in great splashes into the fire and onto the dry wooden verandah boards. He stood transfixed, staring into the rolling boiling water. It was his mind that he saw rolling and seething, hissing and bubbling, spitting and spewing its dangerous hot spray in every direction. Here was anger, here was resentment, here was aversion. From somewhere deep within his heart and mind laughter began quietly to bubble up. He could hear it. Gently, silently, he was laughing at himself. Such a fool. Such self-importance. Such arrogance. What an idiot. And like steam, the anger and the foolishness dissolved. Just laughter remained. Ideas, thoughts, and feelings arose and vanished as quickly as steam—my time, my practice, my study, me, mine, what foolishness. Laughter flowed, cooling body heart and mind. What else is there to do now but make tea? He touched the tea leaves and smelled their delicate fragrance. He heard the water as it first touched them within the tiny teapot and felt the soft grinding of the terracotta lid as it settled into its place. Lifting the tray and looking out across the courtyard, he felt that the coolness of evening seemed somehow near in the long shadows that rippled across the dusty ground. Two dogs skulked by in the distance, and sorrow tinged with something else arose within him.

Carrying the tray into the room, he was struck by how quiet it had become. Placing the tray to one side, he bowed, placing his forehead to the floor before his master, and his heart was flooded with gratitude and calm joy. Lifting the tray to make the offering and feeling the hands of the teacher taking the tray, he heard the teacher say, "At last we have a cup of tea!"

Placing the tray now in front of himself, the teacher calmly and simply poured some tea into each cup and offered one small cup with both hands to his visitor. The secretary took the cup but, without drinking, placed it politely to one side and announced that he must leave immediately. The teacher lifted the other cup to his lips and, laughing very gently, said, "What a shame. It is a very special tea." Drinking it down with one gulp, he placed it down gently and said, "Enough for one day."

The secretary-monk politely took his leave. As he went down the stairs, they could hear the plop-plop sound of rain striking the banana leaves. Within minutes there was the thunderous roar of tropical rain. He would be drenched before taking just a few steps. Suddenly the room was cool. They went silently to the window. Looking through the teeming rain into the distance toward the now almost invisible mountain, the teacher said quietly, almost whispering to himself, "Beautiful. Cool, so cool."

The Loving-kindness, Compassion, Patience and Wisdom of the thera have grown out of his own experience of living in nissaya/dependence with an elder/director. His personal struggle for freedom from greed, grasping, and unwholesome attachment; anger, hatred, and aversion; and the darkness of ignorance or delusion has taken place in the supportive presence of his own thera. This makes him more compassionate and loving in his encounter with his own student. His vision is whole (*samma*) and he understands well the small incident in the *Samyutta Nikaya* (Part I, Chapter 3.18 "Diligence 2"), where the Buddha corrects the faulty understanding of his disciple Ananda:

> On one occasion . . . the Venerable Ananda approached me . . . and said: "Venerable Sir, this is half of the holy life, that is, good friendship, good companionship, good comradeship."
> When this was said . . . I told Ananda: "Not so, Ananda! . . . This is the entire holy life, Ananda, that is, good friendship, good companionship, good comradeship."

The director or thera in this tradition is not self-selected. He is not a theoretician, someone who knows something about the spiritual life. He is a practitioner who has plunged into its depths. Through his own hard-won wisdom, he is able to lead the student along the path to freedom. He is knowing, loving, and compassionate. He is extraordinarily ordinary.

In the words of a great thera, the Most Venerable Tahnchaokhun Phra Visalsalmanagun, "In the spiritual life you cannot teach anyone what you know, simply show them what you yourself are knowing."

Suggested Reading

Digha Nikaya: The Long Discourses of the Buddha. Translated by Maurice Walshe. Boston: Wisdom Publications, 1995.

Heart Treasure of the Enlightened Ones (Thog mtha bar gsum du dge ba'igtam by Patrul Rinpoche). Commentary by Dilgo Khyentse Rinpoche. Boston: Shamabala Publications, 1992.

The Samyutta Nikaya: Connected Discourses of the Buddha. Translated by Bhikku Bodhi. Boston: Wisdom Publications, 2000.

The Teacher-Student Relationship by Jamgon Kongtrul the Great ('Jam-mgon kong-sprul blo-gros mtha'-yas). Translated by Ron Garry. Ithaca: Snow Lion Publications, 1999.

The Visuddhimagga of Buddhaghosa. Translated by Bhikku Nanmoli. Kandy: Buddhist Publication Society, 1975.

CHAPTER TWO

The Sufi Path of Guidance

Fariha al-Jerrahi

This chapter explores Sufism as a path of guidance and examines its foundation in faith and revelation and its application as a spiritual science for the well-being of the human family. In the text, the name of the Prophet Muhammad will be frequently followed by the request for divine peace to be showered upon him. The tradition of accompanying his name with a prayer of peace derives from holy Qur'an, which recommends this practice to his community. It is also frequently practiced for all of the divine messengers.

Powerful and tender, Sufism appeared in its contemporary form with the coming of the Prophet Muhammad, may loving peace always flow to him and to all the messengers and incarnations of divine love. Sufism is the essence of the holy guidance he received through direct revelation over a period of twenty-three years, which took form in his teaching and practice of spiritual companionship with the intimate knowers and lovers of reality. Sufism is the heart of Islam; therefore, I will address it as such. It is the most recent incarnation of the ancient mystical relationship of humanity and Divine Being, the Mystery that is always revealing itself. Without the continuous nourishment of Sufism, pulsing with divine intimacy, the outer form of Islam would dry up like an old shed skin. Conversely, without the deep commitment to the holy way of life and practice revealed in Qur'anic teaching, Sufism would wither like a flower cut from its stem.

The Prophet Initiates
the First Adepts of Sufism

During his lifetime the Prophet Muhammad, may divine peace shower upon him, initiated a few of his companions and members of his close family into the mystic path, transmitting to them the most subtle teachings of Islam, the deepest meanings of Qur'an. The close ones who drank from this knowledge and then communicated it to others established the foundation of Sufism, and their way eventually became known as *tariqat*—the inner path of the heart.

The core of Sufism is expressed in the holy utterance "La ilaha ilallah Muhammad rasulallah." In twenty-eight Arabic letters, God affirms the absolute all-encompassing existence of God Reality and, at the same time, the reality of the human being as the secret treasure of God, never separate. "La ilaha ilallah"—divine Reality alone exists; "Muhammad rasulallah"—Reality is ceaselessly revealing and manifesting its hidden treasure, which is perfect humanity. Sufi masters say that sincere repetition and deep contemplation of this glorious sentence is the swiftest path to unveiling truth within the human heart. The Sufis are those constantly immersed in the divine name.

Abu Hurayra was one of the companions of the Holy Prophet blessed with spiritual intimacy. One night in Medina, Abu Hurayra encountered the Prophet praying alone in a garden. The Prophet revealed to him that anyone who sincerely recited the mystic words "La ilaha ilallah" once in their lifetime would attain divine forgiveness and eternal bliss. Abu Hurayra ran to share this extraordinary news with the other companions. One of them, upon hearing these words, knocked him to the ground, exclaiming that he would not accept the message unless he heard it directly from the blessed lips of the Prophet. When the Prophet confirmed the statement, the companion begged him not to spread this knowledge because it could harm the very practice of religion. He feared many people would begin to rely on Allah's mercy alone and become lax in their discipline, causing their downfall. I relate this account to point out that two different streams were already emerging during the lifetime of the Prophet. One, representing a Sufi spirit, relied on the power of the heart and faith, and the other, representing a more orthodox approach, placed the emphasis on a meticulous observance of the law.

The Path

How do we come from a secular, material state of mind, verging on despair, seeing the world and people as the "other" and potentially hostile, to a sacred state of consciousness where we have a stream of spiritual joy flowing through our hearts, where we feel a divine loving presence, and where we view the world and others as intimate aspects of this divine power and of ourselves? Each person who has left the one world and entered the other might say that the change came through grace, either in the person of a holy teacher or through a divine illumination of the heart that then led them to explore its source, engaging them in a path of initiation and transformation. But for each of us it is a mystery, because nothing that occurred previously in our lives seems to necessitate or cause the grace to appear, except perhaps the intensity of our longing. We wanted God, whether we called our desire God or not. Maybe we were only very unhappy with life the way it was, and intuited a greater reality of the heart that was not yet ours.

In the teaching of universal Islam, Sufism, it is said that God desires us before we can desire him, he longs for us and draws us to him. It is God's desire that made us restless and unhappy with our condition, made us thirst for something unknown and painfully absent. The unhappiness and long-ing, the sense of not fitting into the world's confinement, indicates that we are already on our path of return. Then, at some point in the desert of our wandering, the guide, messenger of God's love, appears. This appointed being gives us to drink of the nectar that brings profound relief to our hearts. This nectar is a distillation of divine love; in consuming it, we know that God exists and loves us and is near to us. In the holy Qur'an Allah reveals, "I am nearer to you, O humanity, than your own life vein." We melt in the loving embrace. Love, in the form of the human guide, has been sent to call us back to God, the source of love.

The Teacher/Guide/Shaykh

The guide is both messenger and reflection of the Beloved. The mystical opening of the heart that brings us into divine presence occurs through the bond between disciple and teacher. Therefore, in Sufism the entire path is traversed with the guide. The love and service that the dervish (disciple) offers to the shaykh (teacher) is the water that irrigates the seed implanted in initiation. There are many different forms and levels of service. Service can be a simple cup of tea brought with love, it can be sitting in deep quietude and listening intently to the teachings, it can be praying for the teacher and humanity, it can be loving attention and care for members of the commu-nity. Service can also be rendered in the way we bring the teachings into our daily life. Around my teacher, Shaykh Muzaffer al-Jerrahi, the newer dervishes often jostled each other in their eagerness to bring the tea or water to him—I was among these—while the senior dervishes sat like big cats in contemplation, watching the play of the younger ones but always alert and ready to leap if necessary. There was no room for heedlessness. At the time

of Shaykh Nur al-Jerrahi (Lex Hixon), who had received the responsibility
for the guidance of the American community from Shaykh Muzaffer, the
formality was less pronounced. It was American style, more casual and
familiar, but no less intense. American dervishes were not trained in outer
service, but they had a spontaneous capacity in expressing loving affection.
So the dervish landscape around Nur was openly the divine play of love.
The community around the great shaykhs is the royal court of Allah.

Initiation, 'Taking Hand' with the Teacher

At the beginning of the relationship between seeker and teacher, the seeker
might have a dream of the teacher, or the teacher of the seeker. This dream
would be a confirmation of the deeper bond between them and a confirmation of the appropriateness of the path for the seeker. The next step is for
the seeker to "take hand" with the guide. This is the act of initiation into
the particular mystical community overseen by the teacher. In a larger sense
it is the entrance into the river of light that radiates from the heart of the
Prophet Muhammad, peace be upon him, flowing through fourteen centuries of enlightened human beings and culminating as a ray of light in the
heart of the initiate. Initiation is a very real event on the level of the soul,
not simply a psychological or emotional one. A flood of light enters into
one's being and alters its foundational structures, just as a flood of water per-
manently changes the course of a riverbed. Shaykh Nur al-Jerrahi (Lex
Hixon) poignantly describes the Sufi initiation rite:

> The initiation is called taking hand. It sacramentally replicates the
> historical event in the life of the Prophet when certain compan-
> ions, already loyal to the holy way of life, ceremonially clasped his
> right hand, marking a vast intensification of their commitment.
> This act of taking hand creates a unique bond with the beloved
> Muhammad, beyond the respect and loyalty devout Muslims feel
> for their noble Prophet, upon him be peace. The right hand that is
> offered and received in this reenactment, therefore, is ultimately
> the right hand of the Prophet. . . . When the lovers of Love linked
> the right-hand side of their being with the Prophet of Love, upon
> him be peace, the mystic right hand of Divine Presence descended
> upon that linking. In this way Allah confirms the original promise
> made to the noble Adam. This promise has been passed in an
> unbroken stream of light through 124,000 prophets to the beloved
> Muhammad of Arabia and transmitted from him through fourteen
> centuries of mystic shaykhs. This is the promise of the soul's union
> with its Lord in the bridal chamber of Divine Love, the promise

that even the veils of soul and Lord will vanish in the supreme realization of identity. . . . Now this Divine Promise, which is good until the End of Time, is again being confirmed. The ceremony (the hand-taking ritual) is a mystic crowning in which the Crown of Light, usually given to the soul in Paradise, is actually conferred here on earth. . . . Receiving this crown enables one to experience Paradise consciousness here and now, during one's prayers and even during the struggles of daily life. The initiated dervishes can now transmit at least a glimpse of Paradise to their loved ones and colleagues, not verbally but directly, thereby elevating all humankind. The dervishes are not seeking their own spiritual bliss but are clearly motivated by the longing to be of service to humanity. . . .[1]

Caretaking the Seed of Light

Practice of Dhikrullah

After hand taking, the return to the Source is spontaneous, like salmon guided upstream. Still, the dervish needs to make a personal effort to nourish and protect what has been given. Through initiation a flame has been ignited—the dervish needs to tend it. The most important practice offered to the new dervish for protecting the holy fire is the daily recitation of divine names. This recitation is called *dhikrullah,* divine remembrance. The Prophet Muhammad has reported that when the lover remembers Allah in *dhikr,* Allah remembers his lover; Allah is making dhikr to the lover. Lover and Beloved are merged in mutual remembrance.

The principle name is *La ilaha ilallah,* called the sword of light because of its power in dispelling illusion and revealing truth. Using this sword, the dervish undertakes the profound journey of return. The journey is a turning toward and traveling through the light, through more and more intense realms of light "located" in the spiritual hearts of the masters of the lineage. The disciple moves, in a series of spiritual ascents, from the light of the shaykh to the light of the founding saint of the mystic order, the Pir, and then to the glorious light of the Prophet of Allah, Muhammad Mustafa, may Allah fill him with eternal peace. Ultimately, the seeker is dissolved in the light of Allah. Each stage is an extinction, *fana,* as well as a birth. On the way, the dervish not only encounters the ones we have mentioned but also a number of other saintly beings and prophets. Many will dream of the Beloved Jesus and Mariam, peace be upon them both. It is recognized that Jesus represents the mystic path, Moses the holy Law, Abraham the station of truth, and Muhammad the spiritual gnosis. Therefore the way of the Sufi is inclusive and all embracing, not limited by a particular theology. The journey that merges the heart of the dervish into the light of Allah can take twenty years or ten, or less. The truly radical vision is that we have already arrived, that we have never departed from the state of unity, and that the journey is a divine play of love within the open space of Presence.

Spiritual Ascent through Seven Levels of the Self

While dervishes are traveling through the different stages of light corresponding to different spheres of divine radiance in the shaykh, Pir, and Prophet, they are also ascending through what has been described in Sufi spiritual science as the seven levels of the self. Each level constitutes a more evolved and wider expression of the human divine reality. Qur'anic revelation states that Allah Most High created seven heavens and seven earths and created the human being as the macrocosm, containing all of the outer creation and the subtle levels of inner creation. Therefore, the seven levels of the self are an archetype of the entire cosmos. The path of human life is the magnificent play of the divine drama within this stage. As their experience of self deepens, seekers encounter the shaykh, the Pir, the Prophet, and the light of Allah within themselves.

I will give a brief review of these seven levels of self because they are an essential part of the Sufi path. The first level is the biological, survival self, whose focus is on fulfilling its primary needs and drives. It is not inherently evil, but through its complete absorption in the limited mechanism of body and psychological "I," it can bring about harm to itself and others. It is called the tyrannical self, and all negative behavior comes from this level. If left ungoverned and unchecked, it can become the source for great destruction.

The second level is that of "the seeker." It is self-critical and struggles against the primal selfish tendencies with the wisdom of the holy traditions and sacred law. It turns the light of faith onto the biological and psychological tendencies, desiring to lift them to a higher level.

The third degree of the self is called "the inspired self," because it is transparent to divine inspiration. It is taught knowledge directly by Allah. It is like the dry piece of wood floating in an ocean that begins to absorb the water around it, becoming more and more soaked. This is the level where the virtuous qualities such as patience, fortitude, gratitude, generosity, contentment, humility, and knowledge are manifested.

The fourth level is called "the tranquil self." At this level, the heart is filled with divine light and experiences the peace and ease of Paradise. The heart desires everything that is pleasing to Allah and forsakes everything displeasing to its Lord. Some of the qualities that radiate from this heart are complete trust in God, pure joy, overflowing gratitude, love of worship, and contentment with what God sends as one's daily bread of experience. On this level, the heart responds only to love.

The fifth degree is called "the self that is pleased with its Lord." At this level, the heart is infused with divine pleasure. This level belongs to the friends of God. The dervish heart is in constant remembrance of God, abstains from all worldliness, and exhibits powers that come directly from the Source of power. At the culmination of this level, Allah says to the servant, "I am the eye with which you see, the tongue with which you speak, the hand with which you reach, the foot with which you move." The dervish has become the servant of God and the representative of God. The log is completely soaked and permeated by the ocean. At this point, the sense of an individual, separate "I" is radically dissolving.

On the sixth level the heart is completely absorbed in Allah's radiance and pleasure. For the dervish at this level there simply is no reality apart from Allah. A mystic verse of the Qur'an speaks, "Wherever you look there is the Face of Allah." Looking in—Allah. Looking out—Allah. Everywhere Allah. The log is drowned in the ocean and cannot find itself. The mystic speaks from this level.

The seventh level is called "the pure self" or "the perfect self." At this level it is said that those who do not know cannot speak and those who know cannot speak. The one who has reached this level is said to be the perfect servant of Allah, having reached complete unity in Allah. This person is camouflaged by his or her very intimacy with God. The person's attributes are Allah's attributes and vice versa. The log appears as a log again but has no identity apart from the ocean. Every cell of the log is ocean, and the ocean appears as log.

However remarkable this model, it is still only a sketch, and it cannot be applied in a rigid way to our life experience. That would be imposing an orthodoxy onto the heart, which is free and mysterious. Usually we are fluctuating from state to state, existing on different levels at the same time. The diagram of the seven levels gives us the general direction of the divine journey. Only Allah knows where we are at each moment of our lives.

The Inner Battle: Jihad

In the initial encounter with the teacher, the seeker is filled with love and bliss, the drunkenness of homecoming. After the flowering of spiritual love comes the second stage, the beginning of the great struggle, inner *jihad*. The bliss of love never entirely leaves the dervish but the going can become fairly rough at times. In a subtle way, the divine confirmation at the beginning sends a message through the inner world of the dervish, like the call of revelation coming into the outer world. All the forces of power, both good and negative, are released. All childhood experiences, all genetic memories, all traces left by the actions of the person on his or her psyche, enter the great arena of the heart to be purified. The goal of the path is complete transparency and total submission to the divine reality within. On the way to this great luminosity no stone is left unturned. Fortunately, however, we do not have to tend to every single thing ourselves. For every step we take many issues are pulled along in the wake. Perhaps the step is addressing a very tiny detail that looks insignificant, yet it covers a mountain of denial and fear. The Sufi path is supremely gentle in handling these moments. The teacher rarely confronts a dervish, but rather draws him or her to realization through a story or living example. It is our experience that the teaching that is needed flows spontaneously without our knowing the precise reasons for it. The inner awareness of each dervish extracts what is necessary for its self-clarification.

At this point on the path, the practices are essential. They are the treasuries of light that we draw on in our struggle of return. In the practice of *dhikr* and prayer, we find Allah. We have already mentioned the recitation of divine names, which is the single most important practice. This is completed by other practices and together they constitute what is called the Five Pillars of Islam. Not every dervish adheres to the full practice, particularly at first, and there is no requirement. Keeping the practices is left to individual discretion. Many prefer to honor the *dhikr* as their main practice, along with a life of loving charity, because no worship is acceptable unless accompanied by charitable thought and actions.

Universal Islam: The Five Pillars, Shariat

Universal Islam is the name inspired to Shaykh Nur al-Jerrah to describe the generosity, vast openness, and universality of the path of Islam. Islam is submission to the Source of love, conscious merging into the Source, and reemerging as pure love moved by the divine will alone, anointed with the beautiful attributes of the Beloved. The Qur'an identifies five pillars or fundamental supports of this universal way. In observing these five pillars and in abstaining from negative or harmful actions, one is honoring the divine law or *shariat* of the Prophet Muhammad, may Allah shower him in radiant peace.

FIRST PILLAR: The heart of this great path is awakening into pure unity of being. Allah Most High reveals *La ilaha ilallah* as the essential affirmation of unity and completes it with *Muhammad rasulullah,* humanity is its perfect manifestation. The dervish affirms this truth through *dhikr* and through aligning the heart with the heart of the shaykh.

SECOND PILLAR: Overflowing with the infinite love of *La ilaha ilallah,* the dervish prostrates in adoration. This finds expression in *salat,* the cycle of five daily prayers enjoined upon the lovers of Love by Allah Most High as a way of meeting with him.

THIRD PILLAR: Filled with the gratitude of *La ilaha ilallah,* the dervish longs to share with all beings the bounties bestowed on him or her by the Generous One. This is manifested by *zakat,* sharing a portion of lawfully earned income with those in need. Beyond this is the continuous flow of generous actions, thoughts, and gestures. The Prophet of Allah has enjoined that we offer charity constantly through every limb of our body. A loving smile is counted as a charitable offering.

FOURTH PILLAR: Called to divine nearness through *La ilaha ilallah,* the dervish fasts from the limited self and feasts on divine love alone. Our celebration of the initial revelation of the Qur'an to the heart of Muhammad, peace be upon him, occurs in the noble month of Ramadan. For thirty days we abstain from food, drink, and sexual embrace during the day, and at night plunge into dhikr and prayer. Ramadan is a beautiful embodiment of our burning love for Allah.

FIFTH PILLAR: Intimately guided by the wisdom of *La ilaha ilallah,* the dervish embarks on life's pilgrimage through divine radiance back into the Source of love. Once in our lifetimes we are called to the holy city of Mecca to circumambulate the Kaaba, celebrating and giving thanks for Allah's guidance to humanity revealed through the hearts of the great prophets and divine beings, may they all be showered in holy peace.

When asked, "What is Islam?" Shaykh Muzaffer replied, "Islam is everything beautiful."

The Mystic Path, the Subtle Path, Individual Freedom

The strength these five pillars of light bestow to our faith is inestimable if they are not imposed upon us but rather are offered as a banquet feast with which we can nourish our hearts. The way of simple *shariat,* which is the outer form of the religion, is to tell the practitioner that these actions are obligatory and must be performed to please God. Otherwise practitioners are in rebellion and risk divine chastening. The way of *tariqat,* which is the mystic path of return, is infinitely more subtle. It is infused with the vision of Allah's boundless mercy and wisdom, and it knows that Allah alone desires souls and draws them back into the Source, each one in its own way. In tariqat the shaykh does not impose anything as the dervish is essentially free. The shaykh fulfills a mysterious function, more like the empty center to the fullness of the dervish, the still point around which the waves of the dervish mind swirl and finally come to rest. The shaykh is the connecting point in the electrical current that comes from Allah so that the dervish heart receives the light. The shaykh is the open door through which the dervish steps. In the teaching of universal Islam, the shaykh simply spreads the banquet table.

Some Personal Experiences on the Path

I have been a dervish on the path of Sufism since 1978, formally taking hand in 1979 with Shaykh Muzaffer Ozak. When he passed into the realm of beauty in 1985, I reconfirmed hand with Shaykh Nur (Lex Hixon). He formed a community of lovers of God of independent spirit, creative gift, and universal vision, desiring to experience the mystery of God without borders or preconceptions. I inherited the community when Shaykh Nur passed into the realm of beauty in 1995.

Allah intimately guides the dervishes through the spirits of Shaykh Muzaffer and Shaykh Nur and the light of our lineage. The light of the shaykhs is part of Allah's light, and therefore we do not see them as essentially separate. My teaching is to encourage the dervishes to turn to and to rely on Allah and the light of the shaykhs. My own role is mysterious, even to myself. I come, I speak, I offer communal dhikrullah once a week—we all join in a circle and chant Allah's holy names. I meet with dervishes individually. I pray for them. I interpret dreams. But none of this could account for the amazing transformations that I witness in the dervishes. The closest analogy for what I see is the image of bathers stepping into a river, and the river carrying them to the sea. By the time they reach the sea they have become the water itself. My role is like that of a mirror, a see-er, a signpost, an inspirer, a cup of wine.

The most difficult moment is when two dervishes are at odds with each other and both feel passionately that they are right. This is a tearing of the garment of the mystical body and it is painful to all. Here again, the way of healing is to turn to Allah, for all our efforts at repairing come to nothing if they are undertaken without the awareness that all goodness and healing come from God's grace. We begin by taking refuge in the infinite mercy of our Source and asking for complete forgiveness. By sincerely asking for forgiveness, much resistance and pride, the main obstacles, are cleared away. Then I might sit with the two and listen to the grievance of each. Then we look for the openings where they can better understand each other. I might remind them that in the mystical community the dervishes are polishers of each other's mirrors, and the disagreements serve as this polishing. To see it this way, as hastening our paths rather than as an undesirable problem for which we blame each other, is a great help.

Another resource in difficult moments is to call the community to a circle of counsel in the Native American way. I have found this extraordinarily transformative and healing. The deep listening to each other, the knowledge of being heard by each other, the wisdom that pours through, all are signs of the divine nature of the counsel. It has been the medicine for some of the stormiest situations in our community.

The Guide as Mirror of Self

The subtle function of the shaykh in tariqat makes the relation between the disciple and student all the more important. In one sense, their relation is the path, for in the way of love the path is simply the bond of heart to heart. How we relate to our guide, who is a mirror for our self, is how we relate to our self and to God and how we relate to all beings. This is a principle of the Sufi mystic path. Everything that appears on the outside is really within us, and the path is about coming to our core, which is no longer "ours," rather it is Allah's. We cannot love another, we cannot love Allah, if we do not love ourselves. And to love ourselves we must let go of the walls of fear and anger and mistrust that we have built. This process can be excruciating and sometimes the walls seem to be endless, especially when they become as fine as onionskin. Yet they always melt when we turn to Allah with our burning hearts. The dervish must have trust in the guide, otherwise he or she cannot even enter the dangerous land where the limited ego self meets its death.

This brings up another question. Does the guide have to be a perfected being for the path to be successful? Ideally, yes. In practice, this is rare. The main thing is for the guide to be oriented to the light of truth. Then the current flows through to the student. If intentions are sincere, the light flows. It is also recognized that a sincere dervish can reach perfection even if the guide is a bad one. Allah is the Merciful and Wise.

So the shaykh does not tell the dervish what to do with his or her life. Even though there are "teachings" and talks and counsel, the guidance is mostly on subtle levels. Usually the teaching is within the group, but sometimes the dervish seeks an individual session. One of the means of guidance is through dreams that the dervish brings to the teacher. The dream is like a window into inner states and tendencies, and it can also carry news from the Beloved. The teacher gives an "interpretation" that seals the good of the dream and shields the potential harm.

Community

After the bond to the spiritual guide, community is the most important foundation for spiritual growth on the Sufi path. Although it is possible for the heart to blossom without a surrounding community, it is more difficult.

The dervishes are the mirrors for each other, and they support, nourish, inspire, and challenge each other. The community is the mystic body, living the divine life of Moses, Christ, and Muhammad, peace be upon them all. The union of souls within this body transcends space and time. What is for one is for all. All together they enter the gates of Paradise, all together they hold open the gates of Paradise for humanity. In a special way, the dervishes are also among the disciples of Jesus, who are known by the love that radiates from them, by the love they shower upon each other, and by the love they have for the human family. The community provides the opportunity to practice sincerity and commitment to one's path.

The Prophet Muhammad, May He Be Showered in Peace

In Christian mysticism, Christ is the Word, the Logos, the first manifestation of the hidden divinity, and the power by which creation is brought about. In the Islamic mystical tradition, this same function is given to the primordial Muhammad, called the Nur Muhammad. The Nur Muhammad is said to be the First Light from which all the other levels of light evolve—the divine Throne, the mystic Pen, the original tablets of revelation, all human souls, all heavenly and angelic realms, all of the natural creation. Everything in manifest existence, on material and subtle planes, derives from this original light. Everything shares the same fundamental divine nature of light.

Here we see the same universal event taking on a different name and form. The main challenge among the religious traditions is in recognizing a similar divine dynamic underlying the manifold revelations. Divine reality never ceases to reveal itself. Naturally, each tradition sees itself as the divine center and eye. Otherwise, it could not be a complete path to the truth. The blinder and the cause of painful conflicts, however, is to think that our path is the only path or the only truth.

In the unfolding of historical time, the Nur Muhammad took form as the living man Muhammad, peace be upon him, Prophet and messenger of God in the sixth century C.E. This magnificent human being, whose true greatness is still a mystery, became the vessel of the outpouring of divine mercy and wisdom for humanity, known as the revelation of holy Qur'an.

Outwardly the Prophet lived a humble life. He owned nothing except for a few items of clothing. He never raised his voice except in the Friday sermon, nor did he ever harm or wish harm to anyone, even his most violent opponents. His nature was so gentle that a child could approach him while he was deeply engaged in discussion and lead him away by the hand. Inwardly, he was an ocean of radiance and divine power. The holy Qur'an states that if the revelation had descended upon a mountain that mountain would have crumbled, as did the mountain of Moses. Yet the heart of

Muhammad was able to bear the weight of revelation over a period of twenty-three years. A few of his companions could perceive him with the inner eye. They saw a luminous pillar extending from the earth to the heavens, showering light, mercy, and protection on the inhabitants of all realms. This exalted station was mostly a secret between Muhammad and his Lord.

In the Sufi tradition, he is the shaykh of all shaykhs on the path of return. The light of all the guides comes from his light. He is the threshold of human and divine, and the door to God. He is called the Perfect Human Being and Ocean of Mercy to humanity. Whoever comes to know him through the heart is astonished and bewildered. Throughout fourteen centuries, great Islamic mystics have been inspired with chants of praise for him, and a large body of these now exists. They are called *salawats,* meaning something like blessings or prayers. Both Muslim and dervish practitioners recite these every day out of pure love. Mystic tradition states that if we recite one salawat upon the Prophet Muhammad, may the divine peace always shower upon him, Allah Most High will recite ten over us. Therefore, they are said to bring blessings and peace to the heart of the one who offers them. Once, when I was a new dervish, suddenly plunged into mystical community life, I asked my shaykh where these salawat came from. His answer was immediate, "From the tongue of Truth."

The Prophet's teachings speak from every level, from the simplest to the most exalted. Like the noble Moses, he received a sacred law, shariat, and like the beloved Jesus, he taught the mystical path of the heart. Therefore, he transmits teachings for the large community in its covenant with God and also for the adepts of the heart in their ardent longing to merge into God. He instructs humanity that cutting a tree uselessly is like killing a person. He counsels that what we desire for ourselves we should desire for all our sisters and brothers. He alerts us that true religion is sincerity of heart. He reveals to us that to meet God we must die to our ego self.

Love for the Prophet is the lifeblood of the dervish, and this love instills a burning and longing for God in the dervish that is shared with Christian and Jewish mystics and with mystics from all traditions. Love is the religion of the dervish. Nothing has dominion over dervish hearts but love. Their desire is love, their call is love, their path is love, their goal is love, their God is love. When all is placed in the fire of reality, only love remains. Therefore, all that we have been speaking of is the dance of love—the steps of initiation, the seven levels of self, the path, the shariat, tariqat—all are forms of love. This is why Allah declares in the holy Qur'an that there is no coercion in religion. Love alone calls back to the source of love.

In the infinite ocean of love where all beings exist, there are unending kingdoms and realms of love. The lovers' desire is to plunge ever deeper. They have died to the self and have found their Beloved, yet still their hearts are thirsting for more, seeking the Essence and endless faces of Love.

CHAPTER THREE

The Guru and Spiritual Direction

Christopher Key Chapple, Ph.D.

One distinguishing feature of spiritual life entails the need for a guide or preceptor in order to shape the formation of an individual seeking self-understanding and self-betterment in relationship to the transcendent. The spiritual director provides a map of the path toward a deepened spirituality. In the religious traditions of India, the teacher is generally referred to as a guru, acarya, or swami. The Sanskrit term "guru" means heavy or weighty, in the Quaker sense of someone who is grounded with deep knowledge. The root of acarya is *car* and denotes dignified comportment. "Swami" means someone in full possession of one's self (*sva*), an allusion to the inner spirit or *atman*.

In the Indian tradition, the teacher or spiritual preceptor takes on sanctified status, as indicated by the term "guru-deva," or divine teacher or teacher of divinity. The *Yoga Sutra*, a text on meditation written more than fifteen hundred years ago, claims that all teachers have been instructed by a special unencumbered soul (*isvara*) who has been untouched by afflictions or attachments.[1] The idealized teacher symbolizes a state of perfection, and from that vantage point can offer counsel and model techniques for meditative acuity.

The *Guru Gita,* a medieval text on the relationship between the teacher and the student, lists many benefits that accrue from following the instructions of the preceptor, including good health, long life, happiness, and prosperity. Two modern classics likewise speak eloquently about the quest for and the commitment to following one's guru: *The Autobiography of a Yogi* by Paramahansa Yogananda (1946) and *Remember Be Here Now* by Baba Ram Dass (1971).

The spiritual preceptor within Indian religious traditions (Hindu, Saiva, Vaisnava, Buddhist, Jaina, Sikh) generally grounds his or her teaching in a textual tradition. For instance, the Hare Krishna movement relies extensively on the stories and teachings of Krishna as found in the *Bhagavata Purana* and the *Bhagavad Gita*. The Dalai Lama conducts workshops on the texts of Nagarjuna. Many prominent teachers of yoga, such as swamis Rama, Iyengar, and Deshikachar refer frequently to the *Yoga Sutra* of Patañjali. Siddha yoga training includes daily recitation of the *Guru Gita*. The followers of Laksman Joo rely heavily upon the Siva Sutras.

In addition to using an authoritative theological source, the guru also provides direct instruction in meditation techniques and often gives personal counseling or advice. In some instances this can be conducted in a mass conveyance of *darsan,* particularly if the movement is quite popular and the sheer number of adherents prohibit individual instruction. Often a guru will deputize key disciples to assist in this aspect of the work.

This chapter will primarily discuss the development of the guru tradition in the United States, with reference to several foundational movements such as the Vedanta Society and the Self Realization Fellowship. It will also include a personal narrative of my relationship with Gurani Anjali, a teacher from Calcutta who in 1972 established a small meditation center in Amityville, New York, for spiritual direction within the path of classical yoga. Drawing from some literature on the advantages and disadvantages of the guru-disciple system, the chapter will close with some reflections on the theology and psychology of this important tradition.

Defining the Guru

One of the most well-read books on the topic of finding and following one's guru is Baba Ram Dass's *Remember Be Here Now*. This book, which had sold nearly a million copies by the time of its forty-third printing in 2001, was published in 1971, has been read widely and, although not generally recognized as fitting within the realm of academic scholarship, was in fact written by a former Harvard professor of psychology, Richard Alpert, whose guru bestowed on him the name Ram Dass, or servant of Lord Ram. Richard Alpert found his guru, Baba Neem Karoli, while traveling in India, and remained devoted to his teachings even after Karoli's death in 1973. Ram Dass writes:

> At certain stages in the spiritual journey, there is a quickening of the spirit which is brought about through the grace of a guru. When

you are at one of the stages where you need this catalyst, it will be forthcoming. There is really nothing you can do about gurus. It doesn't work that way. If you go looking for a guru and you are not ready to find one, you will not find what you are looking for. On the other hand, when you are ready the guru will be exactly where you are at the appropriate moment.[2]

Paramahanasa Yogananda describes such a moment in his autobiography, when Sri Yuktesvar suddenly appears to him on the street in Banaras.[3] Their "chance" encounter forever altered Yogananda's life, and eventually led him to establish the Self Realization Fellowship in Los Angeles.

Yet, despite Ram Dass's words recounted above, not every disciple meets his or her guru; he himself notes: "There have been many saints who realized enlightenment without ever meeting their guru in a physical manifestation."[4] Devotion to a chosen deity (*ista devata*) as mentioned in the *Yoga Sutra* (II: 44–45) might substitute for the actual presence of a living spiritual preceptor. In such instances, however, a community of fellow believers will help form the support network required to stay balanced on the path.

In the Hindu faith, the guru can become identified with divinity. Ramana Maharshi wrote: "Guru, God, and Self are One."[5] It is not uncommon to see graffiti in India that proclaims "Gurudeva!" an expression that attributes divine status (*deva*) to the spiritual teacher. Within the context of India, this makes sense. The conventional world occupies continuous space with the spiritual world. Special places and natural objects such as trees, stones, groves, and river systems are said to possess spiritual power (*sakti*) which abounds, permeates, and pervades what otherwise would seem ordinary. The attribution of divine qualities flows freely in India, where one's parent's are proclaimed to be gods, a wife's husband is said to be a god, and one's teachers are proclaimed to be gods. We must remember, however, what is intended here by the term god. Divinity comfortably finds a home in India's saints and in the epic stories of the *avatiras,* heroic figures sent forth by Vishnu the Lord of Preservation to restore order to a world in chaos.[6] The continuity in the Indian worldview between spirit and nature allows for certain places and individuals to be seen as infused with divinity.

Perhaps the first guru to be widely known in America was Swami Vivekananda, whose address to the Parliament of World Religions (Chicago, 1893) has become legendary in ushering in a wave of tolerance of religious pluralism. He wrote several books that are still widely read, including *Raja Yoga,* an analysis of the classical Yoga of Patañjali. Though he died at a young age, fellow swamis of the Ramakrishna-Vivekananda order established centers and monasteries throughout the United States and Canada.

In the middle of the twentieth century, Paramahansa Yogananda's Self Realization Fellowship, under the competent leadership of Daya Mata, built both a network of congregations in southern California and a very successful mail-order training system. Through nearly all of the twentieth century, Krishnamurti, dividing his time between Ojai, California, Banaras, India, and England, served as a sort of anti-guru, providing spiritual advice that included an insistence on self-reliance.

In the years immediately following the publication of *Remember Be Here Now*, a number of gurus appeared on the scene and some longtime spiritual teachers such as Krishnamurti saw a resurgence in their own popularity. Some of these teachers found fame and grew large organizations. These include Swami Muktananda, Swami Rama, A. C. Bhaktivedanta Swami Prabhupada, Sri Chinmoy, and Maharishi Mahesh Yogi. Some fell into infamy, such as Bhagavan Rajneesh, Da Free John, and the American-born Fred Lenz. Others worked quietly to build small communities of spiritual practitioners following an array of methods (*sadhana*), such as Eknath Easwaran and Gurani Añjali. More recently, a number of very popular women gurus have emerged, including swamis Chidvilasananda and Ammachi, continuing the sixteenth-century tradition of Mirabai and the twentieth-century precedent set by Ananda Mayi Ma.

Finding the Guru

In writing about the role of the guru, I must confess that I am not a neutral or objective assessor of the phenomenon of spiritual gurus. In the late sixties and early seventies, while still in high school, I set out on a spiritual quest. I was involved with Quakerism and religious theater, performing at church services regularly with the Wakefield Players, a troop recognized by the Episcopal Church. I augmented this with a bit of Zen meditation as learned from Philip Kapleau and some yoga that I picked up from the Sikh Kundalini community (also known as 3HO: Happy, Healthy, Holy). In 1972, as I was setting off to college, I had an important dream in which Meher Baba introduced me to a gracious Indian woman. A few months later I entered formal yoga training at Yoga Anand Ashram in Amityville, New York, under the guidance of Gurani. During our undergraduate years, through graduate school, and for our first years of employment, my wife and I participated in yoga training under the guidance of this rather remarkable woman, who had devoted her life to helping others. During this time we helped to establish a vegetarian restaurant, comanaged a bookstore, helped the editing and publication of Añjali's book *Ways of Yoga,* and supported the spiritual and ritual life of the community, which generally numbered no more than one hundred people.

The Call to Discipleship

The invitation to contribute to this book offers me an opportunity to reflect on my experience in the overall context of the guru-disciple tradition. What attracted me to the ashram? In his 1977 book *Turning East: Why Americans Look to the Orient for Spirituality and What That Search Can Mean to the West,* Harvard Divinity School theologian Harvey Cox explores several paths of alternative religious experience and outlines six "types" who join such communities. The six reasons are: 1) a search for friendship; 2) to "experience life directly"; 3) to be delivered from "overchoice" through the leading of an authority; 4) to live a more simple or natural life; 5) to escape male domination; and 6) for environmental reasons.[7] My own reasons include three of the six: a quest for immediacy, simplicity, and ecological integration. I will explain below how my ashram experience moved me toward those three areas. Three of Cox's categories did not fit my situation: I had plenty of great friends before my ashram life, I did not crave an authority figure to mandate the details of my life, and I did not feel particularly oppressed by male domination. Notably absent from Cox's list are the prime reasons given in Indian texts as to why people pursue a religious quest: desire for knowledge (*jijansa*) and desire for liberation (*mumuksu*)[8] Religious communities of whatever faith might provide some fulfillment of the six needs listed by Cox. Most, however, will offer some approach or avenue to a religious experience that transcends the somewhat conventional or psychologized needs articulated above.

So in what follows, after reflecting on my quest for immediacy, simplicity, and integration, I will attempt to articulate some additional reasons, drawing on personal experience to explain the allure of the guru-disciple relationship.

The path taught at Yoga Anand Ashram grounds itself in the classical or raja yoga found in the *Yoga Sutra* of Patañjali. The text defines yoga as "the restraint of fluctuations in the mind" (*yogas-citta-vritti-nirodhah*). After defining five different states of mind, Patañjali gives more than two dozen techniques for bringing the mind to equanimity. These range from reflection on auspicious dreams to different styles of meditation to breathing techniques, postures, devotionalism, ethical behavior, and clear thinking. In one way or another, all these methods were employed in the course of our yoga training. The result would fit into Cox's first category: an ability to experience life directly. According to yoga psychology, past actions (*samskaras*) cloud a person's ability to see the world clearly; the practices of yoga purify a person's karma, allowing one to see things as they are, to stop expecting or projecting, and to move into a mode of acceptance and absorption (*samadhi*). Some have criticized this practice as a form of escapism. In my experience, it could only be attained through a rigorous self-analysis and a difficult process of self-correction. For me, yoga has been more of a confrontation of myself than an escape.

Ram Dass has written that the guru serves as a mirror. In a very informal style, he explains the guru as follows:

> He has no attachment either to life. Or death. And: if he takes on your karma it is your karma. That he should take on your karma. Simple as that. You see: You are the guru . . . and that's what you finally know when you are hanging out with one of these guys. You hang out with yourself because there's nobody at home there at all. So to the extent that there's hanging out (in the interpersonal sense) all you can be seeing are your own desires. He is a perfect mirror since there's nobody there.[9]

My own experience was that Gurani Añjali would reflect back to me my own moods, a process that was quite painful after the initial excitement of beginning yoga training. I struggled with thoughts and behaviors that, while not pathological, were uncomfortable, and I sought purification and improvement. At times, she would mirror to me my own expectations and attachments. For instance, after one singing practice she praised everyone in the room, but ignored me. For me, accustomed to being rewarded for good behavior, this was devastating, until I realized the source of my attachment, struggled through the foul mood that overwhelmed me, and surrendered into an unspeakable place of acceptance. Simultaneously, I felt the concern and compassion of her desire for me to rise to a higher state and I felt my grade-school engendered search for praise and acknowledgement loosen. It was a transformative moment.

The second aspect discussed by Cox entails simplicity. In his book, Cox includes an extended critique, perhaps inspired by Chogyam Trungpa, of spiritual consumerism. Citing Veblen's famous essay on conspicuous consumption, he describes a "new gluttony" that, in the twenty-five years since the publication of his book, has only increased. Cox observes that religion, even "Oriental" religion, has become big business, and satirically refers to "Enlightenment by Ticketron."[10] Eventually, Cox suggests that true spirituality for America should be found within biblical roots, citing the commercialization of non-Western faiths as one reason. In my experience, however, the ethics of yoga explicitly address Cox's concern with gluttony.

Disciplines (*yama*) and observances (*niyama*) constitute the ethical core of Patañjali's eightfold system. At Yoga Anand Ashram, the sadhana classes are given a discipline and/or observance to practice for the week. The first time I heard about this practice was in conversation with Carole Zeiler in the Student Union at the State University of New York at Buffalo. She said that she had received her sadhana in the mail, and she was to practice non-violence or *ahimsa*, which meant, among other things, that she needed to find cookies made without eggs! I became intrigued with the detail of this practice, which was my first introduction to dietary orthopraxy. Participating in a sadhana class several months later after moving to Long Island brought me new challenges each week. How could I make my life more austere? We routinely observed a weekly fast and weekly day of silence as an aspect of austerity (*tapas*). But what more could be done? While practicing not stealing (*asteya*), we worked at not walking off with little things like pencils and on not hoarding intangible things like time. Truthfulness (*satya*) was always a great challenge. How could I resist the temptation to exaggerate? Was my being in the world fully authentic? Although my wife and I shared these practices with one another, the bulk of our days were spent on a university campus where such topics would not be appropriate to bring up in conversation. So we cultivated a life of ethical introspection while engaged in our studies and campus jobs, enjoying the company of our fellow yoga students while in class at night and on the weekends. In little and big ways, we forged a different path than that dictated by the culture, which at the time was promoting disco dancing and the hustle. Perhaps the biggest culture gap came with the practice of nonpossession (*aparigraha*). For our teacher, this meant avoidance of debt. In India, lending policies have historically been draconian; until recently, people even saved to pay for houses with cash. We came to value and stretch our meager resources and live a truly simple lifestyle that we have carried over into our later mid-life years to some extent.

The other aspect of my relationship with my guru that merits mention pertains to Cox's sixth category, regarding those who "had turned to some version of an Eastern tradition as the result of a concern for health, ecology and the conservation of the planet's dwindling resources."[11] Having been raised in a radically rural environment, I carried an innate aversion to settling in the country's largest and most densely populated metropolitan region. In the ritual life of the ashram, however, I found a sense of comfort and connection with the rhythm of nature. Having moved to New York from the tropical climate of Calcutta, Añjali had observed the beauty of the changing seasons. She initiated festivals in honor of each of these changes and eventually asked me, as *pujari,* to organize these events.

Our yoga training also included an intense study of the *mahabhutas,* the five great elements. Over a period of several months we dedicated some time each day to gazing and reflecting upon the power of the earth, then the power of water, of fire, of air, and finally of space itself. This set of concentrations (known in Buddhism as the *kasinas* and in Brahmanism as *bhuta-suddhi*) brought me into that sought-after immediacy, a connection with the fundamental aspects of reality that can be found regardless of the specificity of one's environment. Having been a connoisseur of the sweeping vistas of the Finger Lakes and the glimmering sunsets of the cloud-studded western New York landscapes, I remember commenting to a fellow yoga student that the little bit of median strip along the Grand Central Parkway in Queens included it all: green earth, moist soil, glimmering sunlight, grasses swaying in the breeze. This simple observation brought all my years of wandering through fields and forests into the immediacy of a parkway moment, and helped release my nostalgia and wistfulness for being elsewhere.

In addition to reflecting on the elements, we were also given sadhana that included concentration on the sensory process and sustained observations of animals. These trainings in the elements, the senses, and animals, combined with an ongoing practice of ahimsa, served to anchor some of my later scholarship, including my book, *Nonviolence to Animals, Earth, and Self in Asian Traditions,* and three edited books on issues of ecological concern. With this background and training I learned to revel in seeing Añjali interact with her dogs. She seemed to simply merge with the consciousness of animals who responded to her quiet signals with alertness and eager compliance.

Finding the Guru Within

As my life in yoga matured, my relationship with the guru also changed. When I first came to the ashram, I was in awe, a bit dumbstruck by the power and gracefulness of this woman who had dedicated herself to building a refuge where people from any and all walks of life could learn the joys of yoga. Some of us were college students; some were college educated. Many others were high school dropouts who were drifting through life. She treated all of us equally. I received no special praise for my chosen career in scholarship (though I was told later that she was happy for my work on behalf of elucidating yoga). In fact, much of her time was taken up with helping people in great need: cancer survivors, people attempting to recover from various types of addictions, and those who were sad and lonely. Her generosity seemed endless. I also saw her more human side, as she dealt with her own family issues and worked at finding a balance between motherhood and ashram management. As she became humanized in my eyes, I not only came to a deeper appreciation of her seemingly boundless energy, but also to a fuller recognition of my own gifts and calling in life.

For an extended period I served as pujari of the ashram, which, in addition to organizing the seasonal festivals, meant I was responsible for blessing the ashram each sunrise and sunset with the gayatri mantra, maintaining the flowers and fruits on the *havan* (altar), making certain the incense was lit during Sunday morning meditations and, on two occasions, officiating at weddings. An added duty was to greet the car when the gurani arrived to speak, open the door, and escort her upstairs. To my great surprise, after several months (or years?) of this routine, one day she hopped out, told me to get in, closed the door, and then went through the formalities of opening the door for me! It was all in great fun, but also signaled a lighthearted change in our relationship.

During her lifetime, Gurani Añjali bestowed her final initiation on only four people: Padmani, Indu, Viraj, and Satyam. Though neither my wife nor myself received this honor, our lives have been enriched beyond description by having the opportunity to grow into maturity with her blessing. She modeled a wonderful style of teaching for both of us, encouraging us to meet people, know their needs, be bold, be tactful, and be fun. Her life also spoke to us in lessons unsaid. We learned to be busy but to avoid being overextended, an accomplishment not realized until our move from New York to California. Añjali, reflecting her commitment to Samkhya philosophy and its emphasis on individual souls, commented frequently, "We come alone and we go alone." Our physical parting from the ashram after twelve years of constant involvement shocked the community but did not result in ostracization or resentment. We felt our inner growth propelled us to a new environment. We continue in our own ways to benefit from and give back to the world some of the wonderful lessons we learned from our teacher.

Inauspicious Encounters

Not all the lessons learned in life are happy lessons. Although I encountered my share of power struggles and internal jealousies and sometimes confusing administrative decisions in the ashram, in the process I learned a great deal about the structure of organizations and about human nature, including that not all people have pure intentions. Unfortunately, even spiritual communities can sometimes become a trap, particularly if an individual does not have the fortitude to integrate ethics with power, which is what happened to an acquaintance of ours who set himself up as a guru. After he had studied with a different New York City Hindu guru, Fred announced to us that he had learned how to lecture, mesmerize his listeners, and attract followers. He had also learned how to obtain free publicity. He preceded us in our move to California and, though we never saw him again, some of my university students in Los Angeles were his disciples. His photograph was even displayed with Yogananda and Krishnamurti in the Bodhi Tree Bookstore, the spiritual center of West Hollywood! After a scandal, he was driven from California back to New York. In his ten-year career as a guru, he amassed millions of dollars, beautiful houses, and enjoyed relationships with hundreds of women. Having known this man fairly well, we were surprised and skeptical. We knew that he used flattery to gain followers and had falsified information in a book on reincarnation. Sadly, our intuitions proved correct. He committed suicide on Long Island in 1998, drowning with his dog in his beloved Conscience Bay after overdosing on barbiturates.[12]

Was Fred a sad aberration, or is there something inherently flawed in a system that accords divine status to its leaders? The *Guru Gita* states: "[T]he water of the Guru's feet (has the power) to dry up the mire of one's sins, to ignite the light of knowledge, and to take one smoothly across the ocean of this world."[13] This attitude toward the guru is wonderful and essential for the disciple. Devotion to a guru allows one to be apprenticed to the ultimate role model, one symbolizing the best of all human possibility. All gurus, according to the *Yoga Sutra,* have been instructed by Isvara, the supreme teacher who has been untouched by karma or its afflictions. By ascribing divine qualities to the teacher, the disciple creates for himself or herself a new standard for excellence, a paradigm to be emulated. Feelings of deep love and respect often accompany this devotion or *guru-bhakti.* But what does it do for the guru? If the guru can integrate the adoration and the rigors of being constantly on call, then everything will feel safe. But in some cases, as with Fred, things can go terribly wrong.

Some critics, such as Anthony Storr, seem to categorically condemn gurus. Though Storr acknowledges that some gurus are saints, he also writes that some are simply mentally disordered. Storr attributes a form of narcissism to all gurus, saying they "retain this need to be loved and to be the center of attention together with the grandiosity which accompanies it."[14] He goes on to note that the guru "remains an isolated figure who does not usually have any close friends who might criticize him on equal terms." He cites as his examples Gurdjieff, Rajneesh, and Ignatius of Loyola. Though he does not impugn the basic notion of the validity of religious transcendence and the need for spiritual leadership, he feels compelled to present a typology of pathological behavior among some gurus. Jeffrey Masson has attempted to do a similar analysis in his discussions of Sri Ramakrishna and Gurdjieff.[15] Likewise, Jeffrey Kripal created a great controversy when he attempted to find psychological causes for Ramakrishna's visions,[16] and Joel Kramer and Diana Alstad devote an entire volume to the dangers of blindly following authoritarian mandates.[17] A critical reevaluation of the guru-disciple relationship is being attempted, with, in the case of Kramer and Alstad, the suggestion that the institution be replaced with more democratic, relational structures.

Despite his generally positive assessment of gurus, even after a rather harrowing experience in the eighties, Georg Feuerstein, in writing about "crazy-wise adepts and eccentric masters" states:

To the extent that they can help us free ourselves from the blinders with which we block our Reality and conceal ourselves (or our Self) from ourselves, we would do well to heed their message. At the same time, I feel, they are relics of an archaic spirituality that, sooner or later, will be replaced by a more integrated approach to self-transcendence. This new approach will be sustained by teachers, including holy fools, who place personal growth and integrity above the need to instruct, reality above traditional fidelity, and compassion and humor above all role-playing.[18]

Interestingly, Feuerstein cites Ramakrishna as an example of a guru who established friend-like relations with his disciples, and commends Sri Aurobindo for encouraging frank debate among his followers.

The literature on the controversial aspects of the guru tradition is quite extensive, as the bibliographies in any of the books cited in this chapter will indicate. Our own teacher expressed a slight sorrow at her situation, noting: "It is lonely at the top," "Heavy is the head that wears the crown of thorns," and "Even the therapist sometimes needs therapy." Standing in the vow to help others can be beautiful and liberating. It also can become burdensome. Having witnessed the comportment of many spiritual leaders or gurus of the Hindu, Buddhist, Christian, Jewish, and Jaina faiths, I feel some compassion for them because of the burden they have assumed. Driven by an inner calling to be of service to others, they run the risk of placing their own well-being in peril, as in the tragic cases of Rajneesh, Fred Lenz, David Koresh, Jim Jones, and others.

Revisiting the Guru Tradition

Do these potential pitfalls in any way invalidate the tradition of spiritual leadership? Based on my own experience, I would argue not. Without the commitment of men and women willing to serve others, the world will even more rapidly fall into the consumer-driven pit of gluttony. We need heroic figures like Julia Butterfly to do the unexpected, to demonstrate that the human being can ascend beyond humdrum existence to embrace a higher cause. We can learn from others, as long as our intentions are clear and we hold sight of our own dignity. To my mind, a guru or spiritual advisor must acknowledge an underlying spiritual equality between persons on the basis of which spiritual introspection is possible. For while the guru needs to devise techniques and seize opportunities to awaken the student and move him or her to transcend the constraint of the ego-defined self, at the same time he or she must respect the student. As with many people, for me this training was not always pleasant. Yet I also knew that sadhana was given not to enhance the status of our teacher or even our organization, but for the purposes of my own purification. Since it is by exerting one's will and creativity, not by simply seeking to please one's teacher, that one advances along the spiritual path, I feel that the boundary between teacher and student, guru and disciple, needs to melt.

That the guru tradition arose within the context of a highly hierarchical society helps to make sense of current practice. In traditional India, one's status in the family and caste determines one's expected behavior. Obedience to one's parents and elders, rather than any questioning of authority as found in the United States, is the norm. Texts such as the *Guru Gita* extol the need to submit to the authority of a higher teacher. Seeming inequalities can be seen throughout India's traditional, pre-independence society that stem from this assent to hierarchy, from special privileges accruing to people of high caste, to sometimes crude treatment of women who are not under the full protection of their families as required in the *Laws of Manu*.

Some organizations have questioned the usefulness of continuing the guru-disciple tradition. A change made by one such organization is the institution of a complex governance board for the International Society for Krishna Consciousness and the replacement of Amrit Desai as head of Kripalu, a large yoga center located in the Berkshire Mountains of Massachusetts. However, will these changes diminish the tradition? William Cenkner makes the following potent observations about the centrality of the guru to the Hindu tradition:

> The guru occasions the immediacy of the religious experience of the devotee. For the faith-filled devotee, he [*sic*] is the center of mystery. The sacred center of Hindu life is the living guru . . . his followers experience him as the restorer of the *dharma* order. . . . The guru is the center of sacredness. In his company the scriptures, idols and even liberation paths pale in importance. . . . The guru is the context wherein an individual gathers spiritual resources in order to encounter mystery; likewise, the guru is mystery itself in the faith experience of some devotees.[19]

Though Cenkner primarily refers to India's thirteen hundred-year-old sankaracarya tradition, he also includes within his definition of gurus the many new teachers and religious leaders. Daniel Gold, in his study of north Indian saints (*sants*), notes, "[T]he redemptive power of *sants* of the past is made available through the living guru. His words convey their instructions, explain the meaning of scripture, and make known the will of the highest divine."[20] However, at the same time, Gold comments on the human qualities of the guru: "The earthly embodiment of the guru known to close disciples is a living, changing person whose behavior may seem continually paradoxical, and his outer worship is performed through practical service that is often unpredictable and almost always most mundane."[21] The mercurial nature of the guru seems both to reflect his or her humanity and mysterious allure.

The psychology of India seems well equipped to accommodate the notion of *gurudeva*, the idea that divinity can be reached through one's relationship with a living teacher. Persons generally go to such an individual with an understanding that the spiritual path requires at least two prerequisite elements: a desire to learn about the spiritual path and a desire for spiritual liberation. The *Atmabodha* also suggests that persons on the spiritual path should already be of "diminished sin due to their austerities, peaceful, and free from attachment."[22] In the traditional context, a guru often ascends to his or her status within the confines of a preexisting organization with a number of social controls in place. In the American context, as noted by Harvey Cox, people might approach a guru from a place of a different sort of need. In some instances, these might be similar to those in India. But in others, they might be seeking to replace a weak relationship with authority or might be acting on a desire to be "re-parented." Such a situation complicates the job of the guru, who might not be trained to discern such psychological issues. Similarly, without preordained social constraints and expectations on the part of his or her disciples, a guru might slip into human temptations and manifest behaviors that exceed acceptability within the category of "paradoxical."

In conclusion, the guru-disciple relationship remains one of the most complex and dynamic of possible interpersonal encounters. For me, it gave focus and grounding to my life. Combined with the good guidance of various professors and a wonderful family, my experiences within a traditional ashram context have been formative, informative, and transformational. I see in my own university a desire for many faculty members to mentor their students, to guide them into appropriate career paths, to give them advice from time to time on personal issues. Though seemingly less hierarchical (though perhaps not less expensive), it seems that even in such a seemingly mundane context, the precepts and intentions of improving others through instruction and examples can be found in paradoxically obvious places close to home.

CHAPTER FOUR

The Place on Which You Stand Is Holy Ground

A Jewish Understanding of Spiritual Direction

Zari Weiss

Oe of my directees, Anna,[1] had just come into my office, and after a few brief moments of silence, she confessed how frazzled she was. She said that she longed to experience moments of calm and peacefulness in the midst of her hectic life. I asked her if she had ever experienced such moments, and when she said she had, I asked her to describe one. Anna had at one time been much attuned to her spiritual life and practice, but sadly, over the years, had grown distant from those things that had once given her strength and comfort. It was her longing that had brought her to my office. Recalling the feeling she had once had and still longed for, Anna told me that recently she had been swimming and had allowed herself just to float, letting the water hold the weight of her body. She experienced a feeling of being held, a sense that in that moment, everything was okay. Because of her estrangement from organized religion, Anna had grown allergic to God language; in our sessions, we would often refer in a lighthearted way to God as "The Great Whatever!" Yet I knew that this image of floating and being held was a powerful and rich metaphor for this young woman—reminding her of a meaningful relationship with God that had once sustained and nourished her. Gently, I asked if—in the midst of the hectic pace of her life now—she ever felt held by God. My words seemed to touch something tender inside her. She shook her head sadly. I felt her great longing, as well as her uncertainty about how to reach out to a God from whom she had turned away. And then, I wondered aloud if there might be anything that she could build into her daily spiritual practice that might allow her to feel held in this way. She thought quietly for a moment, and then said that perhaps she could wrap herself in her *tallit,* her prayer shawl, and just sit quietly. Wearing a tallit was new to her, but it was somehow comforting. I suggested that wrapping oneself in the tallit can indeed be like being enveloped in God's loving embrace, and offered her the beautiful passage from the Book of Psalms that often accompanies the blessing for putting on the tallit:

> How precious is your love, O God,
> when earthborn find the shelter of your wing!
> They're nourished from the riches of your house.
> Give drink to them from your Edenic stream.
> For with you is the fountain of all life,
> in your Light do we behold all light.
> Extend your love to those who know you,
>   and your justice to those honest in their hearts." (Psalm 36:8–11)[2]

Anna's whole body seemed to relax with the image; a feeling of calm enveloped her, indeed, filled the room. God's Indwelling Presence, the *Shechina,* had entered our midst.

I have had other, similar sessions in my capacity as a spiritual director or companion. Often, many of the same images and themes arise in my work with Jewish directees—such as the need to heal a relationship with God (and with Judaism!) that has been damaged through the legacy of a patriarchal tradition, the struggle to find one's way to a loving and comforting God, and the desire to reconnect with Jewish ritual and tradition in a way that is spiritually enriching.

For the past eight years, I have been privileged to be a guide and a companion to others as they grow in their awareness of God's presence in their lives, and as they learn how to tend that sacred relationship through prayer, other spiritual practices, and holy conversation.

I have worked with those who are Jews as well as those who are not, but I have most often accompanied Jews on this journey. For most Jews, the work of spiritual direction is new and unexplored territory. As I have watched and participated in this growing phenomenon in the Jewish world, I have come to understand some of its unique challenges as well as its many gifts. In the following pages, I hope to share some of the insights I have gleaned along the way. These are by no means exhaustive; those of us who are exploring this territory are learning together as we go along. In that sense, I am grateful to my teachers and colleagues in this area from whom I have learned so much. But I am most grateful—as the Talmud teaches[3]—for my students (and in this case, my directees), from whom I have learned most of all.

Tending the Holy

For many modern Jews, tending the relationship with God, or the Holy, is a new concept. To many, the God of the Bible is a distant deity, and the God of the medieval philosophers or mystics is elusive or inaccessible. And though some Jews direct their prayers to God every day in the daily liturgy or every week in the prayers of the Sabbath liturgy—or may speak about doing God's work in the world through *tikkun olam* (repair of the world) or *gemilut chassadim* (deeds of loving-kindness)—in actuality, many do not have a personal relationship with God. Many Jews find it difficult to connect their own experiences of the Holy with those of their ancestors, or they fail to recognize their own experiences reflected in the words and images of their ancient tradition. As a result, they all too often question the legitimacy of their own experiences and discount them as inauthentic. Not surprisingly, then, few know how to tend that relationship so that it can be a source of nourishment, comfort, guidance, and understanding.

To find a meaningful path to God, in recent years some Jews have found their way to spiritual direction—a new phenomenon in the Jewish world, a phenomenon that is quickly making inroads across the Jewish denominational spectrum.[4]

When I first begin to work with someone in spiritual direction, I often begin by exploring some of the directee's conceptions of God. Sometimes these conceptions need to be gently challenged and expanded. Only then can a new, deeper, and more meaningful understanding of God/the Holy take root and begin to grow. One directee, for example, had much resistance to overcome before we could even begin a conversation about cultivating a meaningful relationship with God.

A woman in her late sixties, Sondra had grown up in a conventional Jewish family in which education was valued for men but not for women. Not surprisingly, Sondra's attitudes about religion were largely derived from her social and cultural experience. To Sondra, notions of God were limited to those suggested by the Bible: God was male, powerful, wrathful, and often punishing. This was a God to whom Sondra found it difficult to relate. She found it equally hard to be in a satisfying and meaningful relationship with such a God.

I suggested to Sondra that the God of the Bible represents only one stage in Jews' theological evolution: our attempts over the centuries to name that which is ultimately unnamable. In the last few decades, there have been a number of people—inspired by feminist and Postmodern theologians—who have moved beyond the God as conceptualized in the Bible, transforming liturgy and ritual and religious experience as a result. I pointed her to the groundbreaking work of poet and liturgist Marcia Falk,[5] for example, whose theological wrestling led her to create new blessings in which God is imaged not as a Lord, but as a *Eyn Hahayim*—a Wellspring of Life—from which all life flows. As Sondra began to consider the possibility of new conceptions of God—conceptions which are in fact rooted in her own tradition—an opening occurred that began to lead to a profound healing in Sondra's relationship with Judaism and, equally important, to an authentic and meaningful personal relationship with God.

To help Sondra and other Jewish directees begin to tend their relationship with God, I often explain that this relationship—like all other relationships—does not happen on its own. While some people may experience moments of epiphany or transcendence, having a relationship that one can turn to and rely on in time of need requires effort and patience. It takes time to develop trust—trust that God will be there when we need God, trust that we will be receptive to God's whisperings when God calls or whispers to us.

To develop this trust, one has to spend time getting to know God, and allowing God to know us. For many Jews, this way of relating to God—in such a personal and intimate way—is foreign, and perhaps even a bit scary (since it doesn't "feel Jewish"). While God is absolutely central to Jewish experience, the relationship with God has historically been mediated through community. Jews' relationship with God is manifest in one way, for example, through the performance of *mitzvot*. The mitzvot are the laws understood to have been given by God to the Jewish People. They are recorded in the Torah and then further expanded through rabbinic interpretation. They are incumbent upon individuals as members of a community: the community of the Jewish People. The blessing for the performance of a mitzvah praises God—"asher vetzivanu"—"who has commanded *us* to . . ." (i.e., eat *matzah*, light the Shabbat candles, and so on)—not "who has commanded *me*."

The Jew's relationship with God is also manifest through prayer. Whether in the setting of the home or the synagogue, Jews' blessings and prayers to God are most often phrased in the collective. In his superb book *Entering Jewish Prayer*, Reuven Hammer writes:

> Community prayer is also a way of strengthening the ties of the individual with the Jewish community. It is not accidental that the most important of our formal prayers are all given in the first person plural. We pray to "our God." We ask that God's blessing be

"upon us." Even when thanking God, "we give thanks" and bless Him for "keeping us alive and allowing us to reach this time." It is to the events in the history of the Jewish People that we turn in prayer, and it is for the future of this people that we pray. To pray as a Jew, as Heschel put it, is not to turn to Him "as an I to a Thou, but as a We to a Thou."[6]

Even in the Amidah, the central prayer of Jewish worship where the Jew has the opportunity to enter into a more intimate interior dialogue with God, the blessings are most commonly framed in the context of the communal experience. In the weekday service, for example, where the middle thirteen blessings include petitions for success and well-being, the prayers are phrased in the plural.[7] Again, writes Hammer:

> The Amida is a collective prayer, referring in essence to the people of Israel. When the individual recites it, he or she does so as a representative of the group. It is also a fixed prayer, with a text or at least a pattern that cannot be changed. In response to a felt need, the ancient custom was for a person to follow the recitation of the Amida, the prescribed prayer, with a personal prayer in which he was free to express his own feelings. While the Amida is entirely in the plural, any personal prayer was in the singular.[8]

While historically there was an opportunity for individuals to add their own personal and spontaneous prayers, this custom has been lost or reduced to just a few brief moments at the conclusion of the *Amidah* (in the prayer known as *tachanun*—prayers of supplication). The Reform Movement reintroduced time for private prayers with the addition of "The Silent Meditation" at the end of the Amidah. Thus, while there certainly are a few places within the worship service for an individual's personal prayers and petitions to God,[9] most of our prayers to God are of a communal nature.

In addition to the performance of mitzvot or prayer life, the individual's relationship with God has been, for the most part, a private affair. There have been groups or movements within Jewish history (such as the Wisdom Movement, the Hassidic Movement, or the Musar Movement; see below) in which the individual's relationship with God had a more central focus. These days, we are seeing resurgence in the desire to cultivate and tend the relationship with God among people outside of those circles. This resurgence has pointed individual Jews toward the world of spiritual direction. Not only are individual Jews seeking out others with whom to explore and deepen their relationship with God, so too are groups of Jews coming together in Jewish spiritual companioning groups to share their spiritual journeys and explore God's presence in the ordinary and extraordinary moments of their lives. A number of such groups are meeting in various forms inside and outside of congregations around the country.

Carving New Territory

Being a Jewish spiritual director, or a spiritual director for Jews, is groundbreaking work. For those of us called to this work, it is both a privilege and at times a challenge as we carve out new territory and consider the questions and issues that arise in any groundbreaking enterprise.

For Jews, the past is as important as the present and the future. We look to the past for precedence and for guidance. It is integral to a Jewish way of seeing the world to know if the practice is grounded in Jewish texts, history, experience, and values. We are a text-based people. We look to the core texts of our tradition—the Torah, the Talmud, the Codes, Jewish literature—to find precedents for practices that arise in response to developments in our current situation. We are also a people whose identity is based in history. We look to previous eras and movements within Jewish history to find models for new trends that are emerging. We are a people with religious and spiritual practices that have for centuries guided our day-to-day lives and experiences. We draw on these practices even as we shape new ones in the present and the future. Finally, we are a people whose identity is shaped by core beliefs, values, and ideas. As new practices emerge, we must make sure they are congruent with these time-honored core beliefs, ideas, and values.

As Jewish spiritual direction emerges in the twenty-first century, then, we are compelled to ask: Are there precedents within Jewish history, as reflected in the texts of our tradition, for this type of relationship? Are there religious and spiritual practices that inform and influence how we do Jewish spiritual direction? With which beliefs, values, and ideas might it be helpful for a spiritual director to be familiar to better meet the needs of Jewish directees?

Precedents for the Spiritual
Companion/Guide Relationship

Jewish history, as reflected in our sacred texts, does provide some examples of people who have served as spiritual companions or guides to others—though they may not always have been recognized as such. They differ, however, from the model of Jewish spiritual direction that is now emerging.

An early example of spiritual companionship is found in the beautiful book of Ruth, in which two women, bereft of their husbands and separated from their communities and familiar surroundings, form a deep and lasting spiritual bond. According to the story, after her husband and then two sons die, Naomi entreats her daughter-in-law Ruth to return to her mother's home, where she might be taken in and given a second chance at marriage and children. In a moving pledge of loyalty, Ruth tells Naomi that she will not leave her side, even until death:

> "Entreat me not to leave you, or to return from following after you:
> for wherever you go, I will go; and where you lodge, I will lodge;
> your people shall be my people, and your God my God;
> where you die, I will die, and there will I be buried;
> the Lord do so to me, and more also,
> if anything but death part you and me." (Ruth 1:16–17)

Naomi responds with silence, and the two return to the elder woman's homeland.

In return for Ruth's steadfast loyalty, Naomi acts as a loving and caring companion to her daughter-in-law, as their fates become intertwined. Naomi practices a kind of "holy listening," as Ruth tells her what happens when she goes to the field to glean after the reapers, along with the other widows and orphans. Clearly, Naomi is aware that Something Else is at play, and gently guides Ruth as events unfold. Though not explicitly described in the text as a spiritual guide and companion, we can well imagine that Naomi offered her young daughter-in-law spiritual guidance and companionship along her journey.

Concurrent with this story (which takes place during the period of the Judges—approximately 1030 B.C.E.) and continuing for many generations, another type of relationship develops that reflects a different model of spiritual companionship or guidance. The ancient priests provided the community with instruction in the practices of religion (Torah), and the prophets communicated to the people the divine word or visions that they had received. But it was the wise elders, known as the *zechenim* or *hachamim,* who imparted counsel or guidance to their students in the secular affairs of life. The wise elders did not derive their authority from the Torah, and thus, by extension, from God. But they taught what they believed to be true and right—those deeper spiritual truths and insights which they knew were in harmony with Torah and prophecy. The books of Proverbs, Job, Ecclesiastes, parts of the Book of Psalms, the Wisdom of Solomon, the Wisdom of Ben Sira, and Ecclesiasticus are all examples of what is known as Wisdom (*Chochmah*) literature. According to some scholars, the books that comprise this literature were not simply anthologies of wise sayings commonly heard in ancient Israel, but rather were source books of instructional material for use in schools or in private study, for the cultivation of personal morality and practical wisdom. In these Wisdom schools, which existed in Israel and other countries, students would work with teachers, whom we might call today spiritual guides, to cultivate wisdom and other desirable qualities within themselves.

Many years later, the Musar Movement, founded in the 1840s by Lithuanian rabbi Israel Salanter, may have been an extension of the early Wisdom schools. In orthodox *yeshivot* or schools in Lithuania, Musar teachers guided their students in the regular study of moral treatises, daily meditation, and self-examination, to help them overcome preoccupation with worldly matters and move toward greater spiritual perfection.[10] The teacher was specifically interested in helping the students refine their *middot,* or character traits. A more refined character was the vehicle for a deeper relationship with God. The Musar Movement continues to exist today; though it has gained some popularity in non-Orthodox circles, it is found primarily in the Orthodox world. Few Jews outside of the Musar yeshivot, however, work directly with a Musar teacher to deepen their relationship with God.

Like the Musar Movement, the Hassidic Movement, which was founded by the Baal Shem Tov in the mid-1700s, attracted many followers, many of whom sought spiritual guidance of another kind from their *rebbe.* The disciples of Hassidism, known as *hassidim,*[11] would go to their particular rebbe[12] in a session known as the *yehidut,* or interview. During the yehidut, the rebbe would listen to the problems of the disciple and advise him to engage in actions that were designed not only to relieve his suffering but also to align him with God's will.[13] In this way, the rebbe functioned as a *moreh derekh,* or spiritual guide in serving God. In his book *Spiritual Intimacy,* Rabbi Zalman Meshullam Schachter-Shalomi writes:

> Of all the functions ascribed to *rebbes* . . . the *moreh derekh* was the favorite. . . . The Besht [the Baal Shem Tov, the founder of Hassidism] and his successors saw the spiritual direction of their *hassidim* as the central function of their work. R[abbi] Levi Yitzhaq of Berditchev described the *rebbe's* work as representing a living tractate on Love and Awe before God . . . no book could give direction in this area; a living master was necessary."[14]

He continues:

> *Hasidim* came to the rebbe to learn how to generate religious feelings to God. All social and economic preoccupations were only secondary to the service of God. The spiritual life was the Jew's main occupation in this world. In order to justify his existence in the service of God, a Jew needs to know which acts are pleasing to God

and which acts are not. He could not discover the answer in books. Not all commandments deal with outer behavioral actions. Commandments requiring inner attunement and shifts of attitude and context . . . have no Talmudic treatises discussing them in detail. The *rebbe* himself . . . was to be the tractate of Love and Awe."[15]

The *rebbe,* then, functioned as a kind of spiritual director or guide for those who came to see him.

Though we do not have extensive descriptions of the specific form these relationships took, it is assumed that the teacher of Wisdom, the Musar teacher, and the rebbe were all fairly directive with those to whom they offered guidance. They are examples of some of the relationships of spiritual guidance that have existed in Jewish tradition. However, as we shall see, they differ from the role of the Jewish spiritual director as it is currently emerging.

At the present time, only a handful of Jews have been formally trained as spiritual directors. Because a number have been trained in the Christian contemplative model,[16] the kind of direction offered often reflects this training. At the same time, however, Jewish spiritual directors are exploring what it means to craft a uniquely Jewish form of spiritual direction. We are also experimenting with different language to describe this practice: some refer to a spiritual director as a *moreh derekh,* teacher of the way; and others as a *mashpiya ruchani,* or channel or influencer of the spiritual.

The "Jewishness" of Jewish Spiritual Direction

In contrast with the examples described above, most Jewish spiritual directors are not directive in the sense that they do not tell their directees what to do or presume to know what is best for them in terms of their relationship with God or their spiritual practice. The director may at times be directive in that she may offer specific suggestions for spiritual practice or ritual observance, but she would most likely do so in an atmosphere of holy listening: listening deeply to the directee's deepest yearnings in order to help the directee discern how to be more responsive to God in his or her life.[17] The Jewish spiritual director might gently suggest ways that the directee could draw upon Jewish tradition to enrich and deepen spiritual life and practice. There is thus an atmosphere of spaciousness in the relationship. The director travels patiently with the directee, offering guidance along the way, accompanying the directee as his or her religious and spiritual life unfolds.

The Jewish spiritual director (or the spiritual director offering direction to Jews) often hopes, however, to help directees connect in a more meaningful way with Jewish tradition as they explore their relationship with God and deepen their spiritual life and practice. Of course, among Jewish spiritual directors there is tremendous variety and, as the field evolves, we will see the various forms that this guidance or companioning will take.

Right now the particularly Jewish form of spiritual direction that is being practiced by many Jewish spiritual directors is one that often incorporates Jewish practices and themes into the sessions. Following are some examples.

Central to Jewish life and religious practice is prayer—both formal (liturgical) as well as informal (spontaneous). To begin or end a session, then, a Jewish director may offer a verse from the Psalms or the daily or Shabbat liturgy—perhaps first in Hebrew and then in English, since Hebrew is a language that often resonates deeply for Jews—whether or not they speak or understand the language. Or, the director may begin or end the session with a *niggun,* a wordless melody—which for many Jews often stirs the soul, for inexplicable reasons. Likewise, the director may offer a familiar song, perhaps one known from childhood or religious services—connecting the directee to Jewish community and experience. At times, the director may invite the directee to offer his or her own prayer during the session—though for many Jews, this can be unfamiliar and even uncomfortable. Sometimes it may take gentle prodding and a reminder of the teaching of the Hassidic master Rebbe Nachman, for example, who taught of the importance of spontaneous and heartfelt prayer.[18] With one directee, I had to ask several times before she was able to shift from saying, "If I were to pray I'd say . . ." to speaking directly to God: "Dear God, please help me . . ." Teaching Jews to face God directly when praying can be one of the most healing and transformative parts of the work of Jewish spiritual direction.

Just as prayer is central to Jewish life and religious practice, so too is study. Study of Torah—and the many other texts that are inspired by the Torah—is one of the focal points of Jewish life. As one well-known teaching from the Talmud says, "Upon three things does the world rest: on Torah, on service, and upon deeds of loving-kindness."[19] Another teaches, "When two people sit and words of Torah pass between them, the Divine Presence rests between them."[20] Because of the centrality of Torah study, Jewish spiritual directors are increasingly incorporating text study into their sessions. The study may be formal; for example, looking closely at a passage from the Torah or elsewhere in the Bible and using the study as the context (or pretext) for "holy conversation." Or it may be informal, referring to a certain passage, for example, and exploring the meaning of this passage for the directee. (One passage I have referred to a number of times in response to what a directee has shared with me comes from Deuteronomy 30:19: "I call heaven and earth to witness this day against you, that I have set before you life and death, blessing and curse: therefore choose life, that both you and your seed may live." The passage inspires the question: "What does it mean for the directee to "choose life"?). Sometimes the text study extends beyond the session, as when the directee is moved to continue reflecting or journaling on the passage. In such cases, the text can become an important marker for the directee's unfolding journey.

In addition to study, the performance of mitzvot (often translated as "commandments"; I prefer "sacred obligations") is also important in the life of the Jew. The Jewish spiritual director may suggest that the directee consider taking on the observance of some of the mitzvot. In a recent session, for instance, one of my directees told me that she had just been diagnosed with a medical condition that required her to take better care of herself physically. Seeing that this did not come easily to her, I taught her about the mitzvah derived from Deuteronomy 4:15: "Take therefore good heed to yourselves" (*V'nishmartem meod l'nafshoteychem*). Based on this verse, I explained, the great medieval commentator Maimonides taught that it is a sacred obligation to protect one's general health as well as the health of one's society. Knowing that this woman is someone who desires to expand and deepen her Jewish practice, I wondered aloud if she might consider incorporating this mitzvah into her Jewish life, as part of her sacred obligation to God. She enthusiastically agreed, and committed to exploring the performance of the mitzvah as part of her daily practice.

For some Jews—particularly those who don't see themselves as "religious"—their spirituality may be expressed not through the performance of mitzvot, but rather through efforts to bring about a better world. The director can help these Jews see such actions as reflections of core Jewish values—such as concern for the stranger (*ger*), working toward peace (*bakesh shalom v'rodfehu*), fighting for justice for all human beings (*kevod ha'briot*), and compassion (*rachamim* and *chesed*) for the vulnerable in society. Through gentle exploration of the directee's motivations to work toward a better world, the director might also invite the directee to consider his efforts as *avodah*—service—a way to serve God, humanity, the universe. Such exploration is yet one more way that the director can help ground the directee's experience in a Jewish framework, enriching his or her connection to Jewish heritage along the way.

Like spiritual direction in other faith traditions, Jewish spiritual direction may draw on themes or metaphors that are found throughout our sacred texts, using them as prisms through which directees may better understand their life situations. Wandering through the desert, receiving manna from heaven, being liberated from narrow places (*mitzrayim*), entering the Promised Land—to name just a few—are rich and evocative themes that can provide a valuable means to deeper understanding and appreciation of the spiritual journey. All of these are possible points of connection between the directee and Jewish tradition. The director can help

facilitate these connections and thus make the direction experience a richer
and more meaningful one. The director may draw a parallel to the story of
a certain character in Jewish history—conveying the sense that the directee's
story too takes its place in the unfolding chain of Jewish tradition—another
important value for Jews.

Being a Jewish Spiritual Director (or a Director for Jews)

Spiritual direction is a new and growing phenomenon in the Jewish world.
More and more Jews are being trained as spiritual directors, and more and
more Jews are seeking out direction—from directors who may or may not be
Jewish. For those directors who are Jewish as well as for those who are from
other faith traditions, there are a number of things which may be helpful to
know when called upon to serve the needs of this growing population.

First, and perhaps most obvious, is a familiarity with Jewish texts, tradition, and history. As outlined above, the director can help provide a richer
experience for the Jewish directee by drawing from the vast treasury of
Jewish tradition: citing biblical images, metaphors, or personalities; recalling a relevant passage from the Bible or the liturgy; connecting certain
actions to mitzvot or Jewish values.

The director can also affirm for the Jewish directee the importance and
the validity of the spiritual direction experience. For some Jews, the experience of spiritual direction is at first so unfamiliar that they may wonder if it
is "acceptable" to be talking about their spiritual lives in such intimate and
personal terms. The director can help alleviate some of these concerns by
pointing to other models within Judaism of spiritual companionship and
guidance, such as those cited above, as well as by pointing to those Jews (in
this generation as well as past generations) who might be role models for living the "devotional life." The director can also become familiar with some
of the resources in this new field (books and articles[21] as well as the new
training programs that are emerging, and the opportunities for spiritual
direction being offered at the rabbinical seminaries).

Similarly, one who provides direction for Jews might become familiar
with other modes within Jewish experience—for example, the contemplative mode, as reflected in some of the medieval writings (such as Moshe
Chayim Luzzato's *The Path of the Just* or Rabbi Bachya Ibn Pakuda's *Duties
of the Heart*) or the devotional mode reflected in the Hassidic writings (such
as those of The Baal Shem Tov, Rabbi Yaaokov Yosef of Polennoye, Rebbe
Nachman of Bratzlav, and so on).[22]

Finally, it may be helpful for the director to remember—and when
appropriate, to remind the directee—that Jewish spiritual direction is

indeed a new and growing phenomenon. Part of the price of being pioneers in a new field is living through the period of transition that will necessarily take place until spiritual direction becomes more firmly rooted in Jewish life and culture. Those Jews who have encountered the uncertainty or skepticism of their rabbis or members of their Jewish communities when they talk about their experiences in spiritual direction already know this; they also know that the gifts that spiritual direction brings far outweigh the discomfort or awkwardness of the transition period in which we currently find ourselves. They know that spiritual direction offers the possibility of having a deeper and more meaningful relationship with God, and that it offers the possibility of an even richer experience of Jewish religious life and practice. A number of Jews who have been in spiritual direction are now training as spiritual directors. Slowly but surely, as the practice of spiritual direction in its various forms[23] spreads throughout the Jewish community, Jewish life and experience will be transformed. As Jews speak more openly and honestly of their own experiences of God's presence in their lives, as they share with one another moments of transcendence as well as moments of spiritual emptiness, they will support and walk with one another on the spiritual path, the path of life.

Those of us who are called to be companions to Jews in this sacred work know this: we know that the place on which we stand is indeed holy ground. Many of us also have come to trust that the new and growing phenomenon of Jewish spiritual direction is a part of God's mysterious unfolding in the world. And for that, we can only offer our heartfelt and humble prayers of thanksgiving and praise.

For Further Reading

Addison, Howard A. *Show Me Your Way: The Complete Guide to Exploring Interfaith Spiritual Direction.* Woodstock, Vt.: SkyLight Paths Publishing, 2000.

Buber, Martin. *The Way of Man According to the Teaching of Hasidism.* New York: Carol Publishing, 1990.

Buxbaum, Yitzhak. *Jewish Spiritual Practices.* Northvale, N. J.: Jason Aronson, 1990.

Green, Arthur, and Barry W. Holtz. *Your Word is Fire: The Hasidic Masters on Contemplative Prayer.* Woodstock, Vt.: Jewish Lights Publishing, 1993.

Hammer, Reuven. *Entering Jewish Prayer: A Guide to Personal Devotion and the Worship Service.* New York: Schocken Books, 1994.

Ibn Pakuda, Bachya. *Duties of the Heart.* Jerusalem: Feldheim Publishers, 1962.

Lamm, Norman. *The Religious Thought of Hasidism: Text and Commentary.* New York: Michael Scharf Publication Trust/Yeshiva University Press, 1999.

Luzzato, Moshe Chayim. *The Path of the Just.* Jerusalem: Feldheim Publishers, 1974.

Ochs, Carol. *Our Lives as Torah: Finding God in Our Own Stories.* San Francisco: Jossey-Bass, 2001.

Ochs, Carol, and Kerry M. Olitzky. *Jewish Spiritual Guidance: Finding Our Way to God.* San Francisco: Jossey-Bass, 1997.

Schachter-Shalomi, Zalman Meshullam. *Spiritual Intimacy: A Study of Counseling in Hasidism.* Northvale, N.J.: Jason Aronson, 1991.

Weiss, Zari. "Jewish Spiritual Direction." *Presence: The Journal of Spiritual Directors International* 5, no. 2 (May 1999).

PART TWO

Christian Spiritual Traditions

CHAPTER FIVE

How Ignatius Would Tend the Holy

Ignatian Spirituality and Spiritual Direction

Marian Cowan, CSJ

It is with great joy and some trepidation that I will try to explain spiritual direction in the Ignatian tradition. It is a joy because I operate out of this tradition and can only do spiritual direction in the way that is natural to me. It is also intimidating, because I know there are many other Ignatian spiritual directors who would love the opportunity to write this chapter, among them Jesuits of great learning and experience. I pray that I will do justice to Ignatius and his spirit. That being said, I will proceed in joy and hope that my approach to Ignatian spiritual direction will provide opportunity for further exploration and that it may entice some people to make the full Spiritual Exercises of St. Ignatius of Loyola, founder of the Jesuit order.

Let me begin by making a distinction between the terms "Jesuit" and "Ignatian." Although sometimes used interchangeably, these words are actually not synonymous. Jesuit refers to those who make up the Jesuit order, commonly called The Society of Jesus or The Company of Jesus. Since Ignatius founded the Jesuits, all Jesuit spirituality is Ignatian spirituality. But the spirit of Ignatius goes far beyond the religious order that he founded. It includes all people who follow his tradition, whether in the Society of Jesus or not. So the term Ignatian is applied to all those who live out of the Spiritual Exercises. Some of these people are members of other religious communities that have an Ignatian flavor, like the Religious of the Cenacle or the Sisters of St. Joseph. Others are members of Christian Life

Communities, small groups of people throughout the world, all of whom have made the full Spiritual Exercises and who meet regularly in order to deepen the influence of the Spiritual Exercises in their daily lives. Still others are individual laywomen and laymen who are captivated by the power of the Spiritual Exercises in their lives. All these people who live out Ignatian spirituality have had some connection with the Jesuits, at least by making the Spiritual Exercises. Some maintain close contact and collaboration with Jesuits; some do not. But they are all definitely Ignatian.

The common language of those who claim an Ignatian spirituality is the language of The Spiritual Exercises of St. Ignatius, because it is in the Spiritual Exercises that we see most clearly what Ignatian spirituality is all about. The direction of the Exercises, as Ignatius would have us do them, is good spiritual direction, pure and simple. Therefore, it seems appropriate to use the Spiritual Exercises as a way of exploring Ignatian spiritual direction and how this great saint of the sixteenth century would tend the holy today. In order to do this, I need to introduce you to the man himself, whom his parents named Iñigo, and whom we have come to know as Ignatius of Loyola.

Who Is Ignatius of Loyola?

Ignatius was born in the Basque country of Spain in 1491, just about the time Christopher Columbus was setting sail on his momentous adventure resulting in the discovery of a "new world." At the same time, the Moors were being driven completely out of Spain. These two incidents were shaping events in the young lad's life. First, the expanded horizons of 1492 opened up a world of new thinking and paradigm shifts. Second, the House of Loyola had been involved in the freeing of Spain from the invader, and Ignatius wanted to distinguish himself in battle, too.

While still a very young child, Ignatius lost his mother in death. Before many more years passed, the noble House of Loyola came upon hard times, and in about 1507 the boy was sent to join the household of the royal treasurer of Spain. Here he grew up, learning the ways of the court: how to listen with attentiveness and to speak with deliberation, how to be loyal both to king and to companions, how to defend one's honor, and how to conduct oneself in battle. Ignatius learned his lessons well. Eventually the aspiring knight, who wanted to distinguish himself in the service of the king, now in the service of the Duke de Najerá, had his opportunity to lead a battle—the futile defense of the city of Pamplona.

Ignatius emerged from the battle of Pamplona with a shattered leg, abruptly ending his career as a soldier and sending him back to Loyola to recuperate. It was during his long and painful recuperation that the healing of his soul also took place. Having only two books to read, one *The Lives of the Saints* and the other *The Life of Christ,* he used his imagination for enter-tainment. Daydreams filled the lonely hours—first, dreams of knighthood and romance, which later gave way to imagining himself as another St. Francis or St. Dominic. The romantic daydreams delighted him while they lasted, but soon faded and left him restless. The more spiritual ones delighted him also, and they did not leave him dry as they subsided. Taking note of this, Ignatius began to understand discernment of spirits, which later he put into the Spiritual Exercises. He began taking copious notes about what he was experiencing.

When fully healed, Ignatius left Loyola for Montserrat, a place of pil-grimage in northern Spain. Here he made a general confession, laid down his arms before a famous statue of Mary, gave his courtier's clothing to a beggar, and donned the garb of a pilgrim. He walked to Manresa, where he stayed for over a year. It was at Manresa that Ignatius made the next great progress in his spiritual journey. He spent long hours in prayer and was graced with a variety of spiritual experiences, the most notable of which took place as he was sitting by the Cardoner River. It was what he termed "an illumination," in which God opened his mind to divine truths. During this time in Manresa, Ignatius suffered through an extreme case of scruples, which led him to the brink of ending his life. When he realized that such an outcome could not be from God, he was able to overcome the scruples. This experience gave him more insight into discerning the spirits. It was during his sojourn in Manresa that the pilgrim, as he identified himself, began holding spiritual conversations with people and learned how to apply his listening skills in a new way.

Beginning at Manresa, Ignatius saw that his own conversion process was mirrored in many other people's experience, although each was unique. He began to experiment with what he was learning through his spiritual conversations, seeing parallels and finding patterns of spiritual development. Thus, he was led to begin formulating what later became the Spiritual Exercises.

Following an abiding desire, Ignatius went to the Holy Land to convert the "infidel" there. He was filled with a holy zeal that was not sanctioned by God or the Franciscans, who were in charge of the holy places. They did not allow him to stay in Jerusalem, lest he incite riots or even be killed. Returning to Spain undaunted, he once again engaged people in spiritual conversations, which resulted in his being brought before the Inquisition several times. Who was this relatively uneducated layman who was preach-ing the word of God? What gave him the authority to do it? Nothing amiss was found in his theology, but these experiences made him realize that he needed more formal study, so he first learned Latin in order to pursue higher studies. Over the next few years he engaged in the formal study of philosophy and theology, first in Spain and then in Paris. It was in Paris, where he roomed with Francis Xavier and Pierre Favre, that he actually began giving the Spiritual Exercises, developing them and altering them as he experienced the need. This small group of men became "friends in the Lord" and the nucleus of what would develop into the Company of Jesus. The development of the Company of Jesus makes a fascinating story, but is not necessary to recount here. The Spiritual Exercises were already well on their way to their present form.

The Spiritual Exercises as we know them today were finally approved and published in 1548. Conceived and developed while Ignatius was a layman, the Spiritual Exercises still provide to laymen and women, as well as to priests and religious, one of the most powerful opportunities for spiritual deepening. But one does not enter into the journey of the Exercises alone. One needs to be directed through them. The small volume titled the Spiritual Exercises is a manual for the director of the Exercises, filled with instructions on doing direction well. The book has changed the lives of many people and has stayed with them throughout their lives. It is a school of prayer and a school of spiritual direction.

The *Spiritual Exercises*

The Spiritual Exercises are a structured program of prayer, designed to be practiced over a protracted period of time, with the stated purpose of leading persons to interior freedom, opening them to an ever-deepening relationship with God, and enabling them to encounter God in all things. Sometimes the Exercises are given in a thirty-day period, away from one's ordinary milieu, where the retreatant can give undivided attention to God. Obviously, this manner of making the retreat can only be entered into when the retreatant is free to take thirty days away from home and work for this spiritual enterprise. Taking this into account, Ignatius often gave persons the Spiritual Exercises over a period of months, as a part of their daily living, seeing them regularly to direct their prayer. Today this latter practice is more prevalent than its thirty-day counterpart. At any given time throughout the world, hundreds of people are engaged in the Spiritual Exercises in their daily lives. There are many adaptations of the full Exercises, not the least of which is the opportunity for on-line Spiritual Exercises available from Web sites such as that of Creighton University (www.creighton.edu/collaborativeministry/cm0-retreat.html). Although Ignatian spirituality is not attractive to everybody, there are those who find their home in the Exercises. This is where I find myself.

The Spiritual Exercises, whether given in a thirty-day retreat or a retreat in daily living, are divided into time segments: a preparation time, often termed "disposition days," and four "weeks" of prayer. These time segments are not fixed, but are flexible in order to honor the movement of the Holy Spirit within each retreatant. In fact, every part of the Exercises is meant to be adapted to the individual making them, according to a person's age, abilities, and health. They are to be individually directed. Even though Ignatius had a single desired outcome for the person making the Exercises, the ability and desire of the "exercitant" determines the depth to which he or she may be led in this retreat.

Although the expressed purpose of the Exercises is to deepen one's personal relationship with God, they are in reality apostolic insofar as they lead one to follow Christ in deed as well as in spirit. Ignatius was a contemplative in action. His Spiritual Exercises are meant to be the same, having the retreatant spend much time as a disciple walking with Jesus and eventually becoming an apostle of the Good News. The Exercises are not static, but always move the retreatant towards more.

I describe the Spiritual Exercises in some detail because they present most clearly the way Ignatius would "tend the holy." With years and years of reflection on his own personal salvation history, and the uncounted spiritual conversations he had with other people about their journeys to God, Ignatius stands as a recognized authority on spiritual direction. I find, as do all spiritual directors who have made the Ignatian Exercises, that as I engage in spiritual direction, I have the Spiritual Exercises as a backdrop for all my spiritual conversations. I may not allude to them explicitly, but I am aware of the lessons I have learned at the feet of Ignatius, and apply them when I think it will benefit the directee.

In the paragraphs that follow, I will describe various aspects of the Spiritual Exercises and then make application to spiritual direction. I will follow roughly the dynamic of the Exercises, but I will not attempt to go into very great detail in any part, lest I overreach the purpose of this chapter. Let us now take a close look at this work of Ignatius.

Directions for the Director

The little book of the Spiritual Exercises opens with directives about the Exercises and how to lead one through them. Ignatius begins with the admonition that the director, in suggesting a Scripture passage for prayer, should be restrained in presenting the material, simply narrating the facts accurately and giving a summary explanation, so as not to interfere with the movement of the Holy Spirit within the directee's prayer. Ignatius wants the director to let God deal directly with the retreatant.

An important aspect of the director's work is the ability of the director to discern the movements of the spirits both within the directee and within the self of the director. The director needs to assess what is going on in the directee, whether the person is in consolation or desolation, for instance, and when to introduce the topic of discernment into the retreat. Ignatius warns against introducing too much at once, and to raise the matter of discernment only when the spiritual experiences of the exercitant warrant it. If the exercitant is being tempted, either rather grossly or quite subtly, the director proceeds with great compassion and tenderness to open the eyes of the retreatant to the temptation. Discernment also requires that the director recognize the various movements within him or herself as well as those within the directee.

The director must take care not to urge the exercitant this way or that, but remain as "a balance at equilibrium, permitting the Creator to deal directly with the creature, and the creature directly with our Creator and Lord." The director listens and asks questions, but does not try to sway the directee by offering an opinion. A director may desire that the directee make a certain choice, but is not at liberty to push the directee to make that choice. God may choose otherwise. The director may ask many practical questions, but in such a way that the Creator, without any interference, can work directly with the retreatant. At the same time, Ignatius instructs that, if the exercitant is dealing with an inordinate attachment in decision-making, the director should instruct about methods of prayer to counteract the attachment.

Then there is the matter of adapting every part of the Spiritual Exercises to the exercitant. One is never to insist that a retreatant go through the Exercises exactly according to the book, but the director takes a person through the Exercises with an approach that honors where a person is in his or her spiritual journey and according to that person's capabilities.

Are these not all sound spiritual direction practices? Is it not good spiritual direction to tailor one's approach to the directee? To listen carefully for the movements of the spirits, both in oneself and in the directee? To refrain from saying too much, as well as avoiding trying to influence unduly the choices of the directee? These directives for the one leading another through the Exercises are reiterated throughout the retreat, because Ignatius learned from experience the art of listening and engaging another in spiritual conversation.

The Principle and Foundation

The Spiritual Exercises begin with consideration of "The Principle and Foundation" of our lives, assisting us to encounter God as our loving and compassionate Creator. We recall our own personal salvation history, the myriad ways that God has entered into our lives and has drawn us along the path of grace. Usually, when a directee is asked about his or her image of

God, the response will be quite lovely: "God is my loving Creator and Lord. I can always depend on God. God and I have a good relationship." When put to the test, however, we see this is often simply a person's first, stated response to the question "Who do you say that I am?" But what we say about God to another is not always the way we truly encounter God. A second layer of response to that question, deeper than the first, is to answer: "Who is the God to whom I pray? How do I address this God?" This tells me much more about my God and myself than the first question. However, this, too, may be a bit misleading. There is a third and still deeper layer of response accessed by questions like "What do I say to this God? What do people hear me say about this Deity when I am not trying to answer their queries?" Do I find myself blaming God for things, saying such things as "Why is God doing this to me? What have I done to deserve this? God must be punishing me." Or do I find myself saying, "God, you have never failed me yet; you will see me through this." These two responses point out very different operative images of God. It is the unusual directee whose operative image of God is entirely consonant with his or her stated image, although it does sometimes happen. Working through their personal salvation history is a very effective way for exercitants, or any directees, to get in touch with the image of God that is operative in their lives.

This entry point of the Exercises, "The Principle and Foundation," also helps us to get ends and means straight in our lives. The end for which we are created is union with God, through and in our wonderful universe, affecting and being affected by all that is. Everything else, like having health or being ill, having wealth or being poor, living a long or a short life, and so on, is a means to this end.

In our ordinary day-to-day existence, we may easily tend to make an end out of one or another of these means, becoming inordinately attached to some created reality. We need help in getting free of this distortion. Our spiritual director works with us toward this interior freedom, possibly drawing our attention back to our image of God, assisting us to discover whether the image of God that we profess is indeed actually operative in our lives. Getting us in touch once again with our loving Creator, who only wants our fulfillment, and leading us to consider the presence of God within all of reality are part and parcel of good spiritual direction. Thus we see that this introduction to Ignatian spirituality has a parallel in ongoing spiritual direction in everyday life.

The Reality of Sin

In the Exercises, once we experience God as truly a loving Creator who has a deep desire for the fulfillment of all of creation, we are ready to look at what works at cross-purposes with that divine desire. The retreatant looks at sin, first through the Judeo-Christian Scriptures and then with an unflinching look at sin in the world today. We need to know how sin affects us and how we participate in the sin of the world. We claim our own sinfulness, noting not only the specific sins that permeate our lives but, more importantly, the patterns of sinfulness that assail us. Each prayer period or "exercise" ends with our coming before Jesus on the cross, where we encounter the unconditional love of God made visible. Ignatius warns that the director is not to probe for sins, does not even need to know the specific sins of the exercitant. However, most retreatants trust the director so deeply by this point in the relationship that they talk freely about their sinfulness. If this week of the Exercises is entered into well, exercitants will probably be graced with a profound experience of being loved by God within their very sinfulness.

It is obvious that we live in a world of confusion and sin, where an honest look at the reality of sin and our part in it keeps us from living in a dreamworld. Our directees are coping with the real world all the time. They bring to us spiritual directors the impact of sin upon their lives as well as how they are trying to deal with it. They talk about their own weakness, not only about their consolation in prayer. Sometimes they cannot name what is troubling them in prayer: that they are in a spiritual desolation due to some sinful tendency still unattended. Sometimes they are blatantly sinning and call out to us for help. They want us to challenge them, to console them, to encourage them, and, most of all, to love them unconditionally. This is where the spiritual director is clearly not acting like a moral theologian, but is letting God love the directee through him or her. If the role of the spiritual director is always to assist a directee to come to God, then a directee experiencing sin needs to be led into the healing presence of our compassionate and loving God. Sometimes a directee begins to talk about greed or lust or other sexual issues. Sometimes it is cheating at work or fear of standing up for what is right. Sometimes it is just plain selfishness. Whatever the sin described, the director will do well to assist the person to get beneath the actual sins to the sinful tendencies that underlie these actions. Standing in the place of God, whether we want to or not, the way we receive this part of a person's life is crucial for his or her ongoing image of God and self. We learn in spiritual direction that each person is beloved of God, so we treat the person accordingly, with tenderness and mercy. We do not minimize what an individual says, but we help to put it into perspective. We want our directees to know that God loves them, even within their sinfulness, so we do everything in our power to make that clear. Nothing can separate us from the love of God, not even sin. Even without the structure of the Spiritual Exercises, a person can experience the love of God beautifully, even before trying to make everything right. In fact, if a directee feels the need to wash away sins before approaching God, there is work to be done through spiritual direction about the directee's image of God and self-image.

Desire to Follow Jesus

At the end of the first week of the Spiritual Exercises, Ignatius presents an exercise entitled "The Call of the King" as a transition exercise into the second week. Ignatius uses his own experience to present a parable, painting a picture of an earthly king who calls willing followers to join him in driving out the "infidel." He then applies the parable to Christ, who invites all to follow him in the battle against evil in the world. In both the parable and the application, Ignatius suggests that anyone in their right mind would be drawn to follow such a one as this. Because the retreatant has just experienced his or her own sinfulness and the love of God that is not curtailed by this reality, the response is usually spontaneous and wholehearted: "Yes, I see the need; I know the effects of evil; I want to follow you in winning the world for love." The retreatant also realizes that part of the battleground is within the self.

Spiritual direction of Christians builds upon their desire to live a Gospel-based life, a desire that is often the motivating factor bringing them to seek spiritual direction in the first place. Awareness of their sinfulness is no longer a deterrent to listening for the call of Christ in their lives. They have come to see that there is more to life than what the prevailing culture presents and they have become seekers after "the more." As spiritual directors, are we not often assisting a directee to hear the still, small whisper of grace? We pray with and encourage our directees in their seeking, we teach them to interpret possible pitfalls they may be encountering, and most of all we point them in the direction of Jesus, whose call to "the more" they are experiencing.

An Interior Knowledge of Jesus Christ

Following "The Call of the King," the retreatant making the Spiritual Exercises begins to contemplate Jesus in every aspect of his life. Beginning with the incarnation and proceeding through all the childhood mysteries, the hidden life not revealed through the Gospels, the active life of Jesus and his passion, death, and resurrection, the exercitant enters into the time and space of Jesus, asking for grace to know him more intimately, to love him more deeply, and to follow him more closely. Ignatius teaches a kind of contemplation that leads the retreatant to grow in the knowledge and love of Jesus. As we come to know Jesus better, we also come to know ourselves better.

Drawn into the very mystery we are contemplating, we find ourselves discovering more of our strengths and weaknesses, our deeper desires and our attachments, some of which are not ordered to the end for which we are created. In each exercise, Ignatius tells us to ask for what we desire, and then tells us what would be an appropriate desire. Knowing our desires and expressing them makes them more real to us.

An example of Ignatian contemplation would be my own contemplation of part of the Last Supper when I was making the Spiritual Exercises. I had come to the retreat from a difficult situation at work. We were a staff of twelve people and were not in good space with one another at the time. Although I had put that out of my mind while on retreat, it was not out of God's mind. Both God and I had some definite desires for my work situation. Beginning the prayer, I used the words of Ignatius, asking that I might know Jesus better, love him more dearly, and follow him more closely, and then I turned my imagination over to the Holy Spirit to be used in prayer. As I entered into the scene in the upper room, I saw in my imagination something like the traditional pictures of the Last Supper, except that I was there as well. I watched and listened and observed what was going on. We had not been there very long when Jesus rose from the table and wrapped a towel around his waist. He picked up a large bowl and a pitcher of water and began to wash everyone's feet. As I watched, an astonishing thing happened: The twelve apostles suddenly became the twelve of us on staff. I did not make this happen; it just happened. Jesus seemed to want me to pay close attention to what occurred next. As he knelt before each person and took their feet so tenderly in his hands, he looked up into the face of that person and exchanged a few private words. I could not hear what was said, nor did I feel a need to know. I saw the beautiful love that passed between Jesus and the staff person, and that was enough for me. And when Jesus came to me, I was deeply moved, realizing that this scene shift was entirely for my benefit. When I emerged from that contemplation, I had new feelings for the rest of the staff as well as for myself, new respect and new hope that we would work together much better in the future.

In ongoing Christian spiritual direction we keep turning our directees to Jesus Christ. It is an ever-deepening knowledge and love for Jesus that reveals more of the fullness of God and a concomitant understanding of our own humanness. It is Jesus who is the revelation of the Godhead, and it is Jesus who is also the finest revelation of humanity. Although we may not teach each of our directees how to do an Ignatian contemplation, we do encourage them in their response to Jesus' call to intimacy with him. Sometimes I do teach a person how to contemplate Scripture in the manner of Ignatius, even though they may never make the full Exercises. I show them how to set the stage for their contemplation by recalling the context for the specific Gospel passage they wish to pray through. I ask them to turn their imagination over to the Holy Spirit, then how to see and hear and observe what is going on in that moment in Jesus' life. I tell them how to interact with Jesus within the contemplation and how to draw fruit from the contemplation. Most directees, unless they have been introduced to the Spiritual Exercises, find this manner of contemplating to be a new adventure. Some take to it immediately and some are more drawn to the quiet contemplation of centering prayer. Each is equally fine. As a spiritual director, I like to offer my directees a variety of prayer forms if they exhibit such a desire.

Another aspect of this kind of prayer is the reflection afterward. As we make the Spiritual Exercises, we are taught to spend a little time at the close of each exercise to reflect on what happened during the period of formal prayer. We look at what has attracted us, as well as what we preferred to avoid. We pray from these points in the next prayer period. In spiritual direction, we directors know the importance of being reflective, both for ourselves and for our directees. We jot down the things that have struck us in our direction conversation, lest we lose them to memory. We encourage our directees to become reflective over their lives, to journal their ups and downs, and to pray about this.

Discernment of Spirits

At the heart of the Spiritual Exercises is learning how to discern the origin of our desiring. Each of us knows the pull and tug of various urges, some for our well-being and some for our downfall. These pulls, tugs, urges, and desires are movements that come from different sources. One of these sources is God and the other is not-God or, as Ignatius calls it, "the enemy of our human nature." We can tell where a movement is coming from if we can tell where it is leading, says Ignatius. If we can play out in our imagination where a particular desire will lead us—closer to God or farther away from divine love—we can be sure which spirit is behind that urge.

Ignatius calls those movements toward God and toward the deepest truth of ourselves "consolation," and he calls those movements away from faith, hope, and love and into self-centeredness "desolation." Harking back to his recuperation time in Loyola, Ignatius recognizes the movements of the spirits in his own life and wants the retreatant to know the same. Thus we can choose to follow the movements of grace and avoid falling into the temptations of the enemy of our human nature. We come to recognize the patterns of temptation in our own lives as well as the gentle pull of divine grace. As we come to understand the value system of the Gospel more clearly and in greater detail, through contemplation of Jesus, and as we grow in our understanding of the value system of the world, we are equipped to make better choices in our lives.

At the heart of my spiritual direction is assisting directees to discern the movements of the spirits in their lives. As directees grow to trust me, they are willing to look at their weak spots, those places where the enemy would attack. As they talk about their desires and their choices, we look at how God is within those choices and how they may be open to temptation. We learn the subtleties of the enemy of our human nature as they apply to these directees, so as not to be surprised by them when they come to light. Ongoing spiritual direction provides a venue for fine-tuning directees' abilities to discern in their own right. If spiritual direction can assist persons to become adept in this, it is a great gift that will stand directees in good stead for the rest of their lives.

Dealing with Inordinate Attachments

In the middle of the Spiritual Exercises, Ignatius places a note, which at first blush looks rather innocuous. However, I find it to be such a powerful suggestion that I often use it in regular spiritual direction. It is this: If I find that I am inordinately attached to something, I should pray in the following manner. I should honestly acknowledge to God that I would rather not pray this prayer, because I desire so much that to which I am attached. However, if the object of my attachment is really not that salutary for me in my spiritual growth, I ask God to remove it from my life. This, in my words, is the gist of Ignatius's note. Testing it out in my own life, I have realized firsthand that this prayer demands a lot. I have also found two different results from praying in this manner. On some occasions, I found that my attachment was indeed inordinate, and that I needed to be purified of this disordered love. God took the object of my attachment out of my life. Feeling chagrin and lots of pain, I then remembered that this was precisely the point of my prayer. This realization lessened the sting and eventually it gave way to gratitude. On other occasions, I experienced an opposite result: my attachment underwent purification and the object of my desiring no longer occupied the place of God. I became free in my attachment.

Knowing from experience the power of this prayer, I recommend it to my regular directees when a situation warrants it. When I find directees caught in attachments that are leaving them unfree, burdened by distress at the thought of losing that to which they cling yet feeling a bit worried about where this attachment is taking them, I suggest to them the possibility of the use of this prayer form. Most often, the attachment has to do with another person. Directees' initial reaction is usually not entirely positive. Admitting to God that they have a troubling attachment that they are loath to relinquish is not the problem. That step pales by comparison to the next step of asking for the object of their attachment to be removed, if it indeed is not in their best spiritual interest. One can imagine how difficult this is when the object of the attachment is a lover, even when it is an illicit love affair. Sometimes directees put off praying for many months. But when they finally do enter into this prayer, albeit tentatively at first, they do become graced with the balance they so ardently desire.

Making a Graced Decision

As the Exercises unfold, it becomes clear that the call of Jesus involves a *metanoia* on the part of the retreatant. Some people enter into the Spiritual Exercises with the expressed desire to make a decision about their lives, whether to marry or not, whether or not they should enter religious life or leave religious life, and so on. Others have already settled into their life choice and are not seeking a change. Ignatius suggests that these persons look at their lives and see how better to live within the commitment they have made. The call of Jesus would necessarily be within the context of the retreatant's life choice. As a retreatant contemplates Jesus, particularly in his active life, the desire to follow him more closely often begins to specify itself into a particular way of doing so. This is often manifest in a true desire to live the Gospel more visibly and more tangibly, including ideas for concrete ways in which reform of life is needed. Exercitants bring this to the director of the Exercises to get help in discerning if it is indeed their call. Traditionally this has been called "the election" of the retreat, the deep, life-altering call to live Christ's values, no matter what the consequences.

In a tiny volume called *Discovering Your Personal Vocation: The Search for Meaning through the Spiritual Exercises* (Paulist Press, 2001), Herbert Alphonso, SJ, presents a different take on the election. Alphonso points out that a simple retreat resolution does not need the Spiritual Exercises, but can be arrived at in the time frame of a day of recollection, or a short retreat. So the election is not the same as a retreat resolution. What Alphonso indicates by "personal vocation" is not "what I am called to," but rather, "what I am called." Noting that each of us is really a unique, unrepeatable, and irreplaceable expression of the Living God, the question becomes: "What does God call me?" or "What is God wanting to say to the world expressly through me? What aspect of God do I embody and express?" It is Alphonso's conviction that the Spiritual Exercises should lead one to discover this reality. However, it will only happen if the director is attuned to this possibility.

In applying this to regular spiritual direction, I must confess that I find Herbert Alphonso's approach most helpful, although not at all dichotomous to the traditional interpretation of the election. There are two things at work in me here. As I listen to directees talk about choices they need to make, I take out my discernment toolbox and get to work with them. I assess whether they have already made their decisions and are looking for confirmation of their choices, whether they are attracted by each of the options before them, or whether they are working without affect and must make choices by prudent and careful thought. I then show directees how to proceed accordingly, gathering all the data about every possible choice, getting in touch with the affect accompanying each, or, in the absence of affect, weighing the reasons for and against each choice. Sometimes I suggest the use of art to free the subconscious and let it speak. When all the information has been gathered and the choice is made, I ask the directee to ask God for a confirmation of the choice, which will manifest in a deep peace that the world cannot give. This is, in a nutshell, the traditional method of Ignatian discernment. Adding to this the insights of Alphonso, I also point out to directees that they are expressions of God and indicate that every choice should be made in the light of this reality. Indeed, the "right" choice is arrived at not by trying to psyche out what God desires, but by trying to see the situation from God's point of view and making the choice that will most draw one to the truth of oneself as a particular expression of God.

When I first read Alphonso's book, I was thrilled to have this eminent Jesuit applying to the Spiritual Exercises what I have been talking about with my directees for a long time. Particularly when I encounter directees selling themselves short or operating out of a poor self-concept, I invariably challenge them to experience themselves as who they really are. When they hear themselves saying to someone who has just complimented them, "If you only knew, . . ." I suggest they hear God saying to them, "If *you* only knew, you could not help but love yourself, because you are my very energy in human form. You are a burning bush, afire with my presence." It is so easy for us to tell other people that they are made in the image and likeness of God, but oftentimes it is difficult to accept it for ourselves. I point out that it is arrogant to claim to be the only exception to being made in the image and likeness of God. And we talk about what being made in the image of God means—not just a reflection of God but also the very stuff of divinity.

Ignatius puts it this way: We are like sunbeams to the sun. The sunbeam is not the sun, yet it contains everything of the sun in its rays. We are like drops of water to the waterfall. The drop of water is not the waterfall, yet it contains everything of the waterfall within it. We are the sunbeams; God is the Sun. We are the drops of water; God is the waterfall. This whole aspect ties in with the cosmology that teaches us that we all share the same energy, not only with each other, but also with all the rest of creation. Is not that shared energy the very energy of God? More than 450 years ago, Ignatius was talking in terms like this as he wrote the "Contemplation to Attain Divine Love" and added it to the Spiritual Exercises.

Experiencing God in All Things

In the final piece of the Spiritual Exercises, the "Contemplation to Attain Divine Love," Ignatius shows himself to be the mystic we know he had become. This exercise is not well named in English, although various translators try to make it clear. Actually, it is about how God desires to share love with each one of us. The exercise begins with the statement of two presuppositions: first, real love always shows in deeds as well as in words, and second, true love is mutual. Ignatius explains that the lover always wishes to share all with the beloved, material things and insights and all possessions. The beloved experiences the same thing, the desire to share all with the beloved. Thus lover and beloved exchange places in the dance of love: now being lover, giving; now being beloved, receiving. The extraordinary thing about this loving mutuality is that we are talking about the love between God and every human creature. That God desires this mutuality with us is awesome.

The first of the points to be contemplated within this exercise is that God has graced us with all of creation, the entire universe of stars and planets and sky, of earth and fire and wind and water, of rocks and plants and all sorts of living creatures. This is a gift to the beloved, who is moved to respond in like manner, giving all that we have, be it ever so little.

The second point speaks of God who has not kept aloof from all of creation, but informs everything, giving everything life and sustaining all in being. I spoke about this sharing of divine energy above. God does not remain separate from creation, but all that has being is "an epiphany of God, Who is the essence of all living things," as Tom Stella writes in *The God Instinct: Heeding Your Heart's Unrest* (Notre Dame, Ind.: Sorin Books, 2001). This reality, taking root in the consciousness of the retreatant, evokes a like response of not holding back from the gift to the beloved, but of giving the self within the gift.

The third point describes the love of God made manifest as one who labors for us, always offering ways to lead us to our true home in God. We are often unaware of this labor, taking life for granted and chalking up to circumstance what is really divine love at work. As we become aware of love's labor, we are moved to make a like oblation of ourselves, wanting to match love for love.

Finally, the fourth point is about God living within us, giving us everything we need. Like the sunbeam to the sun or the drop of water to the waterfall, God flows through us as energy. Do we need courage? Hope? Perseverance? All comes, not by begging a God who is separate from us, but by letting the divine energy flow from within. The only fitting response to this great love is a like offering of the totality of self. Ignatius puts the words of this prayer on the lips of the retreatant after each point: "Take, Lord, and receive all my liberty, my memory, my understanding, and my entire will— all that I have and possess. You have given it all to me. To you, Lord, I return it. Everything is yours; do with it what you will. Give me only your love and your grace. That is enough for me."

As a director of the Exercises I often find that I need to explain that in this prayer I do not ask God to take *away* from me my liberty, memory, understanding, and so on, but that I am asking God to use these faculties of my being. I offer them to my Beloved to be filled with divine love so I can be effective in whatever way God wishes to use me. All I need is God's love and grace, and I can let God do anything through me.

In ordinary spiritual direction I sometimes encounter directees who are either ripe for this understanding of a God who desires such a mutuality of love or who are already experiencing it. When I use the words of Ignatius, it strikes a chord of understanding. Such directees are advanced in the spiritual life and are attuned to God's presence in all things.

Sometimes, however, I need to explain to directees what is meant by the phrase "finding God in all things." It has nothing to do with reading God into things, blaming God for disasters, saying this or that is God's will. Rather, it involves opening ourselves to an encounter with God in whatever presents itself to us. God is present in all things, seen and unseen. We are invited to experience this presence in nature, in people, in circumstances, in everything. God is the essence of all that is, and God is within all, in ways that will benefit us. So I ask a directee, "Are you able to feel (or know) God with you in this terrible moment?" "Do you realize that what you are describing as luck is really God's grace?" Finding God in all things turns life into a love story between God and the directee. It leads one far from self-centeredness into love of all creatures. It puts one at the disposal of God to bring all of creation one step closer to its fulfillment. Spiritual direction at its finest facilitates this movement.

Conclusion

Ignatian spiritual direction is indeed multifaceted. It takes the whole of the Spiritual Exercises, which are in fact very succinct, to show what spiritual direction is all about in the Ignatian tradition. Some of what Ignatius gives us through the Exercises was not new even to him. After all, he had studied the lives of some of the great saints who preceded him. What was new was his way of putting together these insights, offering a way of transformation that he learned by experience. Spiritual direction in the Ignatian tradition, then, is about facilitating a directee's journey in conversion, in discipleship, and in the movement to becoming an effective apostle of Jesus. It is about helping the directee toward an abiding, interior, felt knowledge of God's love, both personal and universal, and to live into a fitting response to that love. It is about assisting a person in discovering the holy. It is about tending the holy in that person and celebrating the holy in all created reality.

CHAPTER SIX

From a Graceful Center

Spiritual Directions for Evangelicals

Lisa A. Myers

The subject of spiritual direction with evangelicals is a timely one. In the twenty years of my involvement in spiritual direction within a broadly evangelical context,[1] the phone has never rung so consistently with calls for spiritual direction and requests for referrals. In the past, eyes glazed over with boredom or narrowed with suspicion when I responded to questions about my ministry. Today eyes more often light up with recognition and delight. Interest in spiritual direction is quickly gaining momentum among evangelicals. The demand for directors is already beginning to overwhelm and outrun the supply.

At the same time that spiritual direction is moving rapidly towards the center of consciousness in the evangelical community, it is emerging from the margins of academic consideration and pastoral practice in evangelical seminaries and churches, but at a slower pace. There continues to be an urgent need for training, mentoring, and supervision of directors who are familiar with the tradition and are called to work with this population. Also needed are spiritual and theological resources that address the evangelical audience, deal with specifically evangelical issues, and provide creative vision for the effort to renew the historical practice of direction within the current evangelical context.

Already, new programs are being created to train directors. The number of articles and books being written by evangelicals and for evangelicals on the theory and practice of spiritual direction is increasing to meet the emerging needs of this population. At the same time that the necessary work of integration is progressing within the evangelical context, many experienced evangelical directors have already been introduced to spiritual direction and received training in mainline Protestant, Roman Catholic, or ecumenical contexts. Furthermore, many of those seeking direction, training, or supervision as directors will continue by choice as well as by necessity to be enriched and guided by directors whose own spiritual identity and practice are rooted in other branches of the Christian tradition. This makes the present conversation regarding the issues, needs, challenges, and opportunities that present themselves when doing spiritual direction with evangelicals a critical one. Evangelicals and non-evangelicals working with evangelicals in spiritual guidance have the opportunity to develop a dialogue of discovery across their respective traditions, sharing their perspectives with authenticity and mutual respect. It is time to work together to expand and deepen the ministry of spiritual direction in every part of the contemporary church and to make it increasingly available to all those who long for a deeper experience of God.

This chapter is but one brief contribution to the dialogue that is already begun. I write out of my experience as a director—not so much to inform as to invite, not so much to explicate as to suggest. The perspective outlined here is not intended to be a definitive evangelical statement. However, the content and dynamic that I have observed over time with many evangelicals do demonstrate consistent patterns of invitation and response. I suggest that these patterns of invitation and corresponding responses can be identified and described as movements of grace being experienced by the population as a whole that can be mapped and signposted as new spiritual directions being taken by the evangelical tradition.

As I have worked in this field and reflected on my experiences with many individuals, groups, and whole communities, I have come to see these unique individuals and varied groups not only separately, but together, as one whole, composite person who seeks God. From this perspective, I have identified a series of invitations that seem to have emerged progressively over time in the life of this "one" sought and claimed by God for love and life. I see a linkage among these invitations that shows a trail of footsteps that, when looking backward, mark the path already taken, and when looking forward, begin to provide an orientation that may guide the journey into the future. They are the leadings and learnings that have been recognized in the prayer and life of first one person and then another—to me they seem to open out into new paths of discovery and experience with God for an entire community.

So this is an invitation from my experience to yours, to reflect on how God is already doing something among the evangelical population and how it may be important and helpful for us to pay attention to that something. Perhaps these directions diverge from the normal indicators evangelicals and others usually look to when considering the integrity and well-being of the community and the future of the tradition, since my concern is not with theological or sociological trends, program strategies, or cognitive commitments. What I do propose is that the movements of heart, grace, and Spirit so foundational in the context of spiritual guidance are emerging in a significant and unique way at the intersection of evangelical tradition and the ministry of spiritual guidance today.

Evangelicals and the Evangelical Tradition

The directions being offered here have emerged in the context of spiritual guidance given and received by persons in community identified as being part of a large group of denominations, subgroups, and communities that have been accurately described, but less precisely defined, as the "evangelical" tradition. Opened most broadly, the evangelical umbrella includes groups diverse in their expressions of faith and practice that have legitimate historical, theological, or ecclesiastical causes for mutual critique and even recrimination. Pentecostal, charismatic, fundamentalist, and African American churches are all included in the broad category. From a global perspective, evangelicalism crosses every national and racial boundary and constitutes the fastest growing Christian communion in the world today. Evangelical historian Mark Noll provides a definition of "evangelical" and a way of demarcating the evangelical constituency useful for the purposes of this chapter.

In his book *American Evangelical Christianity: An Introduction,* Mark Noll clarifies three points of reference:

> Whatever its other legitimate uses, "evangelical" is also the best word available to describe the fairly discrete network of Protestant Christian movements arising during the eighteenth century in Great Britain and its colonies. Two complementary perspectives undergird this usage. "Evangelical" refers to the heirs of these Anglo-American religious revivals, but it also designates a consistent pattern of convictions and attitudes.[2]

Noll continues: "These evangelical traits have never by themselves yielded cohesive, institutionally compact, or clearly demarcated groups of Christians. But they do serve to identify a large family of churches and religious enterprises."[3] He then describes three methods that have been used independently to demarcate the evangelical population. They are: 1) self-identification,

2) profession of beliefs historically associated with evangelicalism,[4] and 3) membership or attachment to a historic evangelical movement or denomination.

The directions outlined in this chapter draw on my varied experiences of individual, group, and community guidance with two different populations. The first and larger population is comprised of people in churches or in para-church organizations with whom I have done short-term spiritual guidance in retreats, adult classes, and workshops on spirituality and prayer. The second group includes individuals with whom I have done more long-term work in the context of formalized spiritual guidance. Both groups are comprised of persons identified as evangelicals based on one of the three methods provided by Noll. Neither of the groups is a representative cross section of the evangelical population, yet both represent some of the denominational, socioeconomic, and racial/ethnic and national diversity of the evangelical constituency at large.

Each population has an important contribution to make to the discussion of spiritual directions. One primary factor distinguishes the two groups. The group in short-term guidance has often been identified as a "likely" audience and has been "roped into" the experiences of guidance by enthusiastic pastors or fellow church members eager to offer them an opportunity about which they know little or nothing. The group in formal direction is by its very nature an entirely self-selected pool of eager participants. Therefore, although it is this second group that is the primary focus of concern with regard to our discussion, it is important to point out that it is in reference to the first group that many of the patterns and movements characteristic to this population can be more helpfully perceived and evaluated. The differences as well as the similarities between the two groups have been significant in my highlighting some of the patterns and movements and in clarifying their shape and direction over time.

The people in the second group with whom I have worked individually or corporately in spiritual direction share some of the diversity and many of the traits of the larger evangelical tradition of which they are a part, but they also share one distinction: they themselves chose to become involved in spiritual direction when others they knew were not so engaged. Because of their life or prayer, they were invited or impelled to seek companionship and surprised to find it in a less traditional manner. Furthermore, members of this focal group not only sought out a relationship of spiritual direction, but also chose a form of direction clearly contemplative in its orientation and uncompromising in its refusal to become spiritual mentoring, counseling, or discipling—traits quite unusual in the evangelical context until now. Here, silence and shared presence are the norm, and apophatic experience is intentionally valued and encouraged without being preferred over the more commonly affective experience, oriented to word and image, enjoyed by most evangelicals.

The focal group is made up of those I have companioned in individual or group guidance and of those with whom I have shared companionship for six years of facilitated group guidance in community as part of the guidance ministry "Companions in Community" at La Canada Presbyterian Church. Seminarians are represented in the greatest numbers in my private practice of direction, followed proportionally by clergy, church leaders, and other laity. In the Companions Community at the church, the order is essentially reversed. My personal practice includes members of a variety of denominations and independent churches; however, women and evangelical Presbyterians are disproportionately represented in both groups, especially in the Companions Community. As you would expect, the majority has had some experience of prayer, some as "beginners" and some as "proficients." Participants in both groups range in age from the twenty to eighty plus, and most had little or no prior experience of direction.

The Companions Community program intentionally intersects the practices of individual, group, and community guidance in the experience of the participants. As a result, it has provided a unique opportunity for me to compare and contrast the content and dynamics of each of the processes and to reflect on the connections between them. In community it has become possible to begin to notice how the stories of the enlarging circles of community are related and how the threads and themes emerging at each level of community are woven into and through the others. Here again, it is in the contrasts as well as in the comparisons between the different groups that dynamic movements of grace are revealed.

All of the directions offered here began as movements first noticed and named in spiritual guidance. They emerged out of the shared practices of presence, attentiveness, authenticity, and companionship that are core to the spiritual community recognized and received in these intentional relationships. These movements came together and came to life, were questioned and were weighed, in the process of individual and corporate reflection. Tentative and sometimes contradictory at first, these movements stand out to me now as directions discerned and gracefully taken by some individuals and communities within the evangelical context and as indicators of possible future directions for the larger evangelical community as a whole.

Indeed, it seems impossible for any faith tradition to escape crisis in confrontation with the contemporary pluralistic and postmodern realities in which we all live. In every crisis there are issues and needs, challenges and risks, opportunities and invitations that are expressed in different ways for the tradition, for the community, and for the individual. The movements we are considering are contextual movements. They are responses both to

God's initiative in the realities in which we live and to the realities themselves. As a result, each movement has something to say about how God may be present and what God may be doing in crisis. Each movement represents an opportunity or graced invitation that seems to have emerged in relation to an issue or question and involves a challenge that must be met and a risk that must be taken by the tradition or by the community as a whole.

Five Spiritual Directions

There are five directions briefly outlined in this chapter. Each represents a constellation of movements discerned in the context of spiritual direction that I have come to believe signify a direction of change, expansion, or development related to a "center of grace" within the evangelical tradition—one of those wellsprings of life and faith that provides a corporately shared point of reference for conviction and committed action and a source of power for a distinctive evangelical expression of Christian identity or mission. The presentation of each direction begins with the characteristic of evangelical theology or spirituality to which it is connected. The movement itself is summarized from the complex of experience that has constituted it. It is then considered from the point of view of the opportunities and challenges that those within the evangelical tradition must address if they are to recognize within their own experience the direction that has already been discerned and described in the experience of others. Finally, each direction is offered for consideration with regard to its possible significance for the practice of spiritual direction within the evangelical context.

The first direction involves connecting traditions. It begins with renewed appropriation by evangelicals of the role and contribution of the evangelical tradition within the larger church and in the contemporary world. It moves in deepened awareness of its own identity to reinforce connection with the whole history of the church and its many expressions of faith and practice. Direction two involves Scripture and spirituality. It begins with the evangelical emphasis on taking the Bible seriously and moves to broaden the impact of Scripture into new dimensions of personal and corporate life through new practices of biblical engagement and prayer. Direction three concerns spiritual disciplines and the rhythms of grace, beginning with the central evangelical message of the grace of Christ for salvation. It moves to deepened appreciation and experience of the dynamics of grace at work in the life of faith for personal and social transformation. Direction four relates to spiritual community as Trinitarian experience. This movement begins with the strength of the evangelical community's belief in its own spiritual authority and with its emphasis on relationality and practical service in the body of Christ. In contemporary articulations of Trinitarian theology, the evangelical community finds new ways of understanding itself as a spiritual community in the image of God. Direction five is the movement energized by the incorporation of spiritual guidance. It builds on the intentional pursuit of incarnational relationships and practices of personal exhortation and encouragement that have been a foundational part of the evangelical tradition from its beginning. It moves into new ways of understanding the intention and meaning of those relationships and clarifies their limits and possibilities. It refines the framework, increases the options for the practice of personal and corporate discernment, and opens new dimensions of communal contemplative experience.

In summary, the reflection I have done in recent years on my practice of spiritual direction within the evangelical context has led me to two conclusions that shape the presentation offered in this chapter. The first conclusion is that reflection directed over a substantial period of time and across some breadth of experience on a practice of direction that has been focused primarily on individuals and groups who are identified with a particular tradition may make it possible to notice and name movements of significance for the population as a whole. The second is that what has been noticed and named may have value for other directors, directees, and supervisors, especially for those who function similarly for the most part within a single tradition. Although what has been recognized within the evangelical community will most certainly have the greatest value for those connected with spiritual guidance for evangelicals, there may be pieces of what is happening in this context that have relevance for other traditions. In this way, what is presented here may allow the evangelical constituency with whom I work to become a community of reference for other communities of faith. In fact, it may be the dynamic, not the content of the directions, which is of primary importance. A more extended and detailed consideration of the five directions themselves, if merited by the experience and reflection of others, will have to continue in a wider variety of voices and venues than the current presentation permits.

Direction One: Connecting Traditions

For the evangelical community, the first movement is both a question of identity and even of self-preservation as well as an expression of spiritual hunger. It is a digging deep within and a reaching out beyond for the spiritual resources adequate for the needs of the day. It moves in two directions at the same time, and it involves two different challenges. The first challenge is to examine self-reflectively the roots of the evangelical spiritual tradition, to name the strengths and weaknesses of the outgrowth relative to the present situation while preserving the vigor that made evangelicalism such a force in the Great Awakenings and in the global outreach of the Gospel. The opportunity is to reconnect with the roots of the tradition, to identify the new shoots of growth that show promise in the current context, and to prune the growth that is no longer fruitful. The risk for the community in self-examination, as for the gardener in the pruning, is that the very vigor they seek to preserve may be inadvertently dissipated, misdirected, or cut off. The second challenge is to reconnect with the whole church and with the historical Christian tradition in all its complexity and diversity without obscuring the simplicity and focus that at its best is perhaps the greatest strength of the evangelical tradition.[5] It is the simplicity of message and delivery that first made evangelical faith accessible to coalminers in Wales and to common people from all walks of life and that continues to spread it in developing countries around the world. The evangelical focus on the Gospel message of freedom has had the capacity to cut through the many kinds of bondage present at every level of society and discourse.[6] The opportunity is to share in the spiritual riches that belong to the whole church and to experience anew the unity of a faith that transcends time and human barriers.

For the individual, the challenge often surfaces as a question: Where do I belong, and in what community do my spiritual needs get met?[7] A proliferation of options, changing cultural expectations for religious expression, geographical mobility, and consumerism—all may influence the American churchgoer or non-churchgoer and his or her diminishing attachment to a particular faith community. Nevertheless, there is a distinctive character to the mobility among many evangelicals. Their allegiance is to a tradition that crosses denominational boundaries or to the spiritual expression or statement of faith that most closely represents the tradition for them, not necessarily to a denomination or to a community. This allows them to move from congregation to congregation within a denomination, between denominations, or into and out of nonsectarian churches. The question for many of the evangelicals in our population is not so much whether to make a commitment, but what kind of commitment they will make and to what or to whom they will commit. And it is a question that comes up frequently in direction. Many times the ensuing conversation is painfully related to questions of leadership or ordination for persons who do not fulfill a variety of criteria presented by the congregations or churches to which they belong. Just as often, the dialogue may revolve around whether or not the leadership or clergy of the church fulfill the criteria expected by the individual.

It takes time to address the issues, sort out priorities, and reflect on the trade-offs involved in this question of "place." It is in the context of spiritual direction that many people will begin to explore more deeply what it means for them to live in covenant relationships with family, friends, and faith community. They may be invited to consider 1) that their commitments to persons may be as important as their commitments to biblical truths, 2) that those enlarging circles of community are as important in guiding them on the spiritual path as their knowledge of doctrine, and 3) that spiritual maturity comes at the price of both kinds of commitments of self. To assist the directee in locating himself (or herself) within the often perplexing and continually shifting realities of faith in the contemporary context, the director must make space for theological and spiritual reflection that will enable the directee to locate himself within three different traditions. First, he must find his place theologically and spiritually within the denominational or nonsectarian tradition of which he is a part (for example, Presbyterian, or post-denominational charismatic). Second, he must decide where he belongs within the evangelical tradition. Third, he must find his way relative to the broad historical Christian tradition as well as to other faith traditions of the world. Only then can he find his place in the emerging context of contemporary spirituality. Finally, the director can provide the support necessary for the directee to identify and to engage the spiritual resources of each of the traditions in ways that are most appropriate and helpful.

Direction Two: Scripture and Spirituality

The second movement involves what may be the centerpiece of evangelical theology and the keystone of evangelical spirituality: the nature and authority of the biblical text. A movement that currently crosses denominations, traditions, and communions, it could be argued that it is a widespread response to the unrivaled dominance biblical criticism gained and held in the academy in the latter years of Modernity and to the maelstrom of hermeneutical battles associated with it. In this regard, the movement could be described either as a retreat to the "precritical" exegesis of the past or as an advance to the "post-critical" exegesis of the future. Perhaps it is destined to be something of both. The challenges for the evangelical community are many and complex. In the context of what we are addressing here with regard to the spiritual life of the community, the challenge is to respond creatively to the need for a more comprehensive and integrative approach to Scripture, out of which can come theological orientation, spiritual guidance, support for prayer and spiritual growth, and encounter with God. The opportunity is to continue to develop the understanding of Scripture and broaden its use by incorporating a multivalent understanding and holistic experience of Scripture without compromising the evangelical's high regard for Scripture and commitment to Scripture study.

For the individual directee, the issue often emerges at the limit of his or her understanding and experience of the evangelical practice of biblical "study" and prayerful "devotion." Somewhat paradoxically, the "problem" may actually be the unexpected result of too much disciplined study or too intensive a devotion relative to situation of life or stage of prayer. It may involve a too broad focus or an overfamiliarity with Scripture in general that tames and "domesticates" it. Or it may involve a too narrow focus on some aspect of its content or use that reduces it to one dimension; for example, themes of demand and judgment or use as handbook of ethical principles. Either way, the divine and human voice of Scripture is constricted and the text is robbed of both its mystery and its power to speak into the life of the directee in a transformative and life-giving way.

In this regard, intentional "fasting" from the habitual pattern of Scripture use can be helpful. A directee may also be assisted to name the spontaneous "fast," compartmentalization, or guilty rejection of Scripture he has already made and explore the meaning it has for him. More than that, the director can support the directee in multifaceted engagement with Scripture by assisting him in his exploration of other "uses" or "approaches" to Scripture, such as *lectio divina* and the various modes of scriptural prayer associated with the Ignatian Exercises. Seeking out a more diverse community literally and imaginatively in which to hear the text may enable the directee to see and hear through the eyes and ears of others and bring new meaning. Without dishonoring the directee's own convictions concerning the nature, role, and authority of Scripture, the director can assist his theological and spiritual reflection and support him in considering the possibility that Scripture is much more, not less, than evangelicals have often proposed.

Direction Three: Spiritual Disciplines and Rhythms of Grace

The third movement is a movement of deepening appreciation for the ways that grace is at work in the ordinary processes of daily activities as well as in the dramatic events of life. It is also an expression of a need for structure as well as support in the spiritual life. It reorients the evangelical emphasis on one-time conversion and touches the core of the Protestant dilemma regarding our part and God's part in the work of salvation, the nature of human transformation, and the relationship between justification and sanctification. With the resurgence of interest in the spiritual life and the exploration of the historical spiritual tradition has come a reexamination of the role in evangelical spirituality of what some call the "classic" spiritual disciplines as well as a wide variety of spiritual practices and forms of prayer. Without a doubt, there are historical, theological, and spiritual issues involved that need attention, as well as a set of convictions and emotions that must ultimately be sorted out. Nevertheless, there is hope that new perspectives and new paradigms will become possible as the result of real communication and realistic discussion that is taking place within the

Protestant tradition and between Protestants, Roman Catholics, and the Orthodox. At present, the challenge for the evangelical community is to provide instruction and support in the use of spiritual practices and disciplines while continuing the innovative work that will provide the foundation for new integration of theology, spirituality, and psychology. The invitation is to incorporate new and renewed forms of intentional spiritual practice without compromising the call to conversion, diminishing the intensity of devotion experienced in the heartfelt experience of God, or blunting the impulse to action that the evangelical tradition has valued.

For the individual directee, the issue frequently emerges in the struggle to pray, in the concern to be holy, or in the wasteland of burnout following an intensive period of ministry. Different strands of the evangelical tradition have considerably different emphases regarding the proportional value and character of the "inner" and the "outer" journey. In addition, many evangelicals have been "discipled" or formed in the context of para-church movements that have their own vocabulary and accented syllables of holiness, their own images of spiritual maturity. In the confusion, some may respond by taking too much responsibility for their interior life and alternate between hyperactivity and exhaustion. Others, in the absence of adequate definition or direction within their own community, throw themselves entirely into "external" projects of evangelism or social transformation or may even adopt alternative programs of spiritual or psychological development like twelve-step, self-help, or therapy. Of those who abandon concern for growth in holiness, there are some who are "blessed" with uncommon sanctity through no apparent intentionality of their own, some who drift in whatever direction life's circumstances carry them, and some who stay stuck in their conversion experience by repeating it in their own experience or duplicating it in the experience of others.

From the Protestant perspective, creating theological space between justification and sanctification makes spiritual room for grace. However, keeping the room open in the human heart and life is another story. For either the individual or the community, the room once made may become a vacuum that begs to be filled. The question is how to make and protect the space so that only God can fill it. It is in response to this question that the movement toward spiritual practices becomes a movement into contemplation that turns us to God and opens our hands, and a movement of grace that allows us to receive what only God can provide for us.

The attraction to and consistent participation in practices of the kind we are talking about represent a movement of grace and into grace. They are a means of sanity, because through them we are given the opportunity to see ourselves and our condition as human beings accurately. Spiritual disciplines are a means of clarity, because in doing them we are given the opportunity to begin to recognize that the rhythms they structure and the rhythms they reveal are readily available to us in all the aspects of our daily living. They are a means into grace because, when we set our lives to their rhythms, we discover they are God's chosen rhythms into which we are invited. In every rhythm of God's initiative and our response, of receptivity and activity, word and silence, image and imagelessness, being and doing, prayer and action, holding on and letting go, filling up and emptying out, dying and being raised, we are connected to the rhythms of love that form the dance of the Spirit that is God's gift of re-creation to us and to the world.

In the Companions Community we have discovered that it is not only what we agree we believe but what we agree to do together that has enabled us to recognize and participate in the spiritual community God creates in our experience. As a result, the beliefs that we share are embodied in our covenant commitment through practices, processes, and disciplines of spiritual community, and they are expressed in the framework and criteria of our discernment—not in a statement of faith. The practices, processes, and disciplines connect us to the deeper rhythms of grace and make it possible for us to begin to feel the dance and to embrace the identity and purpose that is ours individually and as a community.

For the individual directee, this movement often emerges in the midst of a desert experience in which the spiritual path dwindles to a track or disappears altogether into an apparently desolate and unmarked wilderness. Forward progress seems to stall or slows to a crawl. At a decelerated pace, aspects of the inner and outer landscape that have previously gone unnoticed invite closer inspection and take on new meaning and new possibilities. The director is given numerous opportunities to assist the directee in deepening contemplative awareness and attention to the more subtle dynamics of consciousness and life process, the rhythms and realities that have been previously obscured by the contents of consciousness and the activity of prayer and life. The director can assist the directee in moving "inside" his particular life experience and into Scripture in order to inductively discover and subjectively explore what God is already doing in his or her life. The director may support the directee to both "actively" and "passively" cooperate with the unique manifestations of grace, instead of trying to "direct" his or her own path or growth according to some universal principle or plan.

Direction Four: Spiritual Community as a Trinitarian Reality

This movement emphasizes the interconnection between the individual and corporate experience of God and the profoundly relational character of divine being and human existence. Of the five movements, this movement has taken the longest to become evident; by its very nature, it remains the most difficult to grasp. The most gentle and unassuming in its beginnings, it may very well have hidden within it the potential for the most dramatic impact on the spiritual lives of those it touches.[8]

This movement brings together the theological work that has been done in recent years on the Trinity and the experience of spiritual community that becomes real in the practice of spiritual guidance. Although at first glance it may seem to pair the sublime and the ordinary, there seems to be no other adequate way to understand and put words on the lovely and grace-filled gift of spiritual community that has been and is still being given in those contemplatively oriented relationships. In fact, in reaching beyond the limits of convention to honor and nurture the gift, new connections are being made and new possibilities are opening up. In the shared reflection on experience, when the most familiar metaphors and models for Christian community have begun to fall short, a Trinitarian perspective has provided the language and meaning needed to enable the community to continue to recognize and receive the gift that is being offered and to take the personal risks that are necessary to deepen the reality of intimate communion that they share.

The challenge the evangelical community must meet in order to participate in the progression of this movement involves a twofold shift in thinking and experience: 1) to articulate a Trinitarian and communal understanding of the structure of spiritual experience, and 2) to provide new opportunities for such experience without diluting the redemptive focus of evangelical spirituality, which at its best brings together a Christ-centered focus on salvation and a Spirit-centered focus on empowerment. The opportunity is to incorporate new forms of experience and reflection, which together may lead to deepened understanding and continued participation in the unfolding mystery and dynamic reality of the spiritual community—the heart of the divine life we are invited to share.

For the individual directee, this movement often emerges out of reflection on his or her experience of relationship in spiritual guidance or in some other contemplatively oriented experience of prayer and silence shared in community. It begins with a dawning awareness that he or she is not alone in relationship with God and with a new appreciation for the tangible support experienced through connection with others. The director can provide the stimulus and support the directee in his or her need to recognize and articulate the Trinitarian nature of the shared God experience and to explore new possibilities for worship, prayer, and corporate spiritual practice as ways to extend the new understanding and experience. When requested, the director can further assist the directee to explicitly name and image God as Trinity and to understand himself (or herself) as an individual in relationship with God in community.

Direction Five: Spiritual Direction in the Evangelical Tradition

The fifth movement involves the role of spiritual direction in the evangelical tradition. The fact that the ministry of spiritual guidance is being given an increasingly warm reception by evangelicals is an expression of the need for companionship and guidance on the spiritual journey, even among those who highly value an individual and personal relationship with God. It is no longer a question of whether spiritual direction will be welcomed as an essential part of the ministry of the church, but of how it will be welcomed. The challenge for the evangelical community is to find a place for spiritual direction alongside other forms of soul care and in the spectrum of ministries such as Christian education, spiritual formation and discipleship, and pastoral care, without undermining the primary mission of "making disciples." The way this is done must do justice to the numerous ways, often communally oriented, that spiritual direction and spiritual companionship have been offered historically within the Protestant and evangelical tradition. Spiritual direction also needs to honor the distinctive emphases and values within the evangelical spiritual tradition, especially the refusal to enshrine any method that might support spiritual elitism, "priestly" mediation, or hierarchical status unrelated to call. The invitation is to continue to experience the results of intentional and intensive relationships of spiritual companionship with the persons involved. The opportunity is to celebrate the way that this will change the church.

For the individual directee, this movement expresses itself in both attraction and wariness about becoming involved in spiritual direction. Frequently the directee comes to direction without experience in it and/or without a framework for understanding the pending relationship or what is at stake for directee and director. In a context in which ministry lines are still in the process of being drawn and roles and responsibilities are still being clarified, it is up to the director to assist the directee in differentiating between spiritual direction and personal support or therapy and in deciding what means and forms of spiritual formation, care, or guidance are appropriate. The director can also support the directee in reflecting on his or her experience in direction and in evaluating continued needs as the relationship progresses. Making the process transparent to the directee helps to demystify what is going on and safeguards the interest of both parties.

For the ministry of spiritual guidance and for all of the persons involved, this movement represents tremendous potential and significant risk. Ultimately at stake in each relationship and worthy of protection are the freedom, initiative, and integrity of all parties concerned—the directee, the director, and God—and the integrity of the ministry itself. When each is protected, no outcome can take precedence over interior freedom, authenticity, and responsiveness to God on the part of either directee or director—and God is given a voice that is preeminent above all others. The ministry of spiritual direction cannot be co-opted for any other purpose than attention to God. It retains its subversive edge and its mystical and prophetic dimensions.

Persons and Processes

Having briefly outlined the five directions that I have proposed be understood as movements of grace and invitations to deepening growth in God for an entire community, I believe it is important to add a few more words to my reflection about the persons and processes that together form the subject of the reflection and the foundation for my suggestions. First, my choice to focus on spiritual directions that have emerged in a composite person who exists in spirit and imagination rather than in the concrete and tangible dimensions of everyday life has the potential to obscure the essential fact that there are many individual and very concrete people who make up that reality. Focused attention to movements of grace is one of the primary features that distinguish spiritual direction from every other kind of spiritual care. Nevertheless, it is persons in relationship, not movements, who are the heart of spiritual direction. Second, I believe it may be helpful to say something more about the process of group direction. Many seasoned and knowledgeable directors have chosen to focus their practices on individual direction. As a result, although they may be well acquainted with the practice of group direction, I find that they are often less experienced, and therefore less familiar, with the dynamics of group direction. The directions outlined in this chapter could only have been pieced together and discerned in the context of reflection directed towards the intersecting content and dynamics of both individual and group direction. In addition, the practice of group direction finds deep resonance in the preferences and historical practices of the evangelical population described in this chapter. For these reasons, I want to briefly describe the process of group direction as I have experienced it.

Spiritual movements are not people. They are subtle stirrings, motions of mind and heart and body that carry us closer and sometimes farther from the God at our center and at the center of the universe. They are breezes of Spirit that blow across the chaos and deep waters of our hearts and lives, real people who live in a world that is sometimes all too real in its power to bring life or death to us and to those we love. The movements described in this chapter were first given form and breath in the "yes" to life and to God of individual persons with names and faces and dear, distinctive bodies who have stories all their own, filled with events and circumstances holy and

hilarious that prove the ridiculous and penetrate the sublime. They are dis-
tillations of unnumbered steps of courage as well as anguished moments of
recognition, of incompleteness, inadequacy, and sometimes defeat, but also
of goodness, truth, and beauty, and ultimately of the victory that is ours in
faith. Each movement has meaning and potency only to the extent that it
faithfully represents the decisions and dilemmas of the real people to whom
it belongs and truthfully connects to the countless hours of conversation
and prayerful presence that are at its core.

My understanding and practice of individual and group direction are
based on a simple premise: *always* God is being for us and doing something
in and through us before we know it. Therefore, the task of spiritual direction is not to make something happen, but to become aware of what God
is *already* doing, so that we can respond to it, participate in it, and take
delight in it.[9]

The presence and action of the Trinity is a conviction of Christian faith,
but only an inconsistently and partially realized experience. The presence
and action of God often goes unrecognized. It is dynamic, not static; a
movement, not a position; a gift of ongoing creation, not a possession.
Although it is sometimes quite dramatic, it is more often quite subtle,
imperceptible to all but the most attuned and practiced eyes of faith. It
takes spiritual perception and judgment to uncover and interpret the gentle promptings of the Spirit. The presence and action of God may also be
refused. It takes wonder to awaken to Mystery. It takes humility to follow
Jesus. It takes courage to enter into the dance of the Spirit, to allow the
rhythms of grace to pace and direct our course. We reach our limits as created beings. We are frustrated by the reality of our brokenness and sin. Only
gradually do we enter into the fullness of our promised inheritance as children chosen for glory. We become what we are by invitation and response.

In spiritual direction, God invites us into a shared process of self-giving
and discovery that enables us to better recognize and become a part of what
God is already doing. Often the spiritual director assists the one who seeks
to hear and respond to God's invitations in his or her life by helping to clear
the clutter, sort the voices, deal with the barriers, and nurture the supports that
enable listening and freedom for response. Nevertheless, the primary work of
spiritual direction is giving attention to God. In the patient and intensive
work of contemplative listening and looking, director and directee join
together in the surrender to love that turns us to God and in the prayerful
desire that opens us to receive and share the gift of divine life.

I love the process of individual direction, but nothing that I participate
in as a spiritual guide is more exciting than watching a group process of
direction unfold. In group direction, the work of guidance is shared. Each
member in turn becomes the focus of the process and the group as a whole

acts cooperatively in the role of the director. As a result, the aggregate experience and cumulative wisdom of a community are brought to the process of individual discernment for the benefit of each member of the group. The varied gifts and stories of each group member are folded together, the pieces become more than the sum of the parts, and direction is given and received in unexpected ways. In the process of giving guidance to one member of the group, other members receive guidance for themselves as well. The group members begin to recognize that what God is offering to another individual through the group is frequently being offered in some way to themselves as well.

At the same time, the experience of shared companionship with God is intensified in the context of the community so that certain aspects of spiritual experience gain heightened clarity and deepened expression. The sacrificial giving and receiving of self that happens in the corporate context of group guidance becomes a sacramental reality through which the spiritual community that so frequently remains hidden to us becomes concretely manifest. The connection experienced is obviously different from what we are accustomed to achieving through our preferred modes of social interaction in other contexts. Neither does the connection stay within the bounds of the group but extends in a mysterious way to include the other, continually enlarging circles of spiritual community. In time, the guidance group itself takes on a meaning that transcends its original self-understanding and a purpose that transcends its original intention. Group members begin to recognize that what God is offering to each one through the group, God may also be offering to every one and to the group as a whole—and not only to this group but potentially to every other circle of community to which the group members belong.

For example, one person risks celebrating aloud her sense of God's pleasure in her. Another responds to this as holy invitation by affirmatively expressing herself in new ways. Words and actions break free from dark places of self-denigration and, as the group supports and marvels at them, they too are invited into newness. Silence shared becomes companionship in freedom; as group members are touched at deep levels by another's freedom, they too experience liberation. Words, action, and silence then help group members recognize and support the movement of freedom and celebration of self in others.

The group supports this new meaning and purpose by paying attention to it in the moment as it emerges and by agreeing to respond to it as well as they are able. There may be some consultation about how to do this, some intentional facilitation. More space is made for shared reflection. The individual focus on personal interiority expands more fully to include a communal awareness of being together in community. Connections are made.

First one member, then another, begins to wonder whether what is being noticed in one person's life is related, whether by comparison or contrast, to what is being noticed in another person's life. First one and then another senses the possibility that what God is speaking and doing in one person's life is somehow connected with what God is speaking and doing in another person's life, and then, perhaps, in another's life as well. Threads and themes emerge in the context of guidance for which the group begins to sense a deeper meaning. Dynamics of relationship with God and others are repeated and establish resonance so that the group catches a glimpse of broader applications.

Organically, the questions emerge: How does what we have begun to recognize in one case affect what we notice in another? How might what is already happening for this one and that one be connected with what is happening or will happen in the community as a whole? How might what is happening among us and for us in this process of shared companionship with God reflect or anticipate God's desire for us? There are also times when a sense of conviction emerges even before the questions take shape. The whole group seems to come to a shared recognition at once: "This isn't just about one of us, there is something about this that is for all of us here and for the community or communities of which we are a part." An experience of liberation from self-denigration initiated by the example of one person and shared by the group invites the group to notice the ways they individually refuse their gifting by God and corporately collude in staying blind to their own beauty. They are encouraged to notice how the systems and norms of their faith community support the devaluing of its members by themselves or others. They wonder about how they delight God as a community and look for ways that God is already affirming them. They begin to celebrate themselves and call out the gifts in one another with less embarrassment and with greater hope in the potential of the community to make an impact in the world.

Such directions for the community that emerge in addition to the direction taking shape for each individual do not become the primary focus or alter the process of the group. In my experience, these kinds of surprises happen most authentically, most evidently, and most frequently, when the original intention of group guidance is kept in focus, the process is flexibly maintained, and the respective roles of the members are clearly delineated. In every case the foundation for continued discernment about directions for the community is the spaciousness that allows each member to explore if, how, and to what extent what has been offered in the group will affect his or her behavior in other circles of community or will be offered to those communities for continued discernment. Diversity of understanding is expected. Freedom with authenticity, not consensus, is the highest value.

Any sense of conviction regarding the importance of what is emerging for the community is respected without dishonoring the continued need to wonder about its content, ponder its thrust, and leave its application to the discretion of those involved. The group doesn't decide to define the limits of graced self-acceptance or to orchestrate the participation of one or another of their communities in celebration of the gifts of its members. They simply give themselves to the shared intention of the group to participate in God's delight as each one stays faithful to his or her process and stays connected to the others as they notice and respond to each new movement of freedom and celebration that emerges in their experience together.

There is an additional assumption underlying the group discernment process that flows out of the experience instead of preceding it. The assumption becomes explicit only in retrospect. One way to state it is to say that the individual is a microcosm of the enlarging circles of spiritual community of which he or she is a part. Another is to say that the ways in which God tends to work in and with the individual are very similar to the ways in which God tends to work in and with the community. The themes of content and patterns of movement in an individual's life and prayer during a specific period of time are very often echoed in the themes and patterns of the groups and communities of which they are a part. By attending to the particular movements of one heart and noticing the ways in which they connect in community with the movements of other individual hearts, we may begin to discern movements of Spirit within a small group, a congregation, or even a denomination. In many ways, group direction forms the center of gravity for my practice of direction in the evangelical context. I believe that this appreciation for group direction and its potential to provide guidance for us individually and corporately is both a function of my gifts, my personal history, and my call to care for the church, and a result of the fact that it is persons of evangelical faith whom I have been called to love.

From a Graceful Center

The directions summarized here represent spiritual invitations that have emerged out of word and silence experienced in the intentional relationships of persons of evangelical faith who have been willing to share their desire for a more intimate experience of the God of Amazing Grace. The directions begin with the strengths of the evangelical spiritual tradition and move out from a graceful center in expanding circles. They well up out of deepening individual and corporate self-awareness and intentionality and extend outward to include broader biblical and theological perspectives and new dimensions of spiritual engagement. They flow from critical reflection and prayerful self-examination and result in creative renewal and reinforcement of the distinctive emphases of evangelical spirituality in light of Scripture, tradition, and current context. The currents surge deeper as they reconnect to the spiritual tradition of the historical church. The swells spread and continue to ripple onward as they incorporate insights and practices that reflect the initiative and work of the Spirit in the experience of the whole church today.

CHAPTER SEVEN

Freedom to Souls

Spiritual Accompaniment According to the Carmelite Tradition

Michael Plattig, O. Carm.

"Spiritual directors should give freedom to souls," instructs *The Living Flame of Love* by St. John of the Cross, summarizing the key to Carmelite spiritual direction.[1] In the old literature, the expressions "spiritual direction" and "spiritual director" are used, while modern publications are increasingly using "spiritual accompaniment" and "spiritual companion." In this chapter, the two sets of expressions will be used in parallel because they describe distinct aspects of the process of spiritual accompaniment pertinent to different spiritual stages and different aspects of such pastoral service.

Maturation and Continually Increasing Freedom as Characteristics of Carmelite Spirituality

Descriptions of development in the spiritual life in Judeo-Christian literature are usually historical or biographical in nature. Christian spirituality is characterized by concepts such as development, growth, maturation, progression, advance, pilgrimage, and ascent—all aspects of spiritual life understood as an imitation of Christ. Teresa of Avila explains this in the following words: "If you do not strive for the virtues and practice them, you will always be dwarfs. And, please God, it will be only a matter of not growing, for you already know that whoever does not increase decreases. I hold that love, where present, cannot possibly be content with remaining always the same."[2] There are several steps to this growth in the Carmelite tradition.

Listening in Silence

The first step of the spiritual life is to listen in silence. The Rule of Carmel encourages an attentive listening for God's presence and activity in one's life, and a willingness to be transformed by that love. The original setting of the Carmelites was in a canyon on a mountain ridge. There, ruminating on God's word in Scripture, the Carmelite was led into an inner land, an interior desert, where God accompanied the soul into more life. Rumination was the original form of meditation, a somewhat different way of meditation than today's concept. The practice of rumination was not just a period of time dedicated explicitly to personal prayer, but more of an attitude by which a person ruminated on everything that had occurred, particularly "the signs of the times" in regard to the Lord. Meditation was more or less an atmosphere of peaceful reflection that provided a fertile terrain for true prayer, a type of recollection that prepared a person for prayer. The Carmelite tradition teaches the grace of valuing the present moment and of being content, giving everything a proper value at the right time. This tradition insists that the Lord deals with a person not only in the high reaches of contemplation, but also that the personal history of the individual can become an instrument of salvation and of divine mercy.

The best guarantee of an effective contact with the Lord Jesus is through the words of Christ himself, which fill his follower with purity of heart and the desire to serve faithfully. Yet even more basic than formal prayers, the Carmelite charism invokes a way of life permeated by the living presence of Christ by being open to God. This attitude calls one to put all of one's time and talents at the disposition of the Lord, to allow one's heart to be captured by him and to belong to him, and to enjoy being together with him. It also calls one to confront one's shadow. Indeed, the early Carmelites established a lifestyle that would practically guarantee that confrontation, both by encouraging quiet introspection through the prism of the Scripture and by gathering together to point out the faults of the community members.

The Path of Purgation

This path of purgation, as it is traditionally called, required not only the confrontation of one's own inner realities with the light that comes from God's living in the center of the soul, but also the confrontation with the soul's shadow, which is made up of sins, faults, and fixations. There is a connection between light and shadow; more light means more shadow. The more a person approaches the light, the more he or she will experience his or her own imperfections. Teresa writes in the *The Interior Castle*: "Rather, let's strive to make more progress in self-knowledge. In my opinion we shall never completely know ourselves if we don't strive to know God. By gazing at His grandeur, we get in touch with our own lowliness; by looking at His purity, we shall see our own filth."[3]

This development of the soul also throws light on the soul's illusions. We come to realize how we can take something good and make it a god. When good becomes a god it is distorted, causes us to neglect God, and further diminishes our humanity. God's love initiates a healing process in the soul. First, it illuminates the soul's fixations and illusions, and then that transforming love asks for the soul's cooperation on its journey to purity of heart and freedom of spirit. The Carmelite authors encourage us to stand our ground in trust when God's love is dark, believing that in those times we are being purified and invited to a deeper union with him.

Teresa of Avila taught us to pay attention to the potential of our humanity and to the process of growing into the fulfillment of our baptismal promises. Openness to God's spirit at work in our lives can lead to a transformation of our desires. Eventually, our desires become less and less fragmented and we desire more and more what God desires. Assuming that God desires the well-being of humanity, a person transformed by him then lives in a way that furthers the actualization of that desire of God. Our desires become consonant with God's. Yet this intensification of personal encounters with God is not a matter of smooth, always ascending biographies. On the contrary, breaks, leaps, bounds, detours, and crises necessarily form a part of this concept of growth and are often the needed impetus toward the next step in the maturation process.[4] "In spiritual growth nothing can be forced. Periods of growth occur, as well as creative incubation periods—containing regressive arrests and progressive spurts of growth."[5]

The guide on this way of growth, as in all concepts of Christian spirituality, is God, or rather the Holy Spirit (see Matthew 28:20; Galatians 4:6; 5:18–25; Romans 8:15f., and so on).[6] But to be well guided, we need to learn to discern the spirits: "My dear friends, do not trust every spirit, but test the spirits, to see whether they are from God; for there are many false prophets about in the world" (1 John 4:1). Therefore, St. Paul, who sees the ability to discern the spirits as one of the charisms (see 1 Corinthians 12:10) urges: "[T]est them all; keep hold of what is good" (1 Thessalonians 5:21).

Thus spiritual growth can be more precisely characterized as growth guided by God's good Spirit. It is growth toward freedom and maturity, particularly freedom from various kinds of dependency and slavery. And it is growth that is progressive, a process beginning with the purgative way, continuing with the illuminative way, leading towards the fulfillment in the unitive way. It is like a science of psychological health. Holiness is true wholeness of the human incarnate spirit.

A Liberating Process

St. John of the Cross describes God's guidance in this process with very impressive images. When God sees that the beginners in the way of God have grown a little on the path of purgation, he desires to liberate them from the lowly exercise of the senses and of discursive meditation and lead them into the exercise of their spirit. Through that process, they become capable of a communion with God that is more abundant and freer of imperfections. "He weans them from the sweet breast so that they might be strengthened, lays aside their swaddling bands, and puts them down from his arms that they may grow accustomed to walking by themselves. This change is a surprise to them because everything seems to be functioning in reverse."[7] Becoming a spiritual person therefore means growing to maturity. It is a task of discerning, of separating, particularly of learning to distinguish the longing to return to the womb from creatively giving shape to spiritual childhood in the correct proportion of dependence, freedom, and self-reliance.

St. John of the Cross uses the words "librar" and "más libres" to describe this liberating process. It is a process experienced as a crisis on the spiritual path, because "everything seems to be functioning in reverse." But it only seems that way, because for a person's spiritual maturity and independence to increase, he or she must leave all "childish" behavior behind. That means overcoming all dependencies on structures, images, and forms that are too rigid and narrow and therefore prevent personal and spiritual growth. John of the Cross called this process of mortification and purgation of the soul "the happy night of the purgation of senses."[8]

Very clearly, St. John was not just preaching a kind of material renunciation. Nor did he intend that people close their ears to beautiful music or their eyes to beautiful paintings or sculptures. In fact, he himself was endowed with an exquisite artistic sensibility. He used his poems and masterly prose to raise his own heart and the hearts of others to God. He drew a famous image of the crucified Christ leaning over the world (the inspiration for Salvador Dali's well-known reproduction of that drawing), and loved to carve crucifixes. John did not mean to condemn religious statues or paintings, but rather the "great attachment" that some pious people have to such objects. Moreover, he did not expect mystics to reject their spiritual experiences (those are, after all, God's gifts), because people cannot do anything about them, especially about the deepest and strongest ones. What

John did constantly emphasize is the detachment of the heart in general. As he saw it, the problem lay in the fact that we may easily stop at some created good and become attached to it. If this happens, anything can take the place of God and become an idol. So what St. John of the Cross insisted on was the need for the greatest spiritual freedom.

Spiritual freedom is precisely what John expected of someone who is having spiritual experiences in prayer, and he expected it for two reasons. First, while an attachment to material riches or social status can be easily perceived as a danger, spiritual greed can often go undetected. People may treasure their spiritual experiences to the point of fixing their hearts on them. They may end up primarily loving the gifts of God rather than God, the giver of these gifts. This is a particularly important point to understand in spiritual direction because many visionaries become obsessed with their visions or inner words, constantly reverting to them, speaking or writing about them, recreating them, and in the processing succumbing to an unhealthy self-centeredness. Genuine mystics, on the contrary, though grateful to God for the gifts they receive, continue their search for the invisible God. Every experience leaves them hungrier for God. They go beyond their experiences.

Another, more profound reason for this greater emphasis on the need for detachment from spiritual experiences is that all particular feelings, images, and concepts of God are only finite reflections of the divine. If mystics remain attached to experiences, they will close their spirit to the infinite, transcendent reality to which these experiences point. Attachment to memories holds us anchored in the past, whereas hope opens us up to God and yearns for unity with God—a unity, however, that will never be fully attained in this life. Living out the cross and resurrection of the Lord in a practical way means dying to our own desires, living by "faith alone, which is the only proximate and proportionate means to union with God."[9]

The Path of Illumination

After the liberating crisis of the dark night, the next segment of the spiritual path is called "illuminatio," and refers to a time when the soul has become calm, its passions having been quenched and its desires put to rest. "The soul went out in order to begin its journey along the road of the spirit, which is that of progressives and proficients and which, by another terminology is referred to as the illuminative way or the way of infused contemplation."[10] God himself pastures and refreshes the soul now without any of its own discursive meditation or active help. This illumination in faith has a transforming effect on its recipient and mysteriously changes a person. "In this faith," says John of the Cross, "God supernaturally and secretly teaches the soul and, in a way unknown to it, raises it up in virtues and gifts."[11]

For John, faith, then, is the proximate means to divine union. Those who want to reach union with God could not advance by understanding, by the support of their own experience, or by feeling or imagination, but only by belief in God's being. God's being cannot be grasped by the intellect, appetite, imagination, or any other sense; nor can it be known in this life except by faith.

When the soul is purified, when the person has had some experience of light and the person's faith has grown, the thirst, hunger, and yearning of the spiritual feeling is immense. Since the soul now has deep cavities, the person suffers profoundly for the food it lacks, namely, for God. "This feeling, which is so intense, commonly occurs toward the end of the illumination and purification, just before the attainment of union, where a person is then satisfied."[12] Now God is the only one acting. Indeed, according to John of the Cross, God's search for us is more constant than our own search for God.

The Path of Union

The final stage is one of union with God. Those brought into the life of peaceful and quiet union should remember that it is God who is carrying them more deeply into their mutual love. God embraces us so fully that one is captivated by nothing except God alone. At this stage, the human being no longer desires selfishly, but desires as God desires, in a full, liberating love. The will, which previously loved in a base and deadly way with only its natural affection, is now changed into the will of divine love, for it loves in a lofty way with divine affection, moved by the strength of the Holy Spirit in whom it now lives the life of love. By means of this union, God's will and the soul's will are now one.

God explained the nature of union in a vision, which Teresa of Avila describes in a spiritual testimony: "He said: 'Don't think, daughter, that union lies in being very close to me. . . . Neither does it consist in favours and consolations in prayer, even though these may reach a very sublime degree. Though these favours may come from Me, they are often a means for winning souls."[13] The fruit of the union with God is conformity with God in spirit and will: "I wouldn't know how to describe this experience. It seems to me I was given an understanding that the spirit is the higher part of the will. . . . I understood . . . that there is nothing in the soul that wants to turn aside from God's will."[14]

Finally, in this union, all the movements, operations, and inclinations that the soul previously had from the principle and strength of its natural life are now dead to what they formerly were, changed into divine movements, and are alive to God. By this, John of the Cross clearly affirms that

God delights in all things. Nothing escapes that delight, because nothing escapes the creative beauty God originally placed there. We should note that when John speaks of the transformed person delighting more in the already possessed interior gift (union with God), and of God enjoying more self-delight than delight in his creatures, he is not denying the beauty, wonder, and delightfulness of created things, but is simply saying that the delight in the more fundamental is greater. John affirms both that God loves all created reality and that human beings brought to a union with God share God's delight in all things.

The whole process of purification and dark nights, through which we are brought into union with God, is meant to free us to be fully and perfectly sensual and passionate in our dealings with creation. Since grace does not destroy but builds on nature, humanity and all its characteristics are perfected. I think I may conclude that spiritual life always implies a process of growth and attainment of full maturation. Spiritual life may also be described as a process of becoming more liberated, with the goal of increased spiritual and human freedom.

The process of becoming more liberated, however, does not imply isolation from others. Teresa of Avila wrote that it was difficult for her not to have anyone to talk to about this and thus to be alone with her difficulties and questions. That is why she encouraged her nuns: "I would counsel those who practice prayer to seek, at least in the beginning, friendship and association with other persons having the same interest. This is something most important even though the association may be only to help one another with prayers."[15] Having experienced what she experienced, Teresa could not understand why in her day and age it was not permitted for those who began to truly serve God to talk with others about their joys and trials because of the danger of vainglory. Teresa does not see any sense in fearing vainglory; on the contrary, she says: "I believe that he who discusses these joys and trials for the sake of this friendship with God will benefit himself and those who hear him, and he will come away instructed; even without understanding how he will have instructed his friends."[16]

Spiritual Accompaniment

Discourse between friends, as Teresa describes it, can be important, but "professional" accompaniment is also beneficial to the individual seeking spiritual growth. According to Teresa of Avila, knowing oneself perfectly and proceeding in everything as God's will requires observation by a third person. The depths of the subconscious are hidden from us and its influence makes matters of conscience appear under a false light. As a result, it is impossible for us to guide ourselves according to objective reality to the real will of God. In St. Teresa's thought, spiritual direction is an effective means of gradual liberation from illusions and from the influence of the subconscious: "If one proceeds with humility, strives to know the truth, is subject to a confessor, and communicates with him openly and truthfully, it will come about . . . that things by which the devil intends to cause death will cause life."[17]

Although having a confessor or director is important, the truth is that the real guide in the process of spiritual accompaniment is God alone. Directors must understand "that they themselves are not the chief agent, guide, and mover of souls in this matter, but the principal guide is the Holy Spirit . . . and they themselves are instruments for directing these souls to perfection through faith and the law of God, according to the spirit given by God to each one."[18] John of the Cross, too, stresses that the director's concern should not be to bring souls into alignment with his personal state of development, with his own method and condition, but that he should observe the road along which God is leading the directee. This can put the spiritual director into an awkward situation, as he or she has to act in a situation of relationship in which God is the acting agent. There are two inappropriate ways out of this tension. The first one emphasizes that only God is acting and fails to take the qualification or capability of the spiritual director into account. The other way out of this tension is demonstrated when the spiritual director believes that he/she has to find the path for the directee, give advice, and so on. In a certain way, "training programs to become a spiritual director" also point in that direction. They give the impression that spiritual accompaniment can be learned; all you have to do is complete some courses to be a spiritual director. That is not the intention of training, but the danger of a basic misunderstanding has to be taken seriously and should be a subject of discussion during the training.

The art[19] of spiritual accompaniment is not to remove such tension but to act within it by acquiring certain technical skills—such as a solid psychological and theological education—by having a corresponding talent, and by being able to recognize the heart and discern the spirits. And yet in a profound way spiritual accompaniment is more than certain skills to be learned, but consists in being fully present and able to summon up enough inner and outer perception that God's guidance can take place.

The Spiritual Director According to John of the Cross

The above theses are explained in the Carmelite tradition of spiritual accompaniment and are exemplified by John of the Cross. He never wrote a manual for spiritual directors and his writings are only indirectly addressed to spiritual guides. References to the spiritual director contained in his works are not primarily directed at the people who exercise this pastoral care of souls but rather to contemplatives who often lack adequate direction. Therefore, John goes to great lengths to describe the faults and the errors of poor spiritual masters and to warn his readers against them.

Despite this cautionary depiction, John of the Cross does present a positive picture of the spiritual director, one that is certainly not complete but nonetheless a goldmine of material on this kind of pastoral service. John's teaching on the role of the spiritual guide is firmly grounded in the long and rich tradition of Western mysticism and in his contemporary understanding of the role of spiritual directors. John's teaching makes it clear that he not only memorized and internalized the teaching of the Scriptures, but was quite at home in the classic sources of the teaching on spiritual direction. His great genius was to integrate them into his writings in such a way that they became part of the main message of his teaching.

Blind Guides

John of the Cross clearly described and denounced false spiritual accompaniment. In his work *The Living Flame of Love,* which was written for those advanced on the spiritual path, John emphasized that God is the principal guide of the blind soul, and he warns his readers against blind guides of the blind: "There are three blind guides who can draw it [the soul] off the road: the spiritual director, the devil, and the soul itself."[20] John then provides many pages warning about spiritual directors—all of them priests in his day—who lay their own spiritual concept and human ideal onto the person accompanied. "Thus all their efforts are like hammering the horseshoe instead of the nail; on the one hand they do harm, and on the other hand they receive no profit."[21]

Some spiritual directors, then, according to John, cause great harm to souls by not understanding the ways and properties of the Spirit. Knowing no more than beginners, they do not wish to permit souls to pass beyond those beginnings and these discursive and imaginative ways. They instruct them in other inferior ways, which they themselves have used or read of somewhere. Spiritual directors hinder and delay the work of God by guiding people according to their own tastes and interests and by hindering them from progress due to reason and human thoughts. For John of the Cross, such directors are amateurs and bunglers, who, out of fear and arrogance and lacking reverence and sensitivity—an often occurring fatal mixture—trust less in other people and in the Spirit of God. They set themselves and their own spiritual lives and experiences as the standard of the Spirit, rather than allowing their directees to follow the Spirit of God.

No director, of course, is perfectly advanced in all aspects of the spiritual life and in all skills. It is impossible for any spiritual director to have the all the qualities required for the guidance of everybody. If the director is not humble enough to accept this fact, he or she will tyrannize souls and deprive them of their freedom. "Spiritual masters, then, should give freedom to souls and encourage them in their desire to seek improvement. The director does not know the means by which God may wish to benefit a soul, especially if it is no longer satisfied with the director's teaching."[22]

We can only speculate on the reasons that caused John of the Cross to utter such sharp words against the guides of souls of that time. Certainly his own experiences with the accompaniment of the Discalced Carmelite nuns played a role. Over and over again members of the order—like the reformer Teresa of Avila—had to fight against the prejudice that women were not capable of real contemplation.[23] In the works of Teresa, we find some references to background experiences she and her nuns had with confessors who for the most part were also the spiritual directors of that time. In Teresa's *Book of Her Life* she writes that half-learned confessors did her great harm and that she was unable to find a confessor with sufficient learning: "I have come to see by experience that it is better, if they are virtuous and observant of holy customs, that they have little learning. For then they do not trust themselves without asking someone who knows, nor do I trust them; and a truly learned man has never misguided me."[24]

In the *Way of Perfection,* Teresa warned her sisters: "If you should become aware that the confessor is turning toward some vanity, be suspicious about everything and in no way carry on conversations with him even though they may seem to be good, but make your confession briefly and bring it to a conclusion."[25] In these circumstances she suggested that the nuns speak with the prioress about the problem and change confessors. Besides speaking with the ordinary confessors, the prioress should always ask permission from the bishop or the provincial for herself and for all the others to be able to sometimes speak and discuss their souls with learned persons, especially if the confessors, however good, are not learned, because: "Learning is a great help for shedding light upon every matter."[26] In a letter to the Reverend Father Ambrosio Mariano of St. Benedict, a Carmelite, Teresa wrote: "You made me smile by saying, that you could tell her character by only seeing her. But we women are not so easily known; for, after having been for so many years under the direction of our confessors, they are often surprised to see how little they know about us."[27] She expresses anger and frustration about narrow-mindedness, ignorance, a lack of intelligence, and a lack of a sense of responsibility among the clerics.

For these kinds of directors, disliked by both John and Teresa, the usually calm John of the Cross predicts severe punishments: "God becomes extremely indignant with such directors and in Ezekiel promises them chastisement: 'You ate the milk of my flock and you covered yourself with their wool and did not feed my flock; I will seek my flock at your hand, he says' (Ez. 34:3 and 10)."[28]

The Spiritual Director Needs to Be Experienced, Wise, and Discerning[29]

Near the beginning of his excursus on spiritual directors, John of the Cross writes: "For this journey, especially its most sublime parts and even for the intermediate parts, he will hardly find a guide accomplished as to all his needs, for besides being learned and discreet, a director should have experience."[30] These three qualifications—experience, discernment, and wisdom—help us comprehend John's understanding of the role of the spiritual director.

Experience is very important to John of the Cross, yet in connection with spiritual directors he mentions the word largely out of concern for the one receiving direction, that this one have the ability to judge whether a director is sufficiently experienced to take him under his care. In regard to a spiritual director, experience has a multifaceted meaning. It encompasses the human experience that comes from reflecting on the dailiness of Christian life. It includes experience from the director's own journey on the spiritual path. It is also gained by learning from other people's walk with the Lord, and finds its expression in the director's attitudes toward and dealings with the souls who come for guidance. A director who has experience is known by his external life. He shows an interior sensitivity to the individual who opens his soul fully to him. The experienced guide avoids forcing his solutions on the person and realizes that he is only a servant of the Holy Spirit who is the principal director of the soul.

Although this description of the experienced director begins to bring the teaching of John of the Cross into focus, it is still one dimensional. Familiarity with the text leads one to the conclusion that experience, when it is applied to the highest states in the soul of the being directed, is very close to the term "discernment," and that when applied to ascetical teaching, the word is difficult to separate from knowledge. John himself tells us that he founded his teaching on the Scriptures, the teaching of the Church, his personal experience, and finally, on the experience of others. Experience is necessary to turn the cognitive understanding that comes from reading into an affective knowing. John contrasts the wise director with those who are ignorant, inexperienced, and merely taught.

The works of John of the Cross contain many references to the context of the spiritual director's knowledge. Not only should the guide have a grasp of the truths of the faith, but he should realize that God is the goal of human existence and what the implications of that are. This ministry would include an overview of the spiritual process: how to understand the ways of the beginner and be able to instruct him or her in the principles necessary for spiritual life; how to direct someone more advanced; and how to recognize when a person has passed beyond the range of the director's own ability to direct him or her. A really competent master understands the principles that govern discernment and pastoral practice in regard to the extraordinary phenomenon of mystical life. He should be able to explain detachment from all supernatural apprehensions without showing excessive interest in them or expressing shock when his directees bring that topic up. Comprehending the great grace that God has been giving the soul led into contemplation, he would know enough to avoid impeding or obstructing the progress of one so gifted.

Wisdom in the spiritual parent should be revealed in his understanding of the theological virtues of faith, hope, and charity, and the path to union with God. The wise guide should understand the steps of prayer, and the special place that prayer and true introspection have in the spiritual life. Because in the works of John of the Cross wisdom is seen to be dynamic, there is no doubt that no director, except the Holy Spirit, has all wisdom. This teaching implies that a director is him or herself a person who is growing in the light of God's wisdom, which shines through him or her onto others.

In teaching that the spiritual director must be discerning, St. John of the Cross situates himself soundly within the long Christian tradition of *diákrisis* and *discretio*. For him, discernment is a reality that may be both a supernatural gift from the Lord and a naturally developed virtue. John sees the discerning person as a clear-thinking person with a balance in his judgments founded on solid diagnostic skills. The discerning person can appraise the soul's present state and can penetrate into the very core of motivation. Aware of the human nature, he is cautious about affirming that the hand of God was active in a particular prayer experience and looks for clear signs of confirmation in the life of the person he is evaluating. Distinguishing between the various possible sources of an experience (God, the devil, and the person himself), the discerning director bases his evaluations on the teachings of the Gospels and his ability to reason out a way through the forest of given theological and psychological principles. Prudent judgments are his hallmark; astute unmasking of motivations his forte. Cognizant of the goal of spiritual life and the means which best lead to union with God, the discerning guide takes on the difficult responsibility of evaluating the source of spiritual experiences in prayer with reluctance, and only when necessary. In both his practice and teaching, the discerning master sees supernatural experiences only as a means and never as an end in themselves. Revelations, inspirations, visions, and so on are never to be sought or valued in themselves.

Certainly, experience, knowledge, deep faith, and wisdom are necessary in spiritual direction, but in the actual direction situation, the virtue of discernment gains primary importance. In a specific case the discerning director can draw on his knowledge and personal spirituality to judge and communicate with the person coming for counsel. Therefore, for John of the Cross, the spiritual director needs to be experienced, wise, and discerning.

Summary Portrait of the Spiritual Director According to John of the Cross

- A good spiritual director will have experienced for him/herself at least some of the crises that have to be faced on the journey to God.
- A competent director will be sensitive to the person who comes for guidance. He or she will be careful to avoid blemishing the masterwork God wants to create in the person who comes for direction and will be sensitive to the directee's need for affirmation, confirmation, and instruction.
- A good director will not attempt to bend a soul to him/herself, but will leave it free to consult others and will even recommend such consultation when he or she comes into contact with a soul that is beyond his or her competence.
- This director will not be overly attached to his/her own categories or theories, nor will he or she be tied to his or her own methods, but will respect the unique gifts that have been given to each soul.
- A good guide will not waste a person's time with peripheral concerns or unnecessary discernments but will always lead toward the darkness of faith and detachment from all internal and external realities that do not proceed from God.
- Communication skills are found in the toolbox of every fine spiritual guide, and he/she will realize the dangers of projection, transference, and countertransference in the spiritual dialogue and know how to avoid them.
- A director worthy of the name will be able to unmask motivations that are less than divine and will be cautious about helping a person uproot the bad habits and tendencies coming from the "old man." The director will understand the common faults of a spiritual person and provide practical means for removing them from the soul.
- Confident that faith, hope, and love are fundamental to the spiritual journey, a good director will urge the client not to be sidetracked by what is not-God but will call the soul to totally desire the spiritual goal.

- A good spiritual director will know that his/her role is more paternal and instructive to the beginner. He/she is more a companion and friend to the spiritually advanced. And finally, for those who are at the highest stages of the spiritual journey, the director acts more as a witness.
- In the direction situation, John's ideal spiritual guide would be sensitive to what the Lord is calling the soul to be or do. Here a good director's discernment is used in applying spiritual experience and wisdom to a practical case. Intuition helps discern when and where the gifts of contemplation begin in the directee, as they are so subtle that they could be easily missed.
- The director has to see him/herself as the servant of the relationship between the soul and God. Never should he/she allow the focus of the dialogue to center on himself or on the directee, but should keep focused on directing the soul towards its goal.

Consequences for Spiritual Accompaniment Today

Spiritual accompaniment means to track down the Holy Spirit in a person and to help to find the individual's path. Inevitably, this way leads to tension because the spiritual director simply does not know what the other person's path looks like. Even if it seems reasonable to him/her, giving outside advice always contains the danger of projecting something onto the other person. To bear this emptiness and not to rashly fill it with one's own wisdom, to resist the temptation of giving a simple piece of advice though it be asked for, to consistently look for the Spirit's work in the other person: these are the tasks and the demands of spiritual accompaniment as John of the Cross and the Carmelite tradition understand it.

Spiritual accompaniment takes place in the tension between faith in the work of God in humans, and the professionalism or—in the words of John of the Cross—the intelligence of the master. This tension cannot simply be eased by what the director him/herself would decide or by framing it with a given concept. Whoever believes to know in advance how spiritual accompaniment works and to know how spiritual life basically has to be thereby shows that he/she does not understand anything of spiritual accompaniment.

The reminder of John of the Cross that the Holy Spirit is the ultimate guide and that spiritual directors are instruments in bringing directees into contact with the Holy Spirit also could help to arrange the many counseling tools available today within the overall framework of spiritual direction. Undoubtedly, John would welcome modern methods as helpful for self-understanding and for discovering the particular road one is called to walk on; however, he would also firmly remind us that the Christian spiritual journey itself is one of personal transformation through dark faith and self-transcending love.

Believing in the working of the Holy Spirit relieves the spiritual director of the responsibility for the success or the failure of an individual's spiritual path; the spiritual director cannot do what the Holy Spirit does. Spiritual accompaniment requires the humble recognition that it cannot be manmade and that it is not within the power of the spiritual director to dictate how effective or helpful his/her actions will be. On the one hand, this belief means that the spiritual director does not have to know or produce the solution that is to be found in the other person, but rather should know that this change takes place in the interpersonal "in between" and is a gift of God. On the other hand, the work involves a double differentiation; first, the spiritual director has to differentiate between his/her own preconceived thoughts and ideas and those that pertain to the dialog; then, he/she has to discern between the thoughts and ideas of the person seeking advice and those inspired by the Holy Spirit. For these differentiations, reported experiences in the tradition and psychological aid are to be used. It is well that John of the Cross emphasized the director's responsibility for his/her actions, for only on the basis of that responsibility, sensibility, and attention can the art of spiritual accompaniment grow.

A good way for spiritual directors to find out the openness of their relationship in spiritual accompaniment is to ask themselves the question of whether they would be able to dismiss the directee into the accompaniment of another spiritual guide if the directee required it, or when their own limits as a director have been reached. John of the Cross asks: "When will the statue be complete? When or how will it be left for God to paint? Is it possible that all these functions are yours and that you are so perfect the soul will never need any other than you?"[31]

This does not mean that such a separation could not be painful as well, since closeness, devotion, and empathy also belong to the accompaniment. However, what is being advocated is that a director should not clutch or cling to the directee just because he or she considers him or herself to be the best director and every separation an insult. This means that they "should give freedom to souls,"[32] that they should give the Holy Spirit freedom to act.

One's faith in God's work in people prevents one's having too much anxiety and narrow-mindedness in dealings with directees. A person able to rely on God's working gains the necessary calmness to stay centered, not having to fearfully close doors to certain rooms timorously, but being able to open doors reverently.

Obviously, spiritual directors have to follow their own spiritual paths to contemplation in order to know "true and pure spirit" from firsthand experience; otherwise, they easily become like uncertain guides who try to lead others through a terrain they do not know themselves. A perhaps obvious but nonetheless crucial need in creating an intimate interpersonal atmosphere is the need to continually grow as a person who can experience and communicate genuineness, caring, and understanding in human relationships. These qualities are not only unmerited gifts like healing in the New Testament, they are human attitudes that can be developed with practice. It is possible to learn to be more authentic with oneself and with others, to accept others unconditionally, and to listen with empathy.

Directors must engage in profound study of Holy Scripture, theology, Christian spirituality, and psychology, for these are the basic foundational sciences for the ministry of spiritual accompaniment. Spiritual directors must hone their skills in applying general principles of spiritual life to the specific requirements of the individual, a process fostered by regular participation in case conferences, peer supervision, and consultation with other spiritual directors and professionals.

Developing the qualifications of a good spiritual director is a lifelong process. As a person grows in experience, wisdom, discernment, genuineness, caring, and understanding, his/her effectiveness as a spiritual director increases, because those qualities are particularly useful in helping directees prepare themselves for the completely gracious action of the Holy Spirit, who is the only one who can transform a person into unity with God.

CHAPTER EIGHT

Seeking and Finding God

Love and Humility in the Benedictine Tradition

Katherine Howard, OSB

In this reflection on Benedictine spirituality and what it has to offer us as spiritual directors, I will begin with a general description of the way I see and experience that spirituality rooted in the *Rule of Benedict* and developed by Benedictine communities over many centuries. Then I will address in more detail each of the three major sections of that statement, occasionally interspersing my commentary with ways particular aspects of that spirituality have been helpful for me in my work as a spiritual companion. My contribution to the conversation on this topic is not made as that of an expert in either area, but as one graced by opportunities of living and studying the *Rule of Benedict* and Benedictine spirituality for forty-five years and serving as a spiritual companion for more than twenty years.

An Overview of Benedictine Spirituality

The spirituality of the *Rule of Benedict* is basic Christian spirituality. It rests on the reality and experience, that is, the faith conviction

1. that God not only exists, but is always lovingly present and active in our lives;
2. that God is present with us is in the Risen Christ in the concrete circumstances of our lives;

3. that the Holy Spirit is the dynamic of God's presence within and around us, transforming us in Christ, that is, bringing us to that fullness of human life permeated by the divine life in which we are able to love and be loved without fear.

This is the baptismal reality that draws us into Christian community, the reality we nurture in prayer and in life and celebrate and intensify in Eucharist.

God's love for us and in us is the foundation of Benedictine spirituality. Its goal is the goal of all Christian life: love—love of God and love of neighbor that is solidly founded in a healthy loving acceptance of ourselves. Though we, inspired by the Gospel and cooperating with grace, must make an effort to foster that love in our lives, it can come to full bloom in us only through the transforming presence and action of the Spirit of God in Christ. This work of the Holy Spirit takes place in us—good, ordinary, sinful human persons—in the simple, daily round of human life, both in work and in prayer.

Christ in Scripture, sacrament, and life is central in Benedictine spirituality. We participate in the transforming work of God within us and our world by giving the full assent of our wills to the Christ-life in us. The divine inspiration and capacity to do this come especially through our regular Scripture-based personal and community prayer and worship, which illumine and shape the way we live. However, watchfulness for God's presence and action in ourselves and others in the ordinary events of daily life is as important as it is during our times of prayer. We sometimes speak of cultivating this vigilance as practicing the presence of God, that is, using any helpful means we have to grow in conscious alertness to and gratitude for God's presence in daily life. Nevertheless, unless we cultivate our awareness of God in prayer, we tend to lose our desire and capacity for it in daily life.

Practicing explicit times of Scripture-based prayer, personal and communal, is the backbone of Benedictine spirituality. To be spiritual definitely means we need to spend regular times in prayer. However, a healthy balance of prayer with work and community involvement is an essential component of Benedictine spirituality. Christ is in the kitchen, in the office, in the guest room, in the infirmary, just as truly and fully as in the oratory. Christ is in family and community discussions, present during times of fun and times of tension and trial as well as in times of common or solitary prayer. The "tools of trade" we use daily are as sacred as the vessels of the altar we use on Sundays. There is nowhere God is not! There is no aspect of life that is not spiritual.

Cultivating our awareness of the primacy of God and the centrality of Christ also involves being sensitive to the inner movements of our own hearts, that is, growing in self-knowledge. This can be exhilarating and it can be painful. We come to appreciate gifts of nature and grace we had not been aware of. We also become conscious of some previously unnoticed ways of thinking, being, and acting that do not fit our idealized image of ourselves. We realize with each new fragment of self-knowledge that even though we are basically good, we are not the models of Gospel living—perhaps the loving, disciplined, courageous, kind, or generous persons—we thought we were. But once our inner eye is enlightened and our heart pierced by the truth of God's love for us, which is constant whether in our goodness or in our inadequacy, this growth in self-knowledge is very freeing. We learn to appreciate and accept our gifts of nature and grace and to acknowledge our shortcomings. We learn what attitudes and behaviors of ours make us receptive to God. And we learn to recognize the obstacles that blind us to the divine presence in ourselves, in others, and in the world, and so keep our wills from choosing truly loving responses to others, to the world around us, and also to ourselves.

The height of spiritual growth in Benedictine spirituality is not spoken of in terms of any extraordinary spiritual phenomena, but as the integration of God's love in Christ through the power of the Holy Spirit into every aspect of our being in such a way that "love casts out fear." This love makes us able to enjoy life's gifts with gratitude and to undergo life's necessary suffering with patience, standing firm in the hope that we will share in the reign of God. It is manifested in our ability to use the good things of the world with respect and moderation and in our willingness to live and work in harmony with others, serving with them in the ordinary and extraordinary events of daily life with respectful, accepting, and loving hearts. It is in its deepest reality the union of our wills with the loving will of God, an unshakable basis of a deep and abiding peace. In short, Benedictine spirituality is Gospel spirituality which emphasizes that the transforming work of the Holy Spirit in our lives begins with and remains rooted in our desire for God, a desire which itself grows out of God's desire for us.

Desire for God: The Breakthrough of the Transcendent

The Prologue of the *Rule of Benedict* not only talks about the presence of God, but really opens us to the presence of God, inviting us into the spiritual journey with all its challenges and joys. An engaging exhortation to return to God, the Prologue of the Rule asks us to "listen with the ear of our heart" (verse 1) to Christ's teaching and to faithfully put it into practice by living in harmony with God's loving will for us (verses 1–3). More than some objective teaching about the spiritual life, the words of the Prologue— largely the words of Scripture itself distilled through Benedict's integration of the Word of God in his life and prayer—are an effective sacrament of the Divine Presence. To read the words or to hear them read is to be stirred by the voice of God speaking to us, appealing to our deepest desire to return to our own souls by "listening with the ear of our heart," to return to God by learning to live in harmony with the divine will. It is God's communication with us as the Light that enlightens our spiritual eyes, as the Voice that longs to be heard by our human ears. Our spiritual journey begins with this awakening of our desire for the God who is always longing for us to come to her/him.

Early in the Prologue, God addresses us in the words of Psalm 34:12: "Is there anyone here who yearns for life and desires to see good days?" (verse 15). God is the One who daily walks through the world, the divine vineyard, inviting us to life and good days. This divine Voice of love is always present within and around us in Christ—through the power and energy of their Spirit—stirring up our desire whether from within or through some external circumstance of our lives. William Shannon, quoting St. Augustine's *Confessions,* points out that God is "*interior intimo meo.*"[1] That is, rather literally, "God is more within than my inmost self," or, as we might say in a more ordinary way, "God is closer to me than I am to myself." Couple conviction about this reality with the truth of John the Evangelist's declaration that "God is love" (1 John 4:8), and the impact of God's invitation to us in the Prologue elicits from us, even if only momentarily, a compelling yes. Our realization of the loving Divine Presence within us as we confess our desire for God only increases our desire for that Love who first loves us.

There are moments in each of our lives when this invitation of the transcendent breaks through—moments of love, of joy, of beauty; moments of sorrow, of suffering, of sin, of death. These moments may come when we are engaged in personal prayer or when we are at worship or work. They may come during periods of our lives when we are wandering along with no particular purpose or when we are deeply engaged in meaningful pursuits. They may come during interludes of solitude in nature or during periods of intense relationship; during hours of creativity and joy, hours of boredom, or hours of deep sadness. In all our activities and passivities, it is as if God is watching for any possible place to break into our awareness, to coax us to turn and see, to stop and feel the divine touch. This is true for ourselves as spiritual directors and for those who come to us for spiritual direction.

The faith conviction that God is a loving presence active in our lives, articulated so effectively at the beginning of the *Rule of Benedict* is the foundation stone of any practice of spiritual direction or companionship. Our first responsibility as spiritual directors is to be on the alert for and to be receptive to these moments in our own lives and to be equally alert for and receptive to them in the lives of those who come to us for help in discovering more deeply how the Spirit of God is touching and leading them. It is this—their desire for

God and God's prior desire for them—that I as a spiritual director trust and want to help them get in touch with. These moments of breakthrough are confirmed, renewed, deepened, and expanded in the process of revealing and exploring them with a trusted other.

"What is it that you really desire, long for?" Coming back over and over again to that question when I am listening to another struggling for a sense of meaning, purpose, or direction in life or prayer has been helpful for me. For example, one woman, after talking about her dissatisfaction with her experience during the time of prayer, her feelings that, though she tried to be faithful, God did not seem to be there for her, sighingly declared, "Maybe I should just give up my regular prayer times, stop wasting time at it." I commented, "You sound discouraged, or is it angry, about the results of your prayer—no satisfaction, empty feelings." She said, "Yes, I am both discouraged and mad! I try so hard and God seems to be absent!" Then she remained silent, but her expression changed from one of harshness to one of thoughtfulness. I asked, "What is it you most want in your prayer—good feelings or God? Do you want to stop praying? That really is a choice you can make. What is your deepest desire?" There followed a long silence, then quiet tears, and finally the simple words: "Well, I want both good feelings and God! But mostly I want to be with God. I want God to be with me no matter how I feel. I am attracted to prayer. Somehow, I trust God is here for me. I really do not want to give up my prayer times."

Once we have heard the divine voice, sensed the Presence, our desire for God and our conviction that God is always present can grow. As spiritual directors it is important for us to continue to cultivate openness to these breakthroughs of divine life, light, and love by listening, as Benedict advises us "with the ear of [our] heart" (1). When Benedict speaks about this, his invitation is "to listen . . . to the master's instructions." Although the more immediate meaning of such "instructions" might refer to doctrinal or moral admonitions, the striking phrase "with the ear of your heart" tells us he was speaking of listening from the inner core of one's being—not only with our ears, not only to the superficial level of words that are spoken, not only to the intellectual dimension, the description, the concept, but to the depth dimension that may resonate within us in an intuitive way. We learn to trust our intuitive responses and those of the ones we companion. We also listen to what is unspoken—the tear, the gesture, the sigh, the look of sadness, pensiveness, or joy. We pay attention to this depth dimension of our own experience and to that of those who come asking us "to listen with the ear of our hearts," attending not only to the overt feelings, thoughts, patterns of response, inspirations, but to the more interior, more subtle levels of thought, feeling, experience.

After turning as profoundly as possible to God for help before beginning a spiritual direction session (knowing my own limitations, I sometimes feel like this is death!), I find it helpful to say to myself, "Open the ear of your heart to her/him; move toward him/her; don't close up, stay open. Don't be afraid to ask him/her to dwell on and explore her/his inner thoughts, feelings, responses." During the session I depend on the Spirit at work in both of us—to keep both my outer being and my inner being awake to the outer and inner being of the person with me and to put the other in touch with the inner self. I try to remember that it is often helpful to ask, "What are you feeling?" Or "What is your deepest or strongest feeling?" And to ask it without any preconceived notion of what that is or ought to be. The answer, in fact, may be, "I feel nothing!" Then it is important for me to sit with that and wonder with the person what that might mean. There are many possibilities! These range from spiritual/emotional paralysis, a present inability to know what he/she is feeling, to a deep mystical realization! It may very well be that I do not really know for sure, but can only pray interiorly with deep humility and trust that the Spirit will enlighten this beloved about the meaning of the experience.

Christ

Christ is central in Benedictine spirituality. The Rule begins and ends with the love of Christ to whom we are urged to pray for the help we need (Prologue 4; 73:8). Early on we read that "the love of Christ must come before all else" (4:21), a phrase that is echoed in one of its final statements: "Let them prefer nothing whatever to Christ, and may he bring us all together to everlasting life" (72:11–12). The love of Christ is the hallmark of any Christian spirituality—the ever-present love of the Risen Christ for us and our love for Christ.

Among the challenges I find is that of trying to be in touch with the Spirit's guidance of those Christians who come without any explicit relationship with Christ. They believe in God, pray to God as God, or Father, or Mother, and may pray to the Holy Spirit, but Christ is not a conscious presence in their lives. Since my faith relationship with God is in and through Christ, I am aware that I would like to help others find that explicit life-giving relationship. But it is important for me as a spiritual companion to understand how each person does address God, who God is for him/her, and in what way she/he relates to God. There may be no address at all. Sometimes that might mean a person is spending prayer time thinking or talking to him or herself instead of opening up to the relational interchange of prayer. But then, of course, there is a kind of relationship in which one is so identified with Christ that she/he no longer addresses Christ in prayer, but is praying *in* Christ. Addressing or relating to a God imaged as male, whether Father or Jesus Christ, may be problematic for some. It is not always easy to distinguish what is going on at the level of a person's relationship with Christ. Finding out how someone's personal and prayer life have developed and changed over the years gives some insight. Taking the stance that the Spirit leads each in a unique and timely way, I try not to impose my own way on another, but to ask questions that help a person get in touch with the way the Divine Spirit is attracting and leading him/her at this time in life. It may not be an explicit relationship with Christ. That does not mean God is not at work in her/him.

In Benedictine spirituality an essential way to foster our relationship with and finally our identity with Christ is the Scripture prayer at the heart of the Benedictine life, that is, Liturgy of Hours and *lectio divina,* which, along with work and community life, give each day its shape. Liturgy of Hours or the Divine Office consists largely of psalmody and readings from Scripture as well as ancient, medieval, modern, and contemporary commentaries, homilies or reflections that break open Scripture's meaning for us. These are interspersed with times of silence—times for thoughtful or concept and image-free personal prayer in which we integrate our experience with Scripture or simply identify with and breathe our silent "Yes" to the Word of God.

Lectio divina is that ancient method of individual Christian prayer in which one reads—or better, *listens,* with the ear of the heart—and responds to Scripture texts as a way of deepening one's relationship with God in the Risen Christ present and acting within us and in our world through and in the Spirit. The same kind of process goes on in lectio as in Liturgy of Hours: reading/listening to Scripture, interfacing the Word of God with one's life experience, expressing oneself in affective prayer, and entering into silent rest in God. For someone who is looking for a way to deepen his or her life of prayer, that is, to cultivate the life of the Spirit that is going on within, spending some time with him or her actually doing this kind of Scripture prayer can be helpful. Done in a spirit of reverent faith and trust, this gives me as a director an immediate sense of a person's relationship with God.

You will not find any practical guidance about how to do lectio in the *Rule of Benedict,* which is not intended to be either a treatise on prayer nor a manual of prayer and spirituality. However, the importance of the practice in life is emphasized by the amount of time given to it in the schedule of the day. Monastic tradition previous and subsequent to the Rule continually emphasized the Word of God, and monastic writers through the centuries unselfconsciously demonstrated and gradually articulated more and more about the process of lectio.[2]

Very literally, the words "lectio divina" can mean "reading God," or perhaps better, "reading the word inspired by God," that is, Scripture. This reading is not like other reading because this book is not like other books. The words of Scripture are symbols through which we are put in touch with the living event of God's presence and action going on within us in the various ways related to the way that presence and action is described in the events of biblical history, most particularly in Jesus' dying and rising, which is not only a past historical event but one going on right now in our lives.

Under the direction of the Spirit who always leads us in prayer, the process of lectio is a fourfold one: through regular attentive reading (*lectio*), and thoughtful, penetrating reflection on or use of imagination with Scripture passages (*meditatio*), we are moved to spontaneous affective response in prayer (*oratio*), which draws us sooner or later into simply resting quietly in God's presence, assenting to the divine mystery in Christ beyond words, images, or specific intentions (*contemplatio*). This process is the development of a relationship with God in Christ. Its various levels, in which we progress as we open ourselves more and more to that relationship within us but which we can also move in and out of freely under the guidance of the Spirit in any one prayer period, are much like the levels of a human relationship. We get acquainted through conversation (lectio: reading); we become friendly with one another (meditatio: thinking about, mulling over, attending to, penetrating the self-presentation of the other); we arrive at a love so deep we commit ourselves to fidelity and express freely our affection, our love, our admiration, our sorrow over our offenses (oratio: affective prayer); we are united in love—a union of wills—simply content and at peace in being with our beloved in silence beyond words (contemplatio: resting in God's presence).

Understanding this process of lectio is important in being alert for the particular way a person may be drawn at different times in their prayer. One may be attracted on one day, or during one part of their prayer, or perhaps during one phase of life to regular, continuous, thought-filled reading as he or she integrates the truths of Scripture into his or her life. At another time a person will be drawn to mull over one passage, to think about it, say it aloud, write it, make it his or her own. On another day, during another part of prayer, or at another time in life, the individual will want to move immediately to affective prayer, perhaps in the form of short aspirations of love, longing, hope, repentance, or praise that may be expressed in psalm verses or other short phrases of Scripture, such as "O God, my God, for you I long!" "Have mercy on me, O God, have mercy!" "Only in you is my soul at rest!" "You are my beloved Child!" At another time, perhaps consistently at some period in life, a person may only want or only be able to sit in silence, willing to be open to God's presence and work in him or her.

Exploring with directees the particular movements of their prayer can be a significant way of helping their awareness of the Spirit's direction in their lives grow. People do not necessarily follow this process of lectio in an orderly way; that is, from reading, through reflection, followed by affective prayer, and then finally silent resting in God. Some people may never feel very much at home praying with words but may be immediately drawn to affective prayer. Others may be attracted primarily to inner silence, finding words an aggravation or burden. Others will get a great deal of benefit from much reading and thinking. Here again, I find it important as a spiritual companion to let go of any expectation of how things ought to proceed for any one person. Rather, I listen carefully to how he or she is being led by the Spirit so we can discover together those places where he/she finds peace and joy at the deepest level. I try not to worry about how others might do it, or whether I am doing it right!

Growth in the life of prayer has its tough spots, those experiences of "not being able to pray" or "not being able to pray like I used to." Most often these times of "failure" in prayer are transition points to a deeper level of prayer. What one feels is misery, but what is happening is a blessing. Sometimes a person says to me something like this: "I'm sick of Scripture. I used to love it and look forward to my prayer time with it. Now I simply can't make myself read it. I feel terrible about this. I feel like I'm doing something wrong, that God has left me." After acknowledging how awful the person feels, I might say, "You seem really worried about this. That surely means you care about your relationship with God. And, of course, God cannot leave; it is God's nature to be with us." Then I might ask, "What can you do? What do you feel attracted to do?" If there is some simple way of staying at prayer that attracts the person, I encourage that. But sometimes the response to my question is "Nothing!" An important response to hear. This can be a significant turning point in prayer. If, after exploring how things are going in other areas of the person's life, I see that she/he is generally faithful to times of prayer and to life's other duties and responsibilities and is trying to do his/her best in expressing love in respect for and service of others, I may conclude that "doing nothing" in prayer may be the most appropriate response, and say that. This may be that important transition from more active to more passive prayer, to a prayer of receptivity, the beginning of contemplative prayer, that prayer in which we simply rest in God, letting the divine activity of the Spirit take over in us.

I might say to a person in such a place: "Why not try doing nothing? What helps you, or what do you think would help you stay with your prayer—doing nothing while keeping your inner self open to God?" The person may very well be able to get in touch with how he or she is being led to pray more simply. Perhaps with the repetition of some short phrase or word, whether from Scripture or something that arises from within. Or perhaps a gentle rhythmic walk or stroll, or a purposeless, quiet walk to some natural setting. Maybe gentle rocking in a rocking chair.

Because of the particular historical and cultural context of the scriptural Word of God, as spiritual companions we can expect to face—in some people and sometimes in ourselves—certain resistances; for example, those aroused by its patriarchal character. Working out interpretations based on some of the valuable hermeneutical studies by feminists and other Scripture scholars can be helpful background work for some directors and directees. However, the important thing in the sessions themselves is to hear and explore the directee's feelings and responses to the particular passage. This can be an important process in uncovering the directee's image or concept of God and helping him or her find the freedom to let other concepts and images arise.

In addition to the numerous spontaneous ways the Spirit invites each of us at various times to become quieter and open to a deeper presence, there are some simple general methods that can be learned as a help in receiving the gift of contemplative prayer.[3]

Centering prayer, like other contemplative practices, is not, strictly speaking, contemplation. Contemplation is a gift of God. Centering prayer is a method of reducing the obstacles to that gift, a method of helping the gift of our Baptism come to fruition within us. Among the chief obstacles to contemplation is our clinging to our own mental and psychological activity when we are being invited by the Spirit interiorly to rest in silence. We tend to want to hang on to our activity instead of entrusting ourselves to God's activity within us. We may think that unless we are making something happen, nothing is going on. The realization that the Trinitarian life of God—prayer, our relationship with God in Christ through the Spirit— is a given. It is always going on within us. We need to become receptive to that life, that prayer, that relationship. That is what centering prayer is about. With God's grace, it makes us receptive to that gift—the mysterious gift of divine life in the Risen Christ that lives in us and in which we live. Though not a necessary conscious component of the practice of lectio divina, it can be a help to us in moving from the more active phases of that practice into receptivity to the gift of contemplative prayer, a gift God wants to give all baptized Christians, all people, in fact.

Centering prayer is a method in which we use what is called a "sacred word," that is, a one or two-syllable word to indicate our faith intention simply to assent or consent to God's presence and action in the Spirit of the Risen Christ within us, a presence and action which is interior, global, diffuse. It is introduced into the imagination very gently and is used morning and evening during centering prayer sessions lasting twenty to twenty-five minutes. The sacred word helps us to return from "thoughts" that attract to the simple loving intention to assent to God's presence and action within and around us. In this way we open ourselves more and more to that simplification of prayer which the Spirit will work in us as she gradually takes over our prayer.

People may or may not be attracted to a practice like centering prayer. No matter. What is important is that we as spiritual directors help others to be alert to the inner invitations of the Holy Spirit in prayer; to listen with them to those nudgings from within to be more simple, more still; to affirm them; and to help them explore ways to give their assent to the invitation even though the experience may be one of pain and failure. All prayer, and especially contemplative prayer, draws us into the paschal mystery, Christ's dying and rising, so it is no wonder it sometimes feels like death. The times we spend in prayer, giving ourselves intentionally to this mystery, help us to grow in awareness of its presence and to give assent to it in the rest of our lives. It is by realizing that we are always sharing in Christ's life, death, and resurrection that we are gradually transformed by that same Spirit into truly loving human persons.

When in prayer we realize the depths of God's love and acceptance, we begin to relax and let all aspects of ourselves be revealed. Things that we have held down in our unconscious for years begin to surface, and our interior during the time of prayer may become very noisy. We also begin to be more alert in daily life to deeply ingrained sinful attitudes, whether they are expressed in words or actions or not. For example, we may become much more attuned to our constant battering down of ourselves and/or others with judgmental, even hateful thoughts. This is no sign that we are losing ground. On the contrary, it means progress, although we may "feel" that we are worse than we were before we started! All these repressed and constricting emotions and false ideas about ourselves and about God and others, with God's help, come to our consciousness so that they may be released, so that the love of the Spirit within may truly take over in our lives. During these times of purification, people tend to get discouraged, to think that prayer is not for them, to want to quit. The insight and encouragement of a spiritual director can be very important at these times, which are so significant in coming to a deeper purity of heart, the most essential component of prayer in the Rule (chapter 20).

According to the early monastics, purity of heart, the focus of the sixth beatitude in Matthew 5, is the goal of monastic life, since without it one cannot "see God." It is a kind of total integration of all our spiritual, psychic, and corporeal energy in the love of God. It is manifest in a deep inner calm and stability, the basis of a freedom to love, to let the love of God be manifest in and through us.

Just as the quality of our lives is affected by the quality of our prayer, so is the quality of our prayer affected by the quality of our lives. Michael Casey, an Australian Cistercian monk and insightful author of many articles and books on monasticism and prayer, points out that though Benedictinism is a major factor in the contemplative tradition of the Western Church, the *Rule of Benedict* itself says very little about prayer. It contains neither an explicit theology of prayer nor any practical directives beyond the order of psalmody and readings for the Liturgy of Hours, the times for liturgy and lectio. However, the Rule contains much about the quality of daily life. Casey quotes John Climacus, a Byzantine monk of the seventh century, who tells us that "prayer is the monk's mirror." Now as then, prayer is a mirror for all of us, since it reflects the depth of our receptivity to grace in daily life. Our prayer shows us what condition we are in.[4] And our loving service and compassionate relationships with others prove our prayer authentic. Our life of prayer expresses explicitly in our relationship with God what is at the heart of our relationships in love and service of others—the love of Christ, his love for us and our love for him. The Rule stresses Christ's presence in the abbot/abbess, in the stranger, the guest, the poor, the sick, and in all our sisters and brothers in the community. The love of Christ comes before all else. All other loves are connected with the love of Christ, which "comes before all else" (4.21).

If someone who comes to me is having trouble in prayer, or if I myself am, one important thing to be on the alert for is the character and quality of the interactions and dynamics of daily life. It is neither insignificant nor irrelevant that many people who come for spiritual direction spend a lot of their time reflecting on their relationships with spouses, children, parents, siblings, coworkers, friends, teachers, students, neighbors, associates, clients, customers. These relationships tell us much about our relationship with God. Destructive behavior and attitudes toward self and others blind us and cut us off from the goodness of God, the basic goodness of life. Loving and compassionate behavior and attitudes open us to God. Reflecting on these various daily experiences of ours often deepen our gratitude in prayer or lead us to repentance and compunction.

We are not able to open to this divine dimension of daily life by our own power. Only with Christ's help (Prologue and chapter 73), only through the power of the Holy Spirit (7.70), can we be transformed by love into loving persons who radiate God's love in our world. This is our journey into the paschal mystery. In the Prologue of the Rule, the general pattern of the spiritual journey is given: turn away from evil, do good, seek after peace with the Gospel as our guide, don't lose heart if things are difficult at first because, as we progress in our journey of faith and disciplined practice, our hearts will expand with love and we will run on the way of God's commandments. Patience is of the essence; if we want to share in Christ's reign, we need also to share his suffering. Benedict encourages us as we begin to turn to Christ for help and reminds us that what is not possible to us by nature will be given by grace.

Growth in Love:
The Work of the Holy Spirit as Integration

Life's journey in its spiritual dimension is about finding the inner freedom to become and be who we are intended to be as expressions of the Divine Life in our world. That is what spiritual direction is about. As Thomas

Merton puts it, "The whole purpose of spiritual direction is to penetrate beneath the surface of a [person's] life, to get behind the facade of conventional gestures and attitudes which [s/he] presents to the world, and to bring out [her/his] inner spiritual freedom, [her/his] inmost truth, which is what we call the likeness of Christ in [the] soul."[5]

Benedict describes this journey into freedom and openness to God as our descent into humility, not a favorite virtue for us nowadays. Caught up in expectations that we must be—or at least appear to be—"on top of things," with everything under control, we find it difficult to let go the drive to be "number one" or at least "one up" on somebody. We tend to feel constantly compelled to be more, do more, have more. Of course, this need to be number one, or at least to appear better than another, or, failing that, to berate ourselves, which is a kind of false humility, is built on the varying depths of each person's insecurity and fear, and it makes truly authentic love impossible. We tend to think of humility as a kind of self-putdown. To encourage that in people who already lack self-esteem is lethal! But true humility is, in fact, the opposite of that. It is the most basic self-acceptance and self-love, a welcome of ourselves just as we are with all our gifts and shortcomings. The self-love of true humility gives us the largeness of heart we need to truly love others. We arrive at such self-love only when we realize that we are unconditionally loved.

The way of humility in the *Rule of Benedict* begins with the constant acceptance of our human, fallible reality, fully known by God who embraces us totally in our goodness and in our particular weaknesses and tendencies to sin. It is spoken of as a descent, a coming down from the precarious, ever-threatened heights of unreality, where we strive for security in some false projection of ourselves as superior people or in some shame-filled hiding of what we consider our inferiority. The descent increasingly identifies us with Christ in his acceptance of human suffering and it ends as Christ's descent ends, not in the annihilation we fear, but in God's unconditional love, which frees us from fear. "Coming down to earth," the "earth" of our humanity, we find ourselves rooted in the stable "ground" (the literal meaning of the Latin word *humus*) of Divinity.

With those who come to us for empathetic and enlightened companionship, we watch patiently and trustingly for the signs along the way revealing the Spirit's presence and work within them. These signs include the following:

- Awareness of God's presence; watchfulness over our behavior and inner thoughts—God's and our own.
- The desire, motivated by the love of God, to live in harmony with God's will in daily life as it comes to us through legitimate requests, commands, duties, and responsibilities.

- Inner peace through growing identity with Christ in the midst of life's inevitable suffering, a deep interior tranquility arrived at by working through the anger, depression, and desire to flee that come with life's losses and troubles, especially its injustices.
- The capacity to be honest, to reveal one's inner thoughts, good or bad, to a spiritual elder.
- Realization that without God we are nothing and can claim nothing as our own—no gift, no talent manifest in us. Knowing our own and each other person's goodness as a gift, we feel neither superior or inferior but are able to identify as equals, free to speak and act or to refrain from speaking and acting without excessive concern about another's response.
- Contentment in one's ordinariness and freedom from constant need for special treatment to reinforce self-worth.
- The ability to live and work in community. The capacity to be quiet and listen or stand up and speak—to contribute to and learn from others without calling constant attention to ourselves through loud or excessive talk and laughter or through inappropriate withdrawal.
- An authentic self-presentation conveying the integration of one's inner and outer selves.

Benedict describes the honesty, self-love, love of others and God—which is the fruit of the freedom from fear and the integration of love resulting from a life of humility—as "good zeal." It is manifest in the ability to be consistent in "showing respect to others," in "supporting with the greatest patience one another's weaknesses of body or behavior," in the desire to do what one "judges better for someone else"; in "mutual love" for one's companions along the way, whether family, community members, or coworkers; in "loving awe of God"; in "unaffected, honest and sincere love of those who have some authority in one's life"; and in preferring "nothing whatever to Christ," whom one trusts "to bring us all together to everlasting life" (72.4–12). These virtues are all good touchstones in attending not only to our directees', but also to our own growth into the life of Christ through the power of the Holy Spirit. The trick in using them as any kind of a guide in assessing the quality of one's prayer life is in our staying honest. On the spiritual journey, we are not about *looking like* we have great patience with another's weakness, whether it be a rotten attitude or a physical disability that requires our constant attention, but *actually being* that patient—something we come to not through the efforts we make, but mostly and finally through the work of the spirit of Christ in us. When that is the case, we honestly acknowledge it gratefully and humbly, realizing that of ourselves we could not do what we are doing. As we struggle along the way experiencing our weakness, over and over we "never lose hope in God's mercy" (4.74).

Accompanying someone on this journey into freedom as a spiritual director is an awesome and challenging gift and work. Neither one of us is in the driver's seat. Neither of us can control the speed or timing of the process or its outcome. Given the most basic ingredients on the part of a directee—sincere desire to seek God according to the Gospel; that is, to open to the Divine Presence and action by doing what the directee can and depending on God for the rest, and the willingness to enter into and articulate his or her experience, thoughts, and feelings are, we trust, as Benedict says at the end of his description of the signs of humility, "All this [God's] will by the Holy Spirit graciously manifest in his [worker]" (7.70). We watch with each person for the signs of God's love, that is, the Spirit's work, the living out of Christ's dying and rising, as they strive to be honest no matter where in their journey they are. God's love is there in the midst of experiences of suffering and desperation as well as in those of contentment, peace, and joy.

Often the best way to assure a person of God's unconditional and faithful love no matter what condition they find themselves in is not by being didactic, pious, or preachy about it, but by silently and compassionately being with them in their pain or joy and reassuring them by empathetically reflecting back their own experience. Certainly some appropriate connection of their experience with Scripture can also be helpful for many. The director's acceptance of a person and his or her experience is a sacramental expression of God's unconditional love present in Christ working through the Spirit. In all of the attending to experience, actions, and attitudes that we do with directees as they get to know God and themselves, I have found it helpful to consistently, gently, and compassionately come back to motivations, that is, sources of personal energy, using such questions as: "Where does your strength to persevere in the midst of your sadness come from?" "What is the source of that joy you talked about being present in spite of that failure?"

As spiritual directors we both embody Christ for others and receive Christ in them. In a way we are called to be the quintessential guestmaster of the *Rule of Benedict,* that is, we are to welcome each person "as Christ, for he himself will say: 'I was a stranger and you welcomed me'" (53.1, quoting Matthew 25:35).

PART THREE

Special
Spiritual
Perspectives

CHAPTER NINE

The Spirituality of Nature and the Poor

Revisiting the Historic Vision of St. Francis

H. Paul Santmire, Ph.D.

Get away from it all! That's the constant message of advertising in our era, whether the ads promote beaches in Tahiti or Jaguars in New York City. The advertisers know their business. They speak to some of our most deeply rooted values. Affluent North Americans typically prefer a spirituality of escape, whether or not they give that spirituality conscious expression. Amidst the shrill noises of world politics and the sometimes dissonant chords of their own personal histories, they seek to take flight to far-off places or to turn within, behind the wheel perhaps, maybe even down on their knees, in order to find the peace and the quiet and the sense of spiritual power that they so deeply desire. Ironically, apart from such moments of escape, many of the same overheated, stressed-out, affluent spiritual seekers seem to be just as committed, if not more so, to a sometimes crass, egocentric consumer careerism, a spiritual schizophrenia.

This divided mind and heart—the fervent quest for spiritual escape, on the one hand, and the avid participation in a consumer culture, on the other—have some mostly unintended but nevertheless disastrous consequences. The escapist schizoid spirituality lends support to forces that work to destroy the earth (environmental crises) and that abandon the poor (social justice crises). A modest but illustrative case in point is the SUV. Many North Americans deeply revere sports utility vehicles and eagerly employ them, in their fantasies if not in fact, in order to get away from it all. This they do with apparent obliviousness to the fact that use of the vehicles both adds inordinately to the air pollution that promotes global warming and consumes disproportionate amounts of nonrenewable resources of God's good earth, resources that might otherwise be available to make a better life for the poor of the earth.

The spirituality of St. Francis can show us another, better way. His is neither a spirituality of geographical getting away from it all nor a spirituality of inner withdrawal. Nor, dramatically, is his way of life hemmed in and oppressed by the possessions of this world. Francis's commitment to living according to the last things of God (eschatology) can lead us to a new, ecstatic appreciation for our mundane experience and for nature in particular (materiality), which can, in turn, make our souls sing (spirituality) as we engage ourselves radically with this world, freed from consumer habits and addictions. But we must begin, in the first place, by understanding Francis aright, because his spirituality is elusive.

The Historic Witness of St. Francis

St. Francis, regrettably, has become the captive of a thousand causes, among them the spirituality of escape. The popular domesticated reading of St. Francis, enshrined in backyard statuary and best-selling guides to the spiritual life, reflects the very schizoid spirituality that many North Americans take for granted. Francis is read by Christians and other seekers as the champion of an escapist nature mysticism: someone who can teach us by example how to move beyond the crowded ways of postmodern, computerized existence in order to experience transforming encounters with the beauties and the wonders of the natural world, encounters akin to those that seem to be articulated by Francis's enormously popular "The Canticle of the Creatures." Conversely, among devout Christians, Francis is sometimes read as the champion of spiritual interiority: as one who turns away from this world to seek solace within, exemplified, above all, by the mountaintop story of his spiritual and physical experience of being touched by the cross of Jesus, the stigmata.

These popular readings of Francis have had, as a matter of course, the effect of reinforcing today's schizoid spirituality of escape and consumerism and have, in turn, provided spiritual support to those very forces that are working to destroy the earth and to abandon the poor, both loved so profoundly by Francis himself. To learn from Francis, therefore, we must divest ourselves of our own assumptions about him, such as they may be, and encounter him in his historical otherness.

Francis was born the son of a wealthy Assisi cloth merchant in 1181 or 1182. He shared all the privileges of this rising class, and some of its vices, as well. As a young man he was given to carousing with his friends and, with that, he was taken by the love songs of the troubadours and their sensualities. He also thought of himself in some measure as a warrior. He participated in an armed struggle with the neighboring city of Perugia in 1202, and was taken captive for a year. This was an era in Italy when such conflicts were commonplace.

Francis broke radically with this class and its lifestyle in 1206, however, when, standing publicly before his own bishop, with his father looking on unhappily, he threw off his garments, the signs of his wealth and social standing, and revealed himself to be wearing a hair shirt, the sign of a new commitment to poverty on his part. He then threw off that shirt, too. Thus he began his new spiritual vocation—naked, with no possessions whatsoever. For some time he lived as a hermit, supporting himself by begging and reaching out, on occasion, to the poorest of the poor, even to lepers.

Like others in his time, Francis had been taken by the claim of the poor Christ, the Crucified, whose voice he heard speaking to him as he knelt before a crucifix in an abandoned wayside chapel. More, he was claimed by the words of the same Jesus read at a mass he attended in 1208: Francis heard Jesus calling him, as the Savior had called the first apostles, to take to the highways and byways to witness to the kingdom of God, all without any possessions of his own. That Francis then did, abandoning the life of a hermit he had been living to that point. Francis committed himself to this apostolic vocation strikingly, with the imagined companionship of that glorious friend of Jesus who by then had become a fixture in Francis's chivalric fantasies, Lady Poverty.

In his new apostolic ministry, Francis immersed himself in the emergent urban culture of his time, a setting that the spirituality of the then-declining feudal monasteries was generally ill equipped to influence. In this sense, Francis was an urban minister, first and foremost, not a spiritual recluse or a nature mystic. His mission was not to retreat to a solitary life in the wilderness, a still viable spiritual option in his time. Nor was it to retreat to a protected monastery, where he might have imagined himself to be living anew in Paradise, surrounded by a hostile world, awaiting the coming kingdom of God, also a spiritual option that many in the Christian West had been choosing for centuries. No, Francis's spiritual retreat was in fact an advance into the rising urban culture of his time. His solitary life was in fact a commitment to seek out the lonely and the godforsaken, who were flocking to the cities. Even more comprehensively, the monastery where he awaited the coming of God's kingdom was in fact the whole world, not just its cities. Francis had become a latter-day apostle who believed that he had been sent by Jesus to preach the Gospel to every creature (Mark 16:15).

What message did Francis preach on his apostolic journeys in the cities and along the highways and byways of his world? We have no clear idea about the particulars, since Francis was not a writing theologian. Nor were his sermons recorded in any detail by others. However, we know that his major theme was peace. "He went about the towns and villages," relates his chief biographer, Thomas of Celano, "announcing the kingdom of God and peace." More significantly, Francis lived that witness, very practically. This is the account of another witness, one Thomas, Archdeacon of Spalato:

> That year [1220] I was living in the Studium of Bologna; on the feast of the Assumption I saw St. Francis preach in the public square in front of the town hall. Nearly the entire population had gathered there. His preaching did not at all resemble the lofty flights of sacred eloquence. It was rather a sort of harangue. . . . All through his talk he spoke of the duty of putting an end to hatred and of concluding a new peace treaty. He wore an old habit; his appearance was not at all handsome. But God gave such power to his words that they brought peace back to many families of noble folk that had been torn asunder by long-standing hatred, so cruel and unbridled that it had lead to several assassinations.

Francis also took his message of peace to the courts of the most powerful leaders of his day. Thus, he made an arduous and finally unsuccessful pilgrimage to visit the Sultan in the name of peace. Francis's contemporary, Pope Innocent III, had attempted to mobilize the whole of the Western world in a crusade against the Saracens in order to regain the Holy Land for Christendom. Francis's witness of peace to the Sultan—for that was indeed the chief purpose of his visit, not just to "convert" the Sultan to Christianity, as often has been surmised—stood in radical opposition to the whole project of the Crusades. Francis took Jesus' injunction in the beatitudes, "Blessed are the peacemakers" (Matthew 5:9), literally and with profound seriousness.

If that was his way of life—poverty and ministry to the poor—and if those were his words and deeds—peace and peacemaking—what vision inspired Francis? While in all likelihood Francis never self-consciously thought of his ministry in precisely this way, his witness can be read as a kind of apostolic realization of the biblical vision of the end times, the great peaceable kingdom announced by Isaiah: "The wolf shall dwell with the lamb, and the leopard shall lie down with the kid, and the calf and the lion and the fatling together, and a little child shall lead them" (11:6). Francis was a literalist. Whereas others might have taken the apostolic imperative of poverty as a guide to moral perfection and the commitment of the earliest Christians to "sell their property and possessions, and distribute the money among all, according to what each one needed" (Acts 2:45) as a witness to deeper spiritual meanings, Francis took it all just as it was written. He lived the apostolic life of the coming peaceable kingdom. Therefore, we can say that Francis's deepest inspiration was implicitly—sometimes explicitly— eschatological. His was a vision of the coming peaceable kingdom of God to be lived here and now.

His famous nature mysticism must be understood in this context. Francis did not go directly to nature to encounter God there. Rather, he committed himself to live the life of the coming peaceable kingdom in this world and, as a result, saw the whole world, every creature, in a new light. What is often referred to as his nature mysticism, his immersion in the materiality of this world, flowed from his literalizing eschatology. Yet it was no less powerful for that reason. On the contrary, as one who lived the life of the coming peaceable kingdom in a exemplary way here and now, Francis was able to befriend all the creatures of nature, to relate to them as brothers and sisters, in a way that was, in its heights and depths, perhaps unique in the history of Christian spirituality.

Francis's great hymn, "The Canticle of the Creatures," should be understood in the same literalizing eschatological context. Francis apparently sang the hymn often. He urged his followers to take it with them on their journeys and to sing it along the way. He had the hymn sung to him as he lay dying on the ground, on his beloved earth, naked, just as he had launched his vocation as a hermit and thereafter as an apostle. Think of Francis's canticle as a song of praise emanating from the coming peaceable kingdom:

> Most high, all-powerful, all good, Lord!
> > All praise is yours, all glory, all honor
> > And all blessing. . . .
> All praise be yours, my Lord, through all that you have made,
> > And first my lord Brother Sun. . . .
> All praise be yours, my Lord, through Sister Earth, our mother,
> > Who feeds us in her sovereignty and produces
> > Various fruits and colored flowers and herbs. . . .
> Happy those who endure in peace,
> > By you, Most High, they will be crowned.

The content of this magnificent canticle cannot easily be summarized. It has been subjected to exhaustive study by many scholars. Basically it is a song of praise for—or by—the whole creation. Scholars have argued for each of these translations of the Italian *per*: be praised, My Lord, for—or by—all your creatures. Both translations can be readily justified: "for" arising from the believer's gratitude for all the good gifts of the creation; "by" attesting to the voice of the whole creation offering praises to the Creator. Probably, as at least one scholar has suggested, Francis intended the ambiguity: he used *per* in the sense of both for and by.

Of perhaps greater interest is the structure of the canticle. It is indeed a celebration of God, the Most High, to begin with. But it immediately becomes a celebration of the merciful goodness of God. The poet who has said that he is not even worthy to speak the name of God, in another context, now joins in solidarity with the whole creation, as the brother of all creatures, in a descending movement, as Eloi Leclerc, the eminent interpreter of Francis, observes. The name "Most High" all but disappears after the second stanza on Brother Sun. Leclerc describes this movement this way:

> The abandonment of the name is significant. It does not mean that Francis has ceased to be alert and open to the call of the Most High. It means that henceforth his way toward the Most High will, paradoxically, be a way that leads from heaven to earth. From the heights of heaven where "my lord Brother Sun" radiates his light, Francis in his praise gradually descends to things ever closer to us, ever more accessible, and ever more humble as well. His way now is not only that of the dazzling sun and the "precious" stars but also that of wind and water and finally of earth: a humble journey of return to mother earth. Francis's itinerary in his song of praise brings us back among things and sets us in their very midst.

This is where Francis typically leaves the human creature, in the very midst of all the creatures of God, not above them, but with them as the friend who cares for even the least of these, even subjecting oneself to them. Not long after he had completed the first version of his canticle, Francis added stanzas about forgiveness and peace and then, finally, about death, thus binding his faith to his immersion in this material world even more.

Still, and of critical importance for Francis, he only arrived at this vision of the coming peaceable kingdom and only sought to embody it in everything he did—his ministry of peace, his befriending and celebrating of the creatures of nature—because his life, so he believed, had first been claimed by the merciful, self-emptying love of God in Jesus Christ. True, Francis devoted all his powers and faculties to the imitation of Christ (*imitatio Christi*) and to the quest to serve Lady Poverty, Christ's own constant companion, in Francis's view. But that was secondary for Francis, a kind of spiritual reflex, compared to God's great act of salvational humility in sending his Son to us. A view of God's self-emptying love—the Greek word is *kenosis*—gave Francis his deepest identity, as announced by Paul in Philippians, regarding Christ: "Who, though he was in the form of God, did not regard equality with God as something to be exploited, but emptied himself, taking the form of a slave, being born in human likeness. And being found in human form, he humbled himself and became obedient to the point of death—even death on a cross" (2:6–8). That view of God's self-emptying love gave Francis his deepest identity. The kenotic Christ, for Francis, was indeed the way and the door to life in the coming peaceable kingdom, here and now.

In a certain sense, for Francis the heavens had emptied. Although he often referred to God as "the Most High," as in his canticle, that was more a way of speaking of the mystery of God, an apophatic statement, than an articulation of how or where God is to be encountered. Rather, Francis's deepest theological intuitions were kenotic in character. They had to do with the merciful self-emptying of God, as we have already seen in the structure of the canticle. For Francis, God is to be known in the outpouring of God's life, here and now, in the material world, above all in the descent of the Son of God into the flesh, in the spirit of Paul's great hymn to the incarnation and crucifixion in Philippians. "The humility of the incarnation," Celano writes of Francis, "and the charity of the passion occupied his memory particularly, to the extent that he wanted to think of hardly anything else."

Undoubtedly this preoccupation with "the humility of the incarnation" on Francis's part was shaped profoundly by yet another facet of his spirituality, which numerous modern interpreters have neglected: his eucharistic piety. Francis made it a practice to participate in the Mass, the sacrament of the body and blood of the Crucified Christ, daily. The kenosis of the incarnation was thus made existentially real for Francis in the ritual milieu of this down-to-earth, sacramental materiality. Francis's most celebrated mystical experience, his being marked by the wounds of the Crucified, the stigmata, on Mount Alverna in 1224, reveals precisely this kind of kenotic vision. As historian of mysticism Ewert Cousins has pointed out, in the prophetic and apocalyptic visions of the Bible, such as Isaiah's contemplation of the holy God above at the time of his call and in the testimony of Christian mystics throughout the ages, the visionary is *lifted up* to heaven. In contrast, in Francis's Alverna experience heaven *descends* to earth: the heavenly seraph comes down to manifest the union of the divine and the human in the crucified humanity of Christ.

But the mountaintop experience of Alverna, dramatic as it was, and the daily experience of the Eucharist, critical as that was for Francis's spirituality, were not, as such, the testimony he wanted as his legacy, although those factors surely and profoundly shaped that legacy. He actually tried to divert public attention away from the Alverna experience, in particular. In contrast, when Francis wanted to dramatize his most fundamental convictions—

his implicit but nevertheless deep commitment to embodying the life of the peaceable kingdom, his profound dependence on the kenosis of God on the cross, mediated in the Mass—Francis did something else: he enacted an end-time drama of the Crucified in the midst of the peaceable kingdom. This is the deeper significance of his often-misunderstood dramatization of the Nativity of Christ toward the end of his life.

Although medieval Christians had, on occasion, created Nativity scenes with the figures of the magi and the shepherds and the animals before Francis's time, he more or less invented the Christmas tableaux as a ritual enactment in the context of the eucharistic liturgy.

Francis had been given to dramatic gestures and enactments all along. Throwing off his clothes in public as a young man, before his bishop and his father, while announcing his conversion to a life of poverty, was but the first of many such public enactments. Toward the end of his life, it appears that Francis decided to make a great summary statement, one last gesture of gestures, announcing more poignantly than he had ever done before what he had stood for since the days of his conversion. It was December 1223. He was in the town of Greccio, preparing to celebrate Christmas. His health was failing markedly. He had nearly been overwhelmed by the trials of shepherding what had become by then a new order of friars, with many hundreds of members in many countries. A definitive Rule for his order had just been approved by the papacy. Undoubtedly, he must have felt, given the state of his health, that this festival would be his last, or nearly last, Christmas on this earth.

Francis spoke with a friend in Greccio, a person of some means and much property. Francis was able to use his friend's mountainous land for a new kind of celebration of Christmas to be held in a grotto there. Francis invited the people of the whole region, rich and poor, as well as friars living in nearby hermitages, to this special Christmas Mass. Francis also brought domestic animals from nearby to gather near the altar. The human participants carried torches as they walked to the grotto, halfway up the mountain. Under the overhanging cliff, a manger had been built. Francis himself, never a priest, served as the deacon, chanting the Christmas Gospel and preaching. The Mass was celebrated. It turned out to be a moment of liturgical ecstasy, even cosmic illumination, for all the participants. According to Celano's account:

> There simplicity was honored, poverty was exalted, humility was commended; and Greccio was made, as it were, a new Bethlehem. The night was lighted up like the day, and it delighted men and beasts. The people came and were filled with new joy over the new mystery. The woods rang with the voices of the crowd and the rocks made answer to their jubilation.

The sense, rooted in the prophet Isaiah, that God was present and doing something new must have been palpable. The sense, likewise rooted in the witness of prophets like Isaiah, that God was there inaugurating the salvation of the whole creation, when the lamb will lie down with the lion and a little child will lead them, must also have been palpable. Here eschatology and materiality came together for Francis in a way that announced the meaning of his spirituality more deeply and more expressively than at any other single point in his life.

St. Francis as a Spiritual Guide

Remarkable as Francis was, can he be our spiritual guide today? Some might say that his is an impossible ideal and that therefore Francis's example can practically be of little use to most of us. But what if we were to try, by the grace of God, to claim his vision for ourselves? What, indeed, if we were enabled, by the grace of God, to take that proverbial first step with which the journey of a thousand miles must always begin, even several first steps? Perhaps in some measure, miraculously, Francis's elusive spirituality might be made our own.

The support of steadfast and insightful spiritual directors along the way could make it much easier for us to take those first, undoubtedly hesitant steps. Spiritual directors, who have encountered Francis in his historical otherness themselves, could also by the grace of God serve as midwives who could stand with all of us who are seekers today, especially with those of us who are affluent North Americans, as we, in turn, inspired by the example of Francis, struggle to overcome the deadening schizoid spirituality of our own world. If the goal is now not to follow the promptings of our culture to get away from it all, but rather the promptings of Francis's example to get into it all, how could those spiritual directors assist us to claim Francis as our guide? What could they tell us? Things like these.

Francis was not a mystic in the usual sense. He did not show his followers the way to lift up their hearts in order to ascend spiritually to heaven, the way to rise above the material conditions of this world to be able to contemplate "the One" in the splendid isolation of the ineffable realm of pure spirit. That mysticism of ascent was not the mysticism championed by Francis. Nor did Francis seek to encounter God by turning within; he was not a mystic of the inner way. He was, rather, a mystic of "last things" in this world of things—a mystic of eschatological materiality.

The meaning of this kind of mysticism was exemplified by the Christmas tableaux Francis choreographed at Greccio, rooted in the liturgical spirituality of historic Christianity. First he focused on the first nativity of Christ and on Christ's sacrificial death, which, Francis believed, opened

the doors of this world to the new world of God to come. He focused likewise on the second nativity of Christ in the Church's historic Eucharist, where
the same Christ comes from the bosom of the Father to be en-fleshed in bread
and wine, thus accessible even to the least sophisticated of believers. Finally
Francis focused on the future coming of Christ when he will fully establish the
peaceable kingdom of God for the whole creation, the new world promised by
the biblical prophets of old. This was Francis's mysticism of eschatological
materiality. Francis was, in this sense, a mystic of the cosmic Christ Mass.

This immediately suggests some practical steps for the seeker. Don't
climb to some mountaintop. On the other hand, don't find a quiet place,
shut your eyes, and meditate, either. You may surely choose to do such
things. Francis did. But first, go to church. Go to the Christian community
that practices the historic Eucharist, and keep going. Francis did that virtu-
ally every day of his mature life. The experience may baffle you. Or it may
uplift you. Either way, stay with it. And, at every opportunity, contemplate
the crucifix that you see before you. Contemplate the image of the God who
empties himself there, taking the form of a servant, so that he can walk with
you and talk with you and die for you and lead you into a new world not
of your own making.

Francis participated in the Eucharist daily, as a matter of course, almost
unselfconsciously. Scholars sometimes think of this kind of faith as a "primary naiveté." For us in the twenty-first century, however, whose minds have
been shaped by the critical questioning spawned by the eighteenth-century
Enlightenment and, undoubtedly in some measure, influenced by the modern and postmodern deconstruction of religion stemming from the works of
thinkers like Karl Marx, Sigmund Freud, and Friedrich Nietzsche, primary
naiveté will not work. We cannot avoid being self-conscious about our faith
and our doubts. Nor can we avoid being scientifically and historically critical of our faith. That goes with the territory of living in our own culture.
But trusting that we have indeed found a good and reliable spiritual guide
in Francis, it will nevertheless be possible for us to do what our spiritual
directors—those midwives of faith whom we also trust—have already done:
enter into a new and fresh kind of faith world called by some interpreters of
religion a secondary or post-critical naiveté.

Martin Luther once talked about faith as following a guide when you
are blindfolded as that guide leads you over a narrow bridge. Francis
undoubtedly could walk over that bridge, trusting in the hand of God to
guide him, almost without being aware that he was crossing the bridge. In
contrast, we will be very much aware of that crossing and of the risks of
falling flat on our faces, if not into much deeper predicaments. For us,
finally, claiming Francis as our spiritual guide will be a matter of risk and
trust: to risk taking hold of Francis's hand as the hand of God reaches out

for us, and to trust that, by the grace of God, Francis will be able to guide us over the bridge.

That is the good news. Now comes the bad news. It wasn't bad news for Francis. Actually, for him this news was a great and liberating joy. But for us affluent North Americans living in the twenty-first century, this news is not easy to hear. We do not truly see the Most High present in the flesh on the cross and in the Christ Mass and, indeed, in our own lives if we do not also know that marvelous figure of Francis's chivalric imagination and become her devoted servant. Meet Lady Poverty.

An irreverent bumper sticker has been seen in a couple of North American locales in recent years: IF YOU LOVE JESUS, TITHE. ANYBODY CAN HONK. Never mind tithing for now; let's talk about your finances. If you are anything like the rest of us affluent North Americans, that's the last thing you will want to talk about. You will talk about your deepest doubts with your spiritual director or even the most intimate details of your sex life. But be honest, wouldn't you resent it if he or she would ask you about your finances? That's your private business, right?

Wrong. Wrong, that is, if you would like Francis to be your spiritual guide. From the point of view of Francis himself, perhaps the greatest spiritual step he ever took was to do what that one affluent young seeker in Jesus' time resolutely refused to do: to sell all his goods and give the gain to the poor, and then to follow Jesus. Francis threw off all his clothes in public, before his father, who had hoped that Francis would help make the family business prosper all the more, and before his bishop, who, well aware that it was to the church's advantage to have prosperous business leaders like Francis's father in church every Sunday, had presumably hoped, secretly if not openly, that Francis would have recanted his earlier announced public espousal to Lady Poverty. To the good bishop's credit, however, he welcomed Francis's rejection of property and possessions, and thereby undoubtedly incurred the wrath of the wealthy father.

Who today in North America, even persons of modest means, never mind the richest of the rich, is going to emulate Francis's model? Some will, of course. Some will give up everything. But they are so few in number that they become figures of public renown, like a Mother Theresa. The name of Dorothy Day is sometimes also invoked in this kind of context. And well should such names be invoked. That kind of all-or-nothing commitment is clearly the most obvious way to emulate Francis's example. On the other hand, it would be all too convenient, would it not, for the rest of us to leave the Francises and the Mother Theresas and the Dorothy Days of this world standing all alone on the pedestals where we have placed them, so that we all could then return to business as usual, confident that their example is indeed impossible for us to emulate in any respect.

Which is sufficient reason, then, for us to return to the mandate of the aforementioned bumper sticker. If, as you consult your conscience and say your prayers, you decide that you are not willing or able at this time to give away all your possessions, would you consider a tithe? Would you consider giving away 10 percent of your yearly income, perhaps more? Would you consider drawing up a plan to allow you to give away 10 percent of your accumulated assets, perhaps more, for the cause of ministering to the poor, over a period of time whose length you could discuss with your spiritual director?

Are you really ready to discuss your finances with your spiritual director? One congregation, the Church of the Savior in Washington, D.C., insists upon such discussions, in this case with congregational leaders who are mature in the faith if not in years. You cannot join the Church of the Savior if you do not discuss your finances and come up with 1) a plan for sharing them with the poor, and 2) a realistic plan for avoiding consumer excesses yourself.

Perhaps the most sensitive and most deeply rooted spiritual challenge faced by affluent North Americans who wish to claim Francis as a spiritual guide is the question of private property. One American wag once asked, at a time of international crisis when some Arab nations in the Middle East were threatening yet another oil boycott: "What is *my* oil doing underneath *your* soil?" The truth from a Franciscan perspective is not only that the oil "over there" is not mine—the oil underneath my own soil is not mine! There is no "mine" from Francis's perspective. That Francis divested himself of all his property and all his belongings was the bedrock of his spirituality.

The idea of property belongs to a world in which people are their own bosses, their own lords, and where they readily "lord it over" one another. The idea of property belongs to a world in which people become so anxious about their status—because of course they trust only in themselves—that they are driven to overcompensate: to amass wealth, to build towers of Babel, to make a name for themselves to reassure themselves that they are of significance in the greater scheme of things. Not for nothing are the richest of the rich, the movers and shakers in North American society, the sports stars, the captains of industry, the TV and film personalities so adulated by so many others. In contrast, Francis knew that his only worth came from the kenotic love of God in the Crucified. Hence, Francis as a matter of course could totally divest himself of property and possessions. It was the most natural thing in the world for him to do.

That total divestment, in turn, invites total detachment for those of us who seek genuinely to emulate Francis. What property and assets we own we do not own. We hold them in trust, for the sake of the poor. This way of thinking emerged prominently in Catholic Worker circles in the United States, which, inspired by the example of Dorothy Day, owed much to the spirit of Francis. Many associated with this movement chose to think of their belongings and other assets as "trusterty," not property. What's mine, in a word, is not mine. I hold it not for the sake of status and worldly security, but in trust, in the spirit of Francis, for the sake of the poor.

Of course, even belongings and assets held as trusterty carry their own weight in this world. To hold things in trust is still to hold them, and to have and benefit from the power that this world accords to wealth. Money talks, of course. How, then, will we use that power? How, then, will we wield that influence? Can we even consider using the power of our money as Francis did, in order to serve the poor of our world? Does my trusterty, as distinct from my property, actually belong to the poor? Is what's mine really theirs? Talk these questions through with your spiritual director. You may find yourself returning to them often. If, then, we choose to make the commitment to let go of the power that goes with our wealth, that commitment will mean at least four things.

First, we who aspire to claim Francis as our spiritual guide must also claim the practice of *philanthropy* as our most important fiscal priority. The first thing we do when a check comes in will be to set aside some generous percentage of that amount to be donated directly or, probably better, indirectly, through agencies that do these things effectively, to minister to the poor of this world. On the other hand, for those of us who choose to think financially more in terms of tithing rather than in choosing to divest ourselves of all our wealth as Francis did, philanthropy is by no means the only step we will need to take. By itself, indeed, philanthropy might end up accomplishing only two things: salving our consciences and helping a few poor people to get through the day. That is not the spirit of Francis. Rather the spirit of Francis requires total commitment.

Hence, if we are truly to let go of the power of our wealth, we will have to move beyond the practice of philanthropy to the practice of *social justice*. Francis lived in a time when cities were emerging in Western Europe. With their expanding economies and growing intellectual pursuits, the cities held great promise, yet they had many problems, too, above all the fact of widespread poverty. We live in a time when urbanization and its companion, poverty, are perhaps the most significant social developments of our era. We will perhaps be best served, as we seek to launch our own practice of social justice, by getting our bearings from people we know and feel that we can trust. Most North American denominations have already developed well-considered moral guidelines for the practice of social justice, here and abroad, in our increasingly urbanized and increasingly impoverished world. The teachings of the U.S. Conference of Catholic Bishops on social justice issues, for example, are typically formed not only by careful social and economic analysis, but by a compelling Franciscan spirit. The practice of social justice, in fact, is not rocket science. It can be done, especially by those who have been claimed by the vision of Francis. So listen to the leading voices of your own faith community. Your spiritual director can show you how to do that.

For the next crucial ingredient in a Franciscan spirituality is the practice of *peace*. This was the hallmark of Francis's public ministry, celebrated dramatically in his Christmas tableaux. Free of entangling alliances with the power of wealth, he invested his energies in peacemaking. He brokered peace deals among the warring factions of his own region—and then had everyone singing! While the whole society was being mobilized by the leaders of the Church, to engage in a "holy" Crusade to remove the "infidels" from power in Jerusalem, Francis instead chose to go and visit the Sultan, in the name of peace!

Who will champion that Franciscan strategy in our era? Who will visit the Israelis and the Palestinians, the Indians and the Pakistanis, the Hutus and the Tutsis, the Croats and the Serbs, the white suburbanites and the African American and Hispanic urbanites, the gangs from the north side and the gangs from the south side, in the name of peace? Who will speak for the rain forests of the planet, which are being ravaged daily by unfettered human greed? Who will call the owners of huge factory complexes, whose facilities are poisoning the air breathed by poor people living nearby who cannot afford to live anywhere else, to sit down with those poor neighbors, in order to make peace with them and with the environment? Such challenges are not easy. When Martin Luther King Jr. visited Chicago in the name of racial harmony, jeering crowds threw stones at him. When he went to Birmingham to be with the garbage workers of that city, he was assassinated. Dorothy Day, likewise, was mocked when, at an advanced age, she sat in the front line of a public protest against the use of napalm bombs in civilian areas in the Vietnam conflict. Francis had less than evident success when he visited the Sultan. But that was the theme of his apostolic ministry nevertheless: the practice of peace.

Lest we throw up our hands in despair at the complexities of the issues facing the world today, let it be remembered that most Christian denominations in our day have issued thoroughly researched and biblically inspired directives for the ministry of peace. With the help of spiritual directors, the directives could be followed, especially by those who claim the witness of Francis as their own,

But that's not all. We have at least one more crucial step to take before we who are affluent can begin to make the example of Francis our own. Along with our participation in the Christ Mass and, growing out of that participation, practicing philanthropy, social justice, and peace, we must adopt a profound change of lifestyle. Call this a commitment to *voluntary simplicity*. Much has been written on this theme in recent years, but it still must be affirmed and lived.

At this point, we come full circle—to Christmas. The celebration of this holiday, as many North Americans experience it, is an orgy of consumerism. Christmas, indeed, can be called the ritual center of the North American consumer economy, with the mall being its temple. Whatever happened to the Christmas tableaux of Francis, where poverty was celebrated and where the hope of the Christ Child, born in a stable for all the poor and all the creatures of nature, was proclaimed?

Perhaps, indeed, your spiritual director could serve as sponsors do in Alcoholics Anonymous. Perhaps the community of faith could function as a kind of Consumers Anonymous: when you have the desire to go out and buy another big-ticket item, you can call up your spiritual director and he or she can talk you out of it. Much has already been written to guide those who aspire to simplify their Christmas celebrations. Now the question is: Is there a Franciscan commitment among the masses who celebrate Christmas—for the sake of voluntary simplicity as well as for the sake of the practices of philanthropy and social justice and peace? Consult with your spiritual director: perhaps the Lord is calling you to take on Christmas in your own community, so that the celebration of this great Mass can reflect more of the Franciscan vision and less of the insatiable fantasies of consumerism.

In retrospect, these kinds of commitment, inspired by Francis, will often fail. You may not achieve what you were inspired to do in the spirit of Francis when you left the celebration of the Eucharist—the practice of philanthropy, the practice of social justice, the practice of peace, the commitment to voluntary simplicity. Francis's visit to the Sultan, it appears, as far as tangible, visible results were concerned, was a complete failure. Although a peace movement led by followers of Francis after his death emerged in northern Italy, that movement was short-lived. The leading families and the small states of the region soon returned to business as usual, the God-awful business of violence and warfare. Churches, meanwhile, continued to amass wealth in Francis's time and beyond, and the more they amassed the more they seemed to become its servants. And the powerful continued to claim the support of the churches for their crusades of various kinds in subsequent decades—crusades that always seemed to be planned to leave the powerful more so. Even the self-conscious followers of Francis sometimes lost their bearings, as the quest for power and wealth and influence all too often proved to be an irresistible temptation.

Is it really surprising, then, that the inaugural inspiration for Francis's vision and the place to which he daily returned was to the sign of perhaps the greatest failure of all times: the cross? Francis himself suffered enormously, not only from a variety of painful illnesses, but also at the hands of physicians, who inflicted much (unnecessary, we can say) pain on him. Francis also must have been stricken, unconsciously if not consciously, by the objectively distressing and depressing sight of his own followers bickering over issues of power in Francis's own order, much as Jesus' own disciples appear to have discussed who would be the greatest in the kingdom of God, who would sit at his right hand once the kingdom had come. No wonder Francis "prayed without ceasing," as the apostle Paul had urged. Francis would not have been the exemplary figure he surely was apart from his inner prayer and discipline that so richly complemented his outer discipline of ministry to the poor and to peacemaking.

If you aspire to claim the example of Francis as your own, prayer will not necessarily be the place where you begin your spiritual journey, although Francis surely began to pray at an early date, perhaps when he was imprisoned for a year in a Perugian jail. Prayer, in any case, is surely where you will be driven by the circumstances of your vocation. We pray because we have no other alternative. No wonder Francis made prayer a regular habit as he pursued his public vocation. No wonder he took time for prayer, to rest his weary bones in the arms of the Lord. He could never have advanced as far as he did, spiritually speaking, with his ministry to the poor and his peacemaking, without having committed himself to a regular pattern of taking time to pray. Prayer is the spiritual way to take one step backward in order to take two steps forward, especially when you have no other alternative. Francis regularly took that one step backward. He was regularly driven to his knees. His culminating pilgrimage to Mount Alverna, important as it was, exemplary beyond all imagination as it must have been, was but one instance of many times when the saint went apart to a quiet place, as Jesus also often did, to pray. Your spiritual director can help you with this, too.

Francis led a life of exceedingly great joy and a life of constant praise of God, a life of blessedness in the midst of the fecund goodness of God's creation, celebrated most forthrightly by his "Canticle of the Creatures." As a citizen of the peaceable kingdom, transported there by his vision and his prayers, Francis could thereafter call every human, however different or distant, and each of the creatures of nature, however alien to human sensibilities, his brother or his sister. He could be a troubadour of a higher order, constantly rejoicing with friends and foes alike, and with birds and oxen and even wolves and worms. The mandate of Christ had claimed Francis's soul profoundly: to preach the Gospel to every creature. This he made remarkable efforts to do, in deed most often and in word whenever necessary. And, notwithstanding all the challenges he experienced and all the pains that were thrust upon him, he found joy in the nearness of God to him in every creature, in his encounters with lepers no less than in his songs of praise with the birds of the air.

Francis found peace and joy in his vocation not by getting away from it all, but by getting into it all. His was a vision and a way of life that is open to all of us by the grace of God, even to the most affluent among us who choose to claim his vision and follow his way: to engage ourselves with this world as if it were the world of the kingdom to come. Ask your spiritual director to help you claim Francis as your own spiritual guide.

For Further Reading

Leclerc, Eloi. *Francis of Assisi: Return to the Gospel.* Translated by Richard Arnandez. Chicago: Franciscan Herald Press, 1983.

McKibben, Bill. *Hundred Dollar Holiday: The Case for a Joyful Christmas.* New York: Simon & Schuster, 1998.

Santmire, H. Paul. *Nature Reborn: The Cosmic and Ecological Promise of Christian Theology.* Minneapolis: Fortress, 2001.

Sorrell, Roger D. *St. Francis of Assisi and Nature: Tradition and Innovation in Western Christian Attitudes toward the Environment.* New York: Oxford University Press, 1988.

CHAPTER TEN

Transforming Institutions

God's Call—A Director's Response

John H. Mostyn, CFC

This chapter is an attempt to put into words one dimension of growth in the art of spiritual direction. As a result of the awareness that institutions themselves have a spirit, spiritual directors have been asked to serve as directors alongside institutions, a ministry I've been involved with in recent years. In this chapter, I'll present some of the things I've learned in my own ministry with organizations.

It is my belief that the engagement of a spiritual director with the spirit of institutions has its source in the Mystery we call God. So I begin the chapter with a description of the theological stance necessary for this work. I then turn to a discussion of the importance of the founding vision of the institution and the impact it has on spiritual direction, suggesting how the spirit of an institution manifests itself, which is different from what occurs in an individual. Next, I look at how one notices the Spirit in this institutional context and make the distinction between group spiritual direction and directing the group spirit. How does the director prepare for work in this setting and what kind of a contract can be expected between director and institution? Finally, for the benefit of others working or planning to work in this field, I describe some lessons of spiritual direction I have learned in my context.

How the Secular Is Sacred: A Theology

The ancient dichotomy between the sacred and the secular is no longer valid in this day and age. All of us are called to be as whole and holy as we can possibly be. The routes we take on this journey are many and varied, and no one route is ontologically better than another. All work is sacred. Each person is gifted with a particular life that gives him or her an avenue to the Mystery we commonly call "God." Regardless of our state in life, our profession, our gender, our orientation, or our race, the avenue is open to the Mystery. All that is required of us is to listen to the inner and outer promptings that come to us, inviting us on our way.

The deepest experience we can have is the experience of self. This deep experience of self contains within it an opening to the divine. All that is necessary for us to do is to trust the experience and enter into it with a companion and without fear. Experiences of self such as being alone, being loved, loving someone else, facing death, fatherhood, motherhood, and other significant normal human experiences all contain this aperture to the divine. These experiences, which appeal to us alone, are the gifts of our humanness. When we accept this essential giftedness in the midst of our responsible choices, we experience freedom. This freedom is the foundation of our ability to co-create the future with the Mystery we call God. Choices not based on the experience of self deny us our freedom and are irresponsible.

The Mystery called God has given us our freedom, has enabled us to claim it and to act out of it. This is how I speak of God as the author of all creation and created things on the planet. This Mystery is so loving and generous that it engages us in a duet of creative actions. We become our true selves when we create, because it is when we are acting most in the image of God. Indeed, we are then creating in partnership with God.

Creativity is one of the royal bonds between the Mystery and us. Inspiration is the core of creativity. Inspiration needs to be put into some form of concrete manifestation. Writers write, painters paint, teachers teach, priests serve, bishops rule, managers manage, mothers mother, leaders lead, capitalists thrive, founders found, mathematicians calculate—the list is endless. All contain the human dimension that embodies openness to the divine, as we know it. Human history is replete with stories of creative human beings whose example inspires us and urges us to be likewise creative.

Some human beings create institutions. As one looks around our world, one sees a myriad of institutions, many of which did not exist a hundred years ago. Start up "dot-coms" come and go like the breezes off the ocean. Longstanding institutions struggle to adapt to the changing times while staying faithful to the visions that founded them. Very large institutions adapt over long periods of time; for example, the Roman Catholic Church has had twenty-one such major efforts at adaptation in its two thousand-year history as an institution, and, like other large institutions, has also had its splits and fractures.

Splits and fractures seem to come with the turf of creativity. Rock groups, for example, go on for a while, and then something happens and the group "splits." AT&T gets split by the U.S. Supreme Court because of a concept called monopoly. The U.S. Constitution divided government into three equal branches so that power would not be in the hands of one person. The framers of the Constitution wanted "checks and balances" between the branches. The human experience of existence, it seems, not only contains an aperture to the Mystery called God but also a tendency toward selfishness. Between these two invisible mountains lies the silent village of life in which we all live and work and have our existence.

In summary, theology needs to be grounded in the lived experience of the folk with whom we are working in spiritual direction. The theological investigation approach of someone like Karl Rahner is well suited for the work of both individual and corporate spiritual direction. There is no dichotomy between sacred and secular in the anthropological-theological approach to the Divine Mystery when the starting point is the lived experience of the subject.

Founding Visions of Institutions

Throughout history human need evokes an inspiration in someone to address the needy situation. When human needs change, so do inspirations and institutions. However, this is at least a three-step process. The first step is the perception of the need or changing needs and the responsive inspirational insight by an individual or a group. The second step is nurturing the insight into the practical realms of life. The third step is making the practical application available to the rest of us. Usually the person inspired is not the one who can make it happen concretely. Thus, a second person takes the original insight, sees its practical implications, and puts it into practice. This second person is the entrepreneur, the one who has the drive to create and distribute wealth for the rest of us. The third step is generally executed by a group of people inspired by the entrepreneur to carry out the practical application. Unfortunately, as the birth proceeds through the three steps, the original inspiration or vision can become blurred or even lost.

As one can see in all three steps, the apparent primary actors and actresses in the three steps are human beings. Institutions are not made by magic or in a vacuum. The first steps might start in garages, on hospital steps, in foreign cities, in an allied profession, or in the company of strangers.

Oftentimes, the original concepts are quite casually recorded—scribbled on the back of an envelope or on a dinner napkin. The second step usually entails inviting a group of people to coalesce around the subject of making the idea a practical reality. Here, the entrepreneur is the "leader," the others, the "followers." Finally, others join the endeavor for various reasons. The more people in the endeavor and the farther one is from the original inspiration, the more difficult it is to maintain the clarity of the original inspiration. Hence, the need for constant and systematic orientations and renewals of the founding vision.

Furthermore, humans possess the freedom to choose between good and bad. Freedom here is defined as a person coming to a self-realization and making a choice. Heredity and environment temper this freedom. In the face of heredity, environment, addictions, illusions, and biases, there is a need for clear thinking and feeling. This move to clarity usually goes by the name of discernment. It is critical to freedom that discernment goes on in the institutional world if only to make the "good" clearer to the people who are choosing the direction of the institution. If they choose to choose the "bad," so be it. The courts, an institution to govern other institutions, will eventually temper the institution at fault. Perhaps today's institutional "whistle blowers" are also today's prophetic voices; that is, they name the truth of the situation as if seen by the eyes of the Mystery called God and propose a just and merciful solution.

Here are four examples of founders of institutions.

1. Edmund Rice was a widower, who in his grief turned to helping those in his society who were more at risk than he was. Over the course of thirteen years, he grieved the loss of his wife and with his sister's help began to rear his invalid daughter. He also found solace in reading the Bible and in helping the poor. In due time, his expertise as a successful businessman was directed to the very poor he started to help after his wife died. He moved to helping the poor boys on the wharves near his business. In a radical step, he sold his business, bought a barn, and started a school for the boys. Soon others joined him in the enterprise and a whole series of schools was begun. This enterprise is now over two hundred years old, and is called the Congregation of Christian Brothers.

2. Agnes Gonxha Bojaxhiu was a nun in the Roman Catholic Church and a successful teacher at St. Mary's Secondary School in Calcutta, India. One day she came upon a dying woman in front of a hospital, and stayed with her until she died. That event galvanized her into action on behalf of the poorest of the poor. For the rest of her life she dedicated herself to them; as a result, many women and men began to do the same. She gained the confidence of Roman Catholic Church officials

and they sanctioned her beginning a new organization in that church. The group is called the Missionaries of Charity.

3. Theodore Vail is one of the parents of the telecommunications industry. His vision, developed over many years in the field of railroad communications, seemed to have one object: he strove for unity and simplicity in all that he did. He seemed always to look for the simplest way to do things for the most people, to bring them together through contact with one another. His work in rural communications was a first. He also built the first paved road in Vermont and established an agricultural school for boys called the Lyndon Institute. One can see in all these activities that others were drawn in and gained wealth and jobs through Vail's vision. When his gift was applied to the telecommunication field, it helped to give birth to the American Telephone and Telegraph Company, popularly known today as AT&T.

4. Bill Hewlett and Dave Packard were students together at Stanford University in Palo Alto, California, and in time became close friends. Their friendship was the source of much productive work. They started their electronics experiments in a garage behind a house and, in time, their practical applications in the field of electronics benefited the rest of us. The business partnership they formed contained elements of their friendship: the openness of their friendship lent itself to a management style that helps shape the way much of the electronic industry does its business today. They also started to manage by setting objectives for their growing number of employees. Thus was built a company culture that has endured to this day and has influenced the rest of the industry. The company is Hewlett-Packard.

These examples show the beginnings of several institutions and mini-cultures that endure to this day, yet these company cultures have changed because it is always a struggle to maintain the original ethos of a founding entrepreneur. Some say the living vision of the founder dies with the founder. Others say it lives on in the people whose hearts are connected by and to the founding vision. It is my observation that the founding vision remains as long as there is a need in the world for the particular vision to exist and a human who responds to it out of his or her freedom.

Each of the people named above is holy in that they seem never to have deviated from expressing the gifts that they had been given and developed over the adult years of their lives. Their lives exhibited the quality of wholeness that is associated with selflessness and faithful adherence to the vision that grasped them. Even though they may have gained much from the experience of following their vision, they also gave much. In rare instances we have been left a record of the inner thoughts and dispositions of founders. In most cases, however, we are left with just the results of their work. From this external record of their lives, we get the sense of goodness at work. Unfortunately, because of the separation of the sacred and the secular in popular culture today, not all of these people are seen as holy. This is to our detriment, because all of us have our story of ordinary wholeness/holiness to tell.

All stories have the power to unite mind and heart in the listener. This union activates the soul to begin or continue its journey toward the good, the true, and the beautiful. Cultures around the world generate stories that contain knowledge and wisdom in a form that everyone can understand and embrace. For our purposes here, spiritual directors need to become aware of the founding story of the group they are going to be accompanying.

In addition, everyone in the group being directed needs to have an intimate knowledge of the founding story. With this knowledge, both the director and the group will be able to help each other make connections between how the policies, procedures, and protocols of today compare with those of the past. The knowledge of the founding story will form one of the bases of discernment for the whole group.

Usually the story of the founding most clearly shows the authenticity of the spirit vision at work. Once the present-day inhabitants of the institution hear the story, the opportunity is created for them to embrace the founding spirit and/or let the spirit vision embrace them. They can then begin to tell the difference between what is helpful in the institution today and what is not. They can observe the original characteristics of the spirit of the founders and the behaviors of the founders. Such is the case of the entrepreneurs mentioned above. Even the name of the institution reflects the founders' spirit. The friendship of Hewlett and Packard; the loving compassion of Agnes Gonxha Bojaxhiu; the simple connectivity of Theodore Vail; the Christian Brothers of Edmund Rice—all are exemplified in name—so the characteristics contained in the name of the institution need to be named by the director and the group at some point in institutional direction.

Once all the participants know the origins, the corporate culture, the founding story, and the name they can then begin to critique, challenge, and perhaps change that culture if necessary. Furthermore, the mental models held by the group today should also be challenged and examined at their deepest level and a renewed mental model put in place if necessary. Without the change of the mental models, all others changes will fail. This is a normal conversion process or *metanoia*. I have found the work of Peter M. Senge, in his groundbreaking book *The Fifth Discipline*, to be an excellent companion resource for this work. One of the disciplines he discusses is that of mental models, their importance, and how to change them.

Characteristics of the Spirit of an Institution

Once a director enters the realm of an institution, he or she must become aware of the particularities of that institution. Here are some characteristics that I have found in my work with groups in institutions.

The first characteristic is openness to the Mystery called God by at least some of the members of the institution. This is a must for this work. Each member of the corporate group needs to be open within him or herself to the realms of the spirit. It is to be noted that not everyone is comfortable with the word "spirit." However, it is necessary for the director to dialogue with the group about the reality of the spirit world and discover language about the spirit that is comfortable for participants to use in the sessions.

The second characteristic is that the spirit of the institution is located in the physical properties of the work. The spiritual director needs to be alert to the actual work carried on by the institution, teaching, healing, making, planning, researching, editing.

The third is for the group to stay human in the face of impersonal pressure. An example of impersonal pressure is the quarterly profit review faced by all companies. This consistent review may have nothing to do with the spirit of the organization or its work and cannot be allowed to diminish the humanness of the group working with the director. For example, if an executive team is as focused as a Wall Street firm on the bottom line each quarter, they may in fact become less conscious of and miss the real goal of the organization. The exclusive focus on making money may distract from making a good product. This exclusiveness and shifting of focus is the critical issue for the director to attend to. Money is one of the great shifters of attention. By becoming exclusively focused on money, the group loses openness and freedom and thereby becomes less human, therefore less whole and holy.

The fourth characteristic is the belief that the spirit drives the institution at all levels. In her book *Leadership and the New Science,* Margaret Wheatley speaks of fractals. This reality from biology indicates the presence of a similar pattern throughout the organism. Once you tap into the deep levels of the employees/participants, you come across the presence of similar phenomena between the individuals and the institution itself. A pattern is present universally within the institution. For example, every department has the spirit. The difficulty for the spiritual director is that the institutional spirit looks different and is described differently by individuals from different departments. For example, the vice president for finance will talk about budgets. If probed, he or she will ultimately describe a deeply felt conviction that serving the poor is the heart of the matter in the institution and that this focus is reflected in the numbers on the budget pages and in his or her advocacy for a certain course of action. The vice president for public relations will talk in advertising lingo and, when probed, will describe serving the disadvantaged as the heart of the matter, explain that it is reflected in the current slogan, and can show with deep feeling and compassion how this is so. The receptionist will do the same type of connecting of work and vision though using different language and behaviors; for example, by being consciously gracious to all who enter the building. He or she provides the first taste of the spirit to the outsider. Keep this in mind the next time you get a human being on the phone when you call a company.

A fifth characteristic is the presence of low morale accompanied by much talk of salaries and perks. This characteristic is a warning to the director that all is not well in the institution. Its presence indicates a modus operandi on the part of the institution that is not in keeping with the founding spirit. It needs to be honored as real and present in the group and then probed for its causes by the group. If the group is more excited about the perks than about product, change is needed.

These five characteristics—openness, the work/product itself, being and staying human, departmental forms of the spirit, and low morale/perks consciousness—are all present in varying degrees at the same time in the institution. The characteristics are invisible to the eye but very visible in behavior. In addition, nonverbal communications, such as smiles, frowns, laughter, quiet or loud talking, folded arms, coughing, sneezing, all alert the director and the participants to the presence of the spirit. The director needs to attend to and, at the appropriate time, point out to the participants these indicators of the spirit. Everyone then needs to enter a dialogue to ascertain the meaning of these characteristics as they affect good directional choices for the institution.

All the characteristics take place in and contribute to the corporate culture. The size of the room, the quality of the furniture, starting a meeting with prayer, construction of the agenda, taking or not taking minutes, parking perks, salary levels, also contribute to the culture. This culture is powerful, quite visible, and even palpable at times. Meanwhile, the invisible spirit of the founding vision permeates the institution and is either helped by the culture or blocked by it. Team meetings, retreats, and so on, facilitate this permeation and help remove the blocks to it.

Noticing the Spirit of an Institution within the Leadership Meeting

In order to notice the spirit of an institution or of an individual, the spiritual director needs to be centered. Time spent alone before the meeting provides an opportunity for prayer and centeredness. It also creates a space inside the director that allows the group experience to be contemplated objectively. The group will sense the receptivity of this space and react positively to it;

the group will be encouraged to be honest because the participants will feel safe, not judged.

The director needs to note on paper, perhaps on the agenda document, the phrases and words used by group members, indicating the tonal quality of the voices used, the feelings expressed or not, during the conversation. At the intervention point in the meeting, the director's ability to be concrete with examples and reminders of physical signs enables the dialogue about the interior movements of the group to go quite deep. It is within this dialogue that the possibility increases for the founding spirit of the institution to come to consciousness. For example, in one of my meetings with a hospital system, at one point there was absolute silence. I called attention to the silence and the group responded that this was the first time that they became aware that there was such a difference in the culture of the two systems seeking to merge. Another example occurred when a group gasped as they realized the pastor was recommending letting go a longtime employee of the parish to solve a budget deficit. When I pointed out the gasp, they came to a realization that galvanized them to search for another solution. Another time, as a group in the process of merging realized that they might all lose their jobs (all but one of the eleven did), they murmured. When I confronted them with the murmur, one of them gave an impassioned intervention on being free to do the right thing regardless of cost. She explained that her freedom to act now for the greater good was based on her experience of being helped to find employment during the course of her career. She had no fear. She named the real spirit in the group, namely, fear and its antidote, freedom, because she was loved. The group became quiet, nodded their heads, and moved on with the discussion. From that moment, they never looked back on the process of the merger.

The physical environment of the meeting room is a telltale sign of the care and support for the founding vision. The placement of the chairs and who sits where needs to be noted. Is a table used? Is the room beautifully appointed or not? Attending to these physical aspects helps the group to center on the spirit present in the room during the meeting. After I began with one group, the meeting room was changed to one wherein the people could be more in a circle, not a long, rectangular, jammed situation. This move alone helped the group come to be more respectful of itself and its need to be more human. The old room reminded them of the former autocratic CEO and was associated with old behaviors and attitudes.

Distinctions between Direction of the Group Spirit and Group Spiritual Direction

I first became aware of the presence of a group spirit in my work on the staff of the Center for Spirituality and Justice in the Bronx, New York. We noticed sometime in 1983 or 1984 that as each group went through the thirty-week program, they had ups and downs "as a group." What really excited us was that one day, we noticed that the movements of the group over the course of the year resembled the movements described by St. Ignatius of Loyola in the Spiritual Exercises for an individual on a retreat. The group was having a spiritual journey as a group! For me, that noticing has become the backdrop for all the subsequent development in this field.

When working with groups of people, it is helpful and necessary to make distinctions between "direction of a group spirit" and "group spiritual direction." First and foremost, the focus is different. Within group spiritual direction, there is one director and perhaps several directees. The director focuses on each directee's experience in turn. There is no focus on the experience of the group as a group. In directing the spirit of a group, on the other hand, the entire attention of the director is on the thinking or affect of the group *as group*. Second, interventions are spaced differently. In group spiritual direction, the conversation with the director takes place with each of the directees in turn. In directing the group spirit, the conversational initiative of the director proceeds either by an agreed-upon plan, when an agenda item is finished, or even at the end of the agenda with an agenda review based on the notes taken by the director. These options in group-spirit directing can and should be talked about ahead of time as part of the agreement between the director and the group. In the direction of the group spirit, one might notice the difference between silence and absolute stillness or the presence of spontaneous laughter. These should be noted by the director and referred to later in the session. It is important to have the plan of intervention agreed on beforehand so that everyone knows the rules of engagement. Then the focus can stay on the intervention example itself and not on the how of the intervention. The focus stays on the group and not on the behavior of the director. Scapegoating the director is kept to a minimum. The focus remains on the contractual agreement of the group going deeper into the Mystery called God.

Corporate culture also plays a role here in the work of directing the group spirit. Some cultures lend themselves to openness and wonder. Curiosity and exploration are the hallmark of others. The director needs to learn very early on in the process what the qualities are of the culture that will be his or her natural allies in the directing process. The old adage that grace builds on nature exists even in a corporation. Some cultures are so far from their original vision, or their vision is so flawed, that the only direction they are headed in is toward extinction. In the United States, the Enron and Andersen corporations are recent examples.

In a final note on distinctions, it is appropriate to note that the traditional mindset of the spiritual director needs expanding. That is to say the mental frame of the director needs to be informed not only by a theology of spirituality and personality development, but also by a deep theoretical understanding of how institutions come alive, stay alive, flourish, or die. A foundational description of an adequate mental frame is set out by Elinor Shea, OSU, in *The Way Supplement* (fall 1985), describing its discovery at the Center for Spirituality and Justice, Bronx, New York. I was on staff of the center from 1980 to 1987, during the time of this discovery. Subsequently I added the category of the environment in my work at Mercy Center, Burlingame, California. This very broad mindset includes the human experience of existence by looking at the simultaneity of the intrapersonal (dreams, inner thoughts, intuitions, inner impetus to a course of action), the interpersonal (relationships, encounters with others), the structural (the job, the position at work, policy governing retirement) and the environmental (nature, physical arrangements of home or office) areas of a person's or an institution's life. It then takes each of these areas and follows them through three levels. The first level is that of regular communication. The second level is that of events that break the flow of the ordinary communication. For example, the birth of a child or a disaster would get our attention and break the regular communication pattern. The third level is achieved when we take the event of the second level, reflect on it, and allow it to show us the ultimate meaning of our lives at that very moment.

Preparation of the Director

When a spiritual director moves toward directing a group's spirit, he or she must be aware of new or different personal preparation needed for this adventure in addition to the traditional preparation of being a spiritual director. Both begin with the contemplative attitude.

The contemplative attitude is just that . . . an attitude. It is, quite simply, the capacity to see, hear, and receive reality as it is, devoid of as much distortion as possible. When you look at a tree, what is seen? Color, size, texture, girth, height, type (hemlock, maple), placement in a garden—these are all aspects of the tree. Sometimes people associate, interpret, find meaning in that tree. These activities would be distortions of the contemplative attitude. The beholder (that is, the spiritual director) of the tree needs to be in an interior place of objectivity in order to behold (experience) the total otherness of the tree (directee). This attitude needs constant development.

Addictions, past traumas, delights, illusions, biases, abound in all of us. All directors need to be aware of their own biases and of the triggers that occasionally set them off. This need is compounded when directing the spirit of an institution. As a result, the need for a very powerful and honest supervisor is critical for every director who works with an institution. The challenges to the director's interior life in this work are enormous; hence, the director also needs a well-informed spiritual director.

The director's preparation also must include the belief that the Spirit of the Mystery we call God is an inhabitant within the institution. Furthermore, the director needs to be a humble practitioner of spiritual direction, recognizing that ultimately the Mystery is the real Director of the institution. The director also must be working on becoming competent in several areas as he or she is working in this field—including spiritual theology, knowledge of the dynamics of institutions, and skill in interpersonal relationships—above and beyond having an active prayer life, being under supervision, and having one's own spiritual director.

The Contract with the Institution's Leaders

Working out the contract with the leader of the institution is the first order of business after the initial contact has been made between the institution and the director. This may take several conversations, depending on the knowledge base of the people involved. Some chief executive officers or department heads may not understand the language of spiritual theology or prayer; conversely, spiritual directors need to become acquainted with the founding story of the institution they plan to work with, its history and culture, and the reason they are being invited into that culture. During this process, the director meets with all the members who comprise the group he or she is going to be working with for the duration of the contract. The entire group needs to come to a common understanding as to what is spiritual direction of the group spirit.

The institution and the director need to arrive at a mutual understanding that the directing of the group's spirit will have two foci: 1) the Mystery called God, and 2) the type, quality, and character of the communication within the relationship with this Mystery. Every relationship is just that, a relationship, and has a form of communication in it. Husbands and wives (marriage relationship) can sit for hours in silence (type of communication) and still be communicating love or hate, tenderness or anger. A mutual, clear understanding of this twin focus is the foundation of the contract. The group needs to acknowledge that there is power greater than themselves at work in the institution. Secondly, the group needs to decide to pay attention to the type of communication between and among this power and themselves.

Another item that needs attention in the contract is how frequently the director will be with the group. Each time the director is with the group, he or she is acting as a spiritual director of the group spirit. There are no separate meetings for "spiritual things." The spiritual is embedded in the regular business meetings. Frequent attendance at these regular meetings during the initial stages will build trust, patience, and confidence in both parties. As time progresses and circumstances alter, the frequency can be adjusted. This can happen in conversation with the group as a whole or with the leader. Sometimes regular business meetings with the director can and should occur away from the normal meeting place. A local hotel, retreat house, or conference center would suffice. When this is necessary, most often the director makes the suggestion for a change of venue. This becomes possible only after trust is built among the members and the director.

Furthermore, conversations need to take place and agreement needs to be achieved on how the interventions of the director are to happen when the director is present at the ordinary meeting of the group. The chair of the meetings is always one of the members of the group. The chair and the director have to choose one of the following protocols for an orderly form of intervention to occur. One way is for the director spontaneously to stop the meeting whenever there is a significant event occurring. A second way is for the director to speak after each agenda item is completed. A third option is for the director to wait until the entire agenda is finished before commenting (hence the need to keep notes). Regardless of the choice of intervention style, there must be agreement that the meeting must include time for the director to engage all of the points mentioned in his or her notes and to engage in a dialogue of meaning about the events.

The director should also insist on being a part of the regular communication process of the group. In this way, the director can keep abreast of the developments within the institution and can keep a contemplative attitude toward them.

The agenda, which usually comes through the regular channels of communication, comes to the director also. As the agendas appear over the months and the director's notes build, the director may spot patterns of communication within the relationship between the group and the Mystery, for example, a continuous challenge to serve the poor. These patterns, which are present in the ordinary meetings, usually in coded language, are brought to the attention of the group at that meeting. These patterns need to be brought to the attention of the group when and if they occur. They also need to be explored for their ability to house an opening to the Mystery called God. The whole thrust of this form of direction is that it is located in the everyday experience of the group at its regular business meeting.

The final task in the contract is to settle the payment schedule. Payment might range from a low of twenty-five dollars an hour to several hundred dollars an hour, depending on the nature and resources of the institution. There could also be a per diem agreement.

Once the contract is set, the director begins the work. Review of the contract should take place every six months or at another regular interval.

Five Examples of Direction of the Group Spirit in Institutional Settings

What follows are actual (though disguised) examples of what has just been outlined, in terms of its being a development from group spiritual direction to the direction of the group spirit. The timeframe is from 1987, when this kind of spiritual direction was quite rare, to 2002. As the examples unfold, changes (subtle or explicit) can be observed both in the practice of spiritual direction and in the nature of the director's contract with the group or institution.

Example 1

The Sisters of the Oval Desk was a group of sixteen or seventeen Roman Catholic sisters who were leaders in their respective congregations. Affectionately called "The Sisterhood Club" among themselves, the sisters began to meet in 1985 as a type of "support" group for each other and as a forum in which to share programs, services, ideas and, in general, things that had or had not worked in their congregations. The idea was to help each other to not reinvent the wheel each time they wanted to initiate something new.

The meetings were held three or four times a year for approximately a day or a day and a half, depending on the agenda. Each member helped create the agenda by contributing whatever she thought would be helpful for the good of the whole. After the first year of meetings, it was decided that one meeting annually should be devoted to a retreat day—a spiritual retreat, not a planning retreat. One sister contracted with the spiritual director for the initial retreat experience, and all of the sisters agreed to and shared in the financial arrangement. Thereafter, whoever had volunteered to host the retreat contacted and contracted with me.

For approximately eight years, the group engaged my services as a spiritual director. I offered suggestions for a "theme," but was open to the wishes of the participants, who expressed some concrete needs they wanted help with in their real world of institutional ministry.

At the first retreat, I introduced the group to the concept and use of dyads (pairs of people in conversation) as a way of conceiving of the sharing and exchange of experiences. Initially, it was foreign for the sisters to be sharing so deeply, but they felt safe with their colleagues in the prayerful setting created by the director. When the sisters returned to the larger group, they were surprised, inspired, and heartened by the experience. In the dyad, one sister had shared that she found it quite difficult to make any meaningful connection between her position as leader and her prayer life. Yet, she could readily see the meaning of the metaphor pointed out to her by her dyad partner, who suggested that perhaps Sister was acting as the "leaven" in her work for the people she was responsible for. Another sister saw her large desk as an altar on which she offered prayer, praise, and sacrifice to God throughout her busy day of meetings, finances, politics, and personnel issues. A third one acknowledged that many times she felt as if she were experiencing her own "Agony in the Garden" as a leader and now had the insight and grace to believe that she was not alone in her trials. In fact, she experienced herself as being invited by Jesus to a form of intimacy by sharing his passion with him. The process began as group spiritual direction. Yet, over the eight years, it evolved to become more a process of direction of the common themes of their work.

The retreat day was structured to include input from the spiritual director, sharing among the participants, personal quiet and reflective time, interventions and observations from the director, recreation, and dining together. The efficacy of these annual retreats was evident by the consistent attendance by all the participants, and the scheduling of the date to accommodate everyone's personal schedule. Even though all group members were Roman Catholic sisters, they acknowledged that each retreat day gave them new insights about prayer. The Mystery called God became more personal and they became more aware of the presence of the Mystery in their institutions. Sharing their faith experiences with each other helped them to get to know each other at a deeper level, both personally and professionally.

After eight years, due to retirements, deaths, and personnel changes "The Sisterhood Club" dissolved. However, deep friendships have endured between pairs of the sisters as a result of the retreat days. One might also say that they became more conscious of being Sisters of the Mystery.

Example 2

In 1989, I was hired as a facilitator at Protestant Seminary. The story is that some faculty wished to develop a spiritual direction training program within the existing spirituality program. Many years and much effort had gone into developing the spirituality program. The new generation of faculty and staff wanted these programs to go further. They invited me to come and help them design the new program.

The seminary is an academic structure with all of the usual protocols in place. Everyone wanted a say in the construction of the new program; hence, the group that convened to begin the project consisted of faculty, staff, administrators, and a board member. A theological reflection process coupled with brainstorming and *lectio divina* was adopted.

Meetings took place over a two-year period. At first, the meetings were all day and occurred every couple of months. This interval allowed the group to do the homework that had come to light during the meeting. As the process deepened, the meetings became more frequent. By the time the brochures were printed and strategies were implemented, the meetings became less frequent.

My role was at first one of facilitation; as the process developed, I found myself more and more acting as a spiritual director of the group spirit. In one memorable session in particular, the group brainstormed the elements of the program from their particular denominational history and filled newsprint with these elements. We then used the "clearness committee" process from the Quaker tradition to sort out the kernels of truth from the newsprint. These were made into a list of ingredients for the program. Everyone was moved by the session as it unfolded. There was a great silence as we looked at the list that had emerged. It was in this process that the experience of the group spirit became clear to me and I began to think of myself as the spiritual director of the group spirit. At the end of this particular session, the group spirit's vision was articulated.

The issue that then surfaced was how to design the program from the vision. This step was enjoyable and lively for all concerned. Then the challenge was to bring the design of the program forward into the culture of the seminary. Much prayer and conversation revolved around the resistance encountered and how to avoid bruising egos of fellow academics.

The style of intervention all throughout the process was one of free-flowing probing of the conversational contributions of each member of the group. The group was of mixed gender, age, background, and roles in the university, yet all were trained spiritual directors, which made my task much simpler—a joy, really.

Termination came about naturally. When the brochure was published, the corresponding application forms designed, and folks hired to teach, my facilitation/direction ended.

Example 3

In 1996 the pastor of a large Roman Catholic parish hired me. This parish had at the time about thirty-two hundred families of mixed and changing ethnic backgrounds. The expressed desire was to learn more about how the parish staff could become a team. I was with them for four years on a monthly basis. This dovetailed with the regularly scheduled staff meetings. We did not meet over the summer months. The fee for the service was about one hundred fifty dollars for the two to three-hour session.

The group was comprised of the professional staff only. It was a group of eight men and women: two lay people, three Roman Catholic religious sisters, and three priests. This staff had developed a wide range of pastoral programs, including service to the poor, shut-ins, and the elderly; a music ministry and a youth ministry; a parochial school, catechism classes, and so on. The community is rich and vibrant and the staff wanted to grow it more deeply.

The contract at first called for input from me on how to improve team communication and function. Again, I used Senge's *The Fifth Discipline* as a text for this part. We then had a meeting and I noted the times wherever they missed using the disciplines we had learned. We ended each session by going into prayer. After the initial process of a year or so, in 1997–1998, the contract evolved as follows.

The pastor received input from the staff on what they thought they needed for instruction. The pastor called me and we conversed about which skill needed to be presented and any issues that had surfaced in the staff since we last met. The meeting began with a brief statement from each person on how they were doing, then and there. Next, the staff answered the question: "How has the Mystery called God manifested Itself to you in your ministry and how has this affected you?" I took careful notes of both the initial brief story and the longer story about ministry/Mystery. At this point, a brief input was given on the skill requested.

The meeting then moved to the agenda items. After the agenda was completed, I offered a contemplative reflection, bringing to the surface any connections between their personal stories, the ministry story, and the agenda conversation. For example, when the pastor put the parish budget on the agenda, he told the group that the budget needed to be balanced and that he had decided the best way to do it was to let the maintenance man go. The announcement exploded in the group, because all of them liked the man in question. This led the group to a wide-ranging conversation about finances and commitment on the part of the parishioners. When I asked the pastor if he had communicated this issue to the parish, his answer was, "Not really." For the next two months, the item showed up on the agenda and became the focus of the group's prayer and conversation within the agenda section of the meeting. Over the course of several meetings, the conversations and the prayer led the group to separate the parishioners into three groups. The staff agreed to the three categories. They took another month to design and approve three different letters to be sent by the pastor to the parishioners. The letters were sent. Almost immediately, the Sunday collection increased considerably and the maintenance man retained. This is an example of a concrete situation being worked through by prayer and discernment. The spirit of the parish came alive in the meeting and was congruent with the name of the parish.

After these types of conversations in the agenda section of the meeting, we stopped for a coffee break and then group members moved into a "circle of silence" for prayer. The circle of silence was the opportunity for the members of the group to connect their initial story and the outcome of the agenda items for the parish. This time of prayer lasted about twenty minutes. Although no one was pressured to speak after prayer, most usually did. The total process took two hours.

Termination came about naturally because I was moving into a new ministry, and we all agreed it was time for a change.

Example 4

About the same time that my contract with the parish was in effect, the pastoral care department of a local hospital hired me. Again, the presenting issue was to help with team development. The agreement I struck with the chairperson was to develop team effectiveness, but also to begin to help them look at how the Mystery called God was at work among them as a team. The team had a director, two Protestant ministers, two Roman Catholic priests, and three Roman Catholic religious sisters.

I went to the hospital one full day a month and was available to the team in the morning for one-on-one direction to explore how the Mystery was active in the ministry. I had lunch with the hospital director to hear what, if anything, had changed since we had last spoken on the phone. After lunch the whole group met to talk about the systemic presence of the Mystery.

One of the major social-structure issues among the team members was the difference between the sacramental ministers and the pastoral ministers. The pastoral ministers felt that they were seeing to the spiritual needs of the patients; the priests felt that they were seeing to the religious needs of the patients. In addition, the time each group spent in the hospital was different. The priests were on call for twenty-four hours a day for a stretch of three days. The others worked regular eight-hour shifts. These divergences of understanding of ministry, time allocation, and the group members' inability to talk meaningfully about each of them created a severe spirit of disunity in the group. We never successfully addressed this disunity and its effects upon the department.

My style of intervention in the group was at times didactic and at other times engaging. No matter which approach I tried, it was difficult to direct the group spirit because of the sacramental/pastoral split. By this time in my development of contemplatively directing the group spirit, it became clear to me that progress could not happen with this group.

Termination came after three years because the direction of group spirit, the systemic change to which I was committed, and the divergent desires of the full staff could not be reconciled.

Example 5

My final example is from the executive team of a hospital system. I was contacted early in 1998. The chief executive officer and I had worked together in the past and he invited me to come and develop the spiritual side of the team. The health system had several hospitals, nursing homes, and clinics as part of its scope.

The team was comprised of the system vice presidents and the chief executive officer. When I joined them, there were three women and seven men on the team, all in various roles . . . finance, law, medicine, nursing, information systems, public relations, mission, and organizational development. The team was very aware of the system's mission to the poor. The system was service-oriented. The culture of the group was one of power, service, and risk. They were all earning salaries in the six-figure range and worked very hard at their respective responsibilities.

The contract called for me to be the spiritual director of the group spirit. I was invited to all of the team meetings and I chose to go as often as my schedule permitted. To implement the contract, I used the *Spiritual Exercises of St. Ignatius of Loyola*. In addition, I used the template created by the Center for Spirituality and Justice from the book *Social Analysis* by Joseph Holland and Peter Henriot, along with Karl Rahner's anthropological theology. This template has been described earlier in the chapter. It proved helpful in this situation because the institution itself was in the midst of a major transition. Discernment of the correct spirit to follow was critical to the life of the institution and required time-honored and effective resources.

The major issue that eventually faced the team was the merger with another system. This merger and all its implications occupied the team at its regular meetings over a period of eighteen months. In this setting, the desire to stay faithful to the mission of serving the neighborhood poor was part of the struggle. At one of our regular meetings, the group listened to the CEO report on the results of his meeting with the other system. Someone observed that the spirit of our system was very different from theirs. People began to consider the implications of the merger in a different light. They began to wonder if their spirit of service to the neighborhood poor would survive the merger. The CEO piped up and said that without the merger, there would be no survival of either institution and no serving the poor. This was another turning point for the group in its acceptance of the movement toward merger. The poor would continue to be served, but services would be funded in a different way.

The style of intervention was free and easy, much like direction of an individual. Trust grew, especially after the whole team spent a day at a retreat house. Some of the team members who were initially resistant to the concept of spiritual direction of the group spirit came to recognize that the experience couched in spiritual language was similar to the language they ordinarily used to describe the same experiences. As a group, they kept their focus on the spirit of serving the poor even in the midst of the merger chaos.

Termination occurred when I needed to move on to other ministry responsibilities, and I was replaced with a full-time spiritual director.

Lessons to Share with Spiritual Directors

Looking back over the twelve years and the five examples cited above, I realize the continuous developments in the field of spiritual direction. When I first started, there were very few of us doing this work. Now, for example, there are many people and many different professions involved in this work, and they go by different names. Traditional spiritual direction is one approach requiring that directors become competent in social justice and organizational transformation. Executive coaches or mentors make up another group of persons who will need to become competent in a theological understanding of their work. Psychologists with a family-systems background have also moved into this work, but they need to address the bias of their profession about things spiritual.

I have come to know that institutions have a life of their own apart from the people who inhabit them. I have watched people enter institutions hoping to change them, but failing because they didn't adequately take into account the culture with which they were dealing. As the years passed, it became clear to me that change could be effected within the culture only if the people currently part of the institution were willing to endure the suffering it took to change the culture. So whenever I joined a new institution as a director, I made it a point to spend my first session simply building trust with and within the group. I accomplished this in various ways depending on the composition of the group and its level of spiritual understanding. I found that it was typically necessary to name the events and feelings that existed between the members of the group, such as the different religious traditions they came from, the presence of gender biases within the group, and different attitudes toward freedom and money. In some cases, this took a long time—in others, it was impossible. Where it proved impossible, the process came to a plateau and the direction of the group spirit never happened. In one organization, the group was still in the same place several years later, to the dismay of most concerned. The lack of trust between members of the group prevented community from happening. I learned that lack of trust is the absence of the reliance of the group on the integrity, ability, and character of its own members. Without believing in and experiencing the integrity, ability, and character of the people in the group, a group cannot become a community.

Belief congruence between the institution's original inspiration and values and the deepest yearnings of the present occupants in the institution is crucial to the life expectancy of the spirit's presence in the institution. Openness to the unknown and unknowable Mystery at work in the transformation of the institution is also a necessary ingredient. I have come to believe and have experienced that the Mystery we call God is more interested in creating a just institution than we are. This gives me the courage to continue the work. In 1971, Roman Catholic bishops declared this truth in the Roman Synod, stating that, in their view, working for the transformation of social structures is constitutive of preaching the Gospel. In my words, if you want to think of yourself as a Christian or as wholly whole, work to make the institutions you inhabit just.

This means that corporate cultures need to be grounded in their original vision so that they become open to the influence of their present-day inhabitants. The policies, procedures, and practices of the institution need to pulse with the power of the still-living original inspiration that founded them. Not everything about the institution has to come from the original vision, nor does everyone need to support that vision, but policies, procedures, and practices do embody the developed spirit of the institution. As the spiritual direction of an institution or a group unfolds, these developed accretions become very clear. It becomes clear that some of the policies, procedures, and practices need to be brought back into line with the original vision. Bringing about this alignment in the present is almost always a very slow process and demands everyone's patience. It is not always successful, and some thought should be given to what might be done if an impasse is reached.

In doing this form of spiritual direction, it has become clear to me that other inspirations are at work in institutions besides the ones from the original story. Greed is often one; timidity, another. Protecting one's turf is a particularly pervasive institutional dynamic. The word spirit itself is a stumbling block for some people; they say it smacks of esoteric things and things not of this world. Much education has to happen over the course of the years for people to become sensitive enough to be able to notice the "spirits" silently at work among them. It is hard for everyone to let go of limited childhood conceptions of the spiritual life to recognize the adult reality of their spiritual lives in everyday clothes at work.

Having a spiritual life is the sine qua non of discerning the difference between the spirits that buffet one throughout the day. The quality and regularity of the personal prayer/reflection/quiet time of the participants typically comes to be seen by all as quite necessary if the group is to direct and transform the institution. Yet as might be imagined, prayer and spiritual life do not mean the same thing to everyone, and there is typically a great variety of spiritual experience within any group. Finding common ground or common understanding is a task in itself.

Having watched the successes and failures of these five very different groups over a period of twelve years, it is clear to me that the Mystery we call God is very active in institutional life. Too many events happened in the stories to be explained by coincidence or serendipity: a merger was successful and the poor continue to be served; a parish increased its income and avoided a layoff; sisters grew closer to the Mystery in ordinary life; a whole new, mostly Catholic dimension was added to a Protestant seminary; a pastoral-care staff was left with a deep theological question about the relationship between ordained and nonordained persons in ministry. And persons of prayer are increasingly being called to tend the holy, which is waiting to be acknowledged within corporate cultures.

For Further Reading

Fleming, David L. *The Spiritual Exercise of St. Ignatius, A Literal Translation and Contemporary Reading.* St. Louis: The Institute of Jesuit Sources, 1978.

Holland, Joseph, Peter Henroit, SJ. *Social Analysis: Linking Faith and Justice.* Maryknoll, N.Y.: Orbis, 1983.

O'Donovan, Leo J., ed. *A World of Grace.* New York: Crossroads, 1984.

Rahner, Karl. "The Experience of God Today." In vol. 11 of *Theological Investigations,* trans. David Bourke, pp. 145–65. New York: Crossroad, 1982.

———. "Experience of Self and Experience of God." In vol. 8 of *Theological Investigations,* trans. David Bourke, pp. 122–32. New York: Crossroad, 1983.

———. "Theology of Freedom." In vol. 6 of *Theological Investigations,* trans. Karl H. Kruger and Boniface Kruger, pp. 178–96. New York: Crossroad, 1982.

———. "Transformation in the Church and Secular Society." In vol. 17 of *Theological Investigations,* trans. Margaret Kohl, pp. 167–82. New York: Crossroad, 1981.

———. "Institution and Freedom." In vol. 13 of *Theological Investigations,* pp. 105–21.

Senge, Peter M. *The Fifth Discipline.* New York: Doubleday Currency, 1990.

Shea, Elinor, OSU. "Spiritual Direction and Social Consciousness." *The Way Supplement* 54 (fall 1985): 30–42.

Wheatley, Margaret J. *Leadership and the New Science.* San Francisco: Berett-Koehler, 1992.

CHAPTER ELEVEN

The Care and Feeding of the Gen-X Soul

John R. Mabry, Ph.D.

So you're thinking of doing spiritual direction—or ministry in general—with those ubiquitous beasts that make up "Generation X"? Beware! While this endeavor is certainly rewarding and often fruitful, it is also fraught with danger as such a safari may take you into wild and unknown territories, and is guaranteed to force the hapless adventurer to rethink his or her reality. It is important work, especially as many of Generation X are now entering midlife and are beginning to ask the big questions—but it is by no means safe.

Perhaps you are seeing a member of this genus in one-on-one spiritual direction; perhaps you have been asked to lead a group of them or are trying to schedule a program that will appeal to them; or perhaps you are doing pastoral work and want to understand how to attract Generation X to your church or social ministry. In these situations, let the reader take heart—this article may serve as a guide to the peculiar habits, gifts, and needs of Generation X, and will point out many potential pitfalls (all drawn from my observances in the field and, of course, on being an Xer myself). Success is not guaranteed—members of Generation X are not tame creatures—but understanding their social structure, underlying worldview, and unique spiritual gifts may help you succeed.

Homo X-ian in Its Natural Habitat

The genus *Homo X-ian*—Xers for short—is a subset of the human species that most sociologists place as having been born between the years 1960 and 1985. Xers possess a distinctive culture, a unique morality, and a sometimes inexplicable sense of humor. Critical to understanding the often-puzzling behavior and culture of Xers is a basic knowledge of the sort of world in which the Xer lives. It is a very different place than most of us are accustomed to, but is easily reached. Simply start down the dirt road of mythological reality (but do buckle your seat belts, as the Middle Ages are a bumpy stretch of road, indeed). At the Enlightenment, take the first paved road on the right towards modernity (a place, the author assumes, most readers are familiar with). From there, take the freeway as far as it goes until it dead-ends at Quantum Close. Make a tight U-turn and park—Postmodernity is just around the corner.

Post-modernity (affectionately known as PoMo by its inhabitants) is initially a frightening place. While modernity has ready answers for most things, and more or less plausible theories for everything else, in PoMo, everything is up for grabs. Conflicting perspectives are not only tolerated— they are encouraged. "A" and "not-A" can frequently be seen strolling down the street hand in hand. While this can be confusing to those who were reared in modernity, for the Xer, it is second nature. Xers are the first generation to fully internalize a post-modern perspective where mythology and science are both useful, but no perspective adequately describes reality in all of its multifaceted glory. There are no ultimate answers in PoMo. All observations are contingent on the perspective of the observer and all dogmas are considered to be arbitrary and suspect. Xers therefore delight in contradiction, rejoice in irony, and can not only hold two conflicting opinions in tension, they can usually add a third and juggle.

Those adventurers who are brave enough to enter PoMo must be willing to check their dogmas and doctrines at the gate (be sure to get a receipt, or you may never get them back). Anyone entering PoMo with an armful of pat answers is subject to ridicule and may be relegated to the unfortunate status of the terminally irrelevant. Remember, this safari is *not* for the faint of heart.

On one's first visit to PoMo, it might strike you as odd that there are more coffee shops than almost any other kind of business. The coffee shop serves a unique and complex function in the lives of *Homo x-ians*. It serves as library, social gathering place, and, curiously enough, as sacred space. Someone looking for an appropriate place to do Xer ministry need look no further. While Xers will eschew civil buildings and avoid churches like the plague, coffee shops provide a comfortable space for everything from informal discussion groups, wisdom circles (spiritual direction groups), and even worship services. Many coffee shops close at six or so, and are easily rented after hours (some benevolent shop owners may even open for you after hours for free, if you can sell them on your cause. Besides, they can still sell coffee to those at your event).

Xers are frightfully easy to spot in a crowd. Currently, they range from seventeen-year-olds to forty-two-year-olds (and climbing), so age is a dead giveaway. They have a penchant for black clothing and blue jeans, and hairstyles run the gamut from short and conservative to hot pink and spiky. They may often be seen lampooning older generations, and actively snarling at Boomers, their generational neighbors, but mostly conversation tends toward the explication of popular culture. If you overhear a conversation on existential themes in *Buffy the Vampire Slayer*, follow the voices—they will most likely lead you to a pack of Xers.

Distinctive Qualities of the Genus *Homo X-ian*

Xers are often maligned as being shallow, but there is much more to them than simply their appearance or environment. Their emergence as a species coincided with the invention of the birth-control pill, and thus they are the first generation to be thought of as being "like headaches, things you take pills to make go away"[1] With the publication of *The Population Bomb* (1968), children began to be seen more as burden than blessing, cramping hippie parents' style and endangering the very survival of the earth by dint of their numbers. This pervasive attitude of "the child as threat" began to make itself known in popular culture. A whole new genre of horror film— the demon-child film—emerged in the late sixties and middle seventies. Films such as *Demon Seed, Rosemary's Baby, The Omen* and its offspring, *It's Alive, Carrie, Children of the Corn,* and many other films depicted children as malevolent and threatening—images and attitudes Xers could not help but appropriate and internalize.

In addition, Xers were raised in an environment of paranoia and despair, viewing explicitly violent images of the Vietnam War (and for later Xers, the Gulf War). Remember that Xers are the first generation to be brought face-to-face with grisly details of war on television, which could not help but make permanent scars on their impressionable young psyches. Add to this the threat of nuclear annihilation during their formative years (especially scary during the Cold War of the Reagan era), and the certainty of environmental demise preached by their science teachers—well, it doesn't take a mathematician to realize that this all adds up to a generation that doesn't have a lot of hope for its future.

While pessimism for humanity's future at large is widespread, an even deeper pessimism struck closer to home. Over 50 percent of Xers are products of failed marriages, some many times over, adding an even more profound sense of dis-ease and insecurity.

While previous generations revered their leaders and institutions (and in the case of Boomers, revered the *idea* of the just institution and social hero), Xers have experienced little but disappointment and betrayal from those in authority. Parents, who were supposed to provide a stable and loving home, didn't; leaders, who were supposed to uphold the ideals espoused by society, didn't (just think of every president Xers have ever known—except maybe for Jimmy Carter); and religious institutions, which are supposed to have our best interests in mind, turned out to care only about their own self-perpetuity.

As a result, Xers are notoriously suspicious of authority, cynical about their own self-worth, and pessimistic about their future. They have no hope that Social Security will be there for them when they need it, that anyone is going to be concerned about providing jobs for them, or that any savior is going to come down out of the sky to rescue them.

All of this, of course, has serious effects on the personalities of individual Xers and on the social structure of Xers at large. The chief result is a fierce self-determination, which may or may not be immediately visible. Xers know that no one is going to be providing stable families for them, so they must create them. They do so by forming very close circles of friends who become surrogate families. Xers are pack animals, and their allegiance to their chosen pack is a very one strong, indeed. Xer packs are more fluid than conventional families (members may be adopted, while others move away or are drawn to another pack), but often Xer packs will survive long into adulthood. Whether these packs are lifelong remains to be seen, but it is clear that intimate friendships play a much more significant role in the lives of Xers than they did in the lives of previous generations.

Xers also know that Boomers are going to be holding on to their jobs for some time; so, if they are going to make it economically, they must invent jobs for themselves. This is precisely what happened in the dot-com boom of the late nineties. While many of these jobs are now unavailable, this entrepreneurial spirit is common amongs Xers, who are painfully aware that their economic survival is entirely up to themselves.

This self-determination extends into philosophical realms as well. Since no idols have gone un-smashed in PoMo, no dogmas un-refuted, no ethic unimpeached, Xers live in a world completely void of transcendent meaning. No one can provide meaning for Xers; instead, Xers must construct their own meaning in an ongoing process of trial, error, and experimentation. Even so, no constructed meanings are absolute; everything is subject to revision with every new piece of data. Since the Xer's perspective is changing perpetually, he or she is likewise perpetually revising his or her paradigm.

Thus, one more or less philosophical constant in Xer society is a realized eschatology. Since the environment is doomed and we'll most likely blow ourselves up—and in the meantime we'll probably get cancer from Nutra-Sweet® anyway—Xers place very little stock in the future and concentrate almost exclusively on the present moment. As far as Xers are concerned, the shining dream of the just society and the hope of eternal reward in heaven that so many of their forebears worked for and placed their hope in are no more than pie-in-the-sky fantasies used by previous generations to coerce people's thinking and behavior. Thus, when dealing with Xers in the wild, it is not helpful to appeal to some future goal, because they will most likely laugh at you.

This pessimism results in a pervasive apocalypticism that finds expression repeatedly in Xer popular culture as Xers collectively reflect on their own impermanence and the vacuum of hope so common to the Xer worldview.

These factors are fundamental to understanding the mindset, goals, and values of *Homo x-ians*. Although older generations may not share their cynical perspective, it is essential that those who want to study and work with Xers have compassion for their experience. This is most difficult for Boomers, who tend to see Xers as simply younger versions of themselves. Boomers must set aside their prejudices and understand that, while they share a common distrust of authority with Xers, Boomers criticized their elders and put forth a vision of how things could be different and better. Boomers are idealists, by and large, while Xers have no such hope that anything better can be built. Boomers are likely to think that existing institutions are corrupt but better ones can be built, while Xers generally believe that institutions are intrinsically evil, and have very little patience with those who work to reform them.

Distinctive Qualities of the Gen-X Soul

Spiritual, not Religious

For all of their cultural uniqueness and their self-distancing from religious institutions, Xers are deeply spiritual creatures. In fact, they are likely to describe themselves as "spiritual" but loathe the designation "religious."

"Religion" conjures for them memories of boring church services and reminds them of the hypocrisy of religious authorities. Xers are quick to distance themselves from spiritual institutions (a designation they would most likely think of as oxymoronic), which they view as being largely irrelevant. As Xer director Richard Linklater says in his film *Slacker:* "Withdrawing in disgust is not the same as apathy," which describes well the Xer attitude towards traditional churches and synagogues. Unlike previous generations, which devoted their lives to building, shaping, and reforming their institutions, Xers could care less whether religious institutions live or die.

"Spiritual," on the other hand, describes the unmediated experiential encounter with divinity that they crave, pursue, and often enjoy. They have an intrinsically mystical orientation, and in true PoMo fashion, are likely to see themselves as in some way connected to "the Whole," and as participating in the life of the Whole. This Hegelian impulse is evidenced in many behaviors in the wild—from their devotion to their pack, to the transcendence evoked in them by recreational drugs and the various musics they enjoy, to the eclectic assortment of spiritual images adorning their walls and ad hoc altars, to their widespread practice of engaged activism.

Eclectic, not Dogmatic

Because of their distrust of authority, Xers are not likely to "settle" into one religious tradition, but will pick and choose from the wisdom of various traditions, scriptures, and iconographies, constructing a highly individualized "pantheon" of images, deities, and teachings that serves both as a guide and a goad to further growth, which, of course, necessitates a revision of their spiritual trajectory with every new epiphany. Thus, their religious journeys are winding, but rich and highly diverse.

Xers are largely allergic to doctrine or dogmatic approaches to spirituality. No formulaic description of deity is going to fly with them. Any catechism or creed will be met with an impatient rolling of eyes. As any true resident of PoMo knows, God is far larger than any of the boxes constructed by the world religions to contain "him." Instead, Xers are more likely to perceive God as Mystery, and learning to live in relationship with this Mystery is the great spiritual journey of the Xer nation.

When working with Xers in the wild, be careful not to state your beliefs in terms that imply that they must share your views. If, however, you can tell the story of your own spiritual journey and own it as yours alone, allowing room for them to express their own unique (and valid) experiences, a fruitful dialogue may develop.

This attitude of mutual sharing is very important, because dogmatic coercion is anathema in Xer society. Xers eschew hierarchy and scorn anyone who deigns to speak "down" to them. If, however, one can approach Xers as equals, as fellow pilgrims, one is much more likely to win their respect, affection, and cooperation.

Authentic and Ironic

Because Xers have overwhelmingly experienced their elders as disingenuous, they have developed a keen sensitivity to authenticity. They have built-in "bullshit detectors," a strategy that has proved to be an invaluable survival mechanism. It is very difficult to put one over on an Xer. Raised in a world of commercials and spin-doctors, Xers know that everyone is selling something, and can spot an agenda a mile away. The fact that you are selling something is fine, so long as you are up front about it. One whiff of a hidden agenda, however, and you've lost them. Xers view commercials as an important and valid art form, but humanitarian ads by tobacco companies aren't fooling anybody. Nor are missionaries who insist they are only there to better the lives of the "natives."

This hypersensitivity to disingenuity also serves as the cornerstone of Xer humor, which is almost entirely built on irony. One has only to view a random episode of *The Simpsons* or *Family Guy* to see an example of this. The clashing juxtaposition of stated values and lived experience is a bottomless well of mirth for this cynical subspecies, who delight endlessly in skewering the sacred cows and Quixotic ideals of their elders.

Mentoring the Gen-X Soul

Directing, mentoring, or facilitating a spirituality group for Xers is important, much needed work, but the pitfalls are many. For one thing, those brave enough to set out on such a safari will need to do so largely on Xers home turf and must know the terrain.

Not long ago, a parishioner approached me and asked me to speak to her son, a last-wave Xer of seventeen who (naturally) had a cynical view of religion. I agreed on the condition that she arranged for us to meet in a coffee shop, and that she not join us for the meeting. True to her word, "Mom" sat at a table at the far end of the coffee shop, allowing "Justin" and me some privacy. Justin was suspicious and trepidatious about this meeting, assuming I had a hidden agenda to somehow magically turn him into a clone of his church-loving mother. He was in for a surprise.

I asked him what he thought of church and religion in general. "It's a crock," he responded instantly. "It is indeed," I agreed. As I am well acquainted with the Xer penchant for iconoclasm, I asked him to describe the God he did not believe in. That got him rolling, and soon we were both laughing. To his great surprise, I agreed with most of his criticisms. After a while, he asked me: "So how can you work with that stuff?" I replied that religion is a lot more about people than it is about God and, in fact, it existed because people needed it, not because God did. I then asked him a question of my own: "What if God is not so much a person or a being, but a process?" That led to a short description of process thought, during which an odd light began to glow in Justin's eyes. At the end of our meeting, Justin realized that religion is primarily about human history, and that there were far more options than simply the standard brand. Justin has been a regular (and very vocal) participant in my adult Bible study class ever since, and is considering studying philosophy at university next year.

I consider my experience with Justin to be a very successful encounter. Although I am certain I have made some mistakes in my ministry with him, I got a few things right. First, I met him as a peer, not as a superior. This is essential in working with *Homo x-ians*. If the playing field is not level, if there is any power disparity—even a perceived disparity, such as in one-on-one direction—you will lose them.

One-on-One Direction and Mentoring

One-on-one direction can work with Xers, but one must proceed with caution. For those looking for a strong authority figure (those who have been wounded by postmodernism and find the range of metaphysical options simply too intimidating), it can work well. But these cases will be rare and you must be careful, because these Xers are those most susceptible to cultic groups, fundamentalist sects, and allowing themselves to be victims of religious manipulation and abuse.

For most Xers seeking one-on-one direction, you might consider a non-traditional meeting space, such as a park bench, a coffee shop, or even a noisy pub. The setting needs to be a place congruent with both the Xer's personality and yours. If your Xer is twenty-two with spiky hair and a tribal tattoo armband and you are a nun in your sixties, your nicely decorated meeting space will probably give your Xer hives, but the noisy pub will probably give you an anxiety attack. A quiet spot on the beach, though, may be perfect for both of you.

Direction Groups/Wisdom Circles

Most Xers, however, will respond best to group direction. This appeals to the pack mentality of the species and to their penchant for processing via mutual mirroring. I have facilitated Xer spirituality groups for ten years, and have found the experience to be nothing short of earth-shattering and transformative for all involved. While most current models for group direction involve a fixed meeting time, strong leadership, and commitment from the members, these elements are all problematic when working with Xers.

I have found the best model for group direction with Xers to be the wisdom circle.[2] In this model, a group does not have a leader but an organizer who participates as an equal with all other group members. Decisions are made on a consensus basis, including whatever theme or program the group will be working on. Groups work best when they are open-ended, allowing room for the group to survive past the initial goal with room to evolve and grow as the needs of the participants change. It is also very important to keep the membership fluid. Xers must feel free to come or go, drop in or out, come late or leave early, as their busy lives dictate. Also, new members should be welcomed at any time. Someone who comes once may never return, yet his or her life might be deeply impacted by the experience, and regular members may be touched by the visit as well.

In a typical wisdom circle gathering, a theme or topic may be chosen (perhaps chosen at a planning meeting held previously). A ritual opening may be employed (probably derived from a religious tradition that nobody in the group actually practices, thus no bad scoobies [feelings, vibes] will be associated with the practice). The participants may take time to get centered or grounded. A series of readings related to the topic may be presented (often in a creative fashion; conflicting readings may even be presented, as in Abelard's *Sic et Non*). After the group has had some time to sit in silence with the readings, open sharing may begin. Participants are invited to share from their own experience, and no cross-talk (comments on or judgments about what another person has shared) is permitted (the ground rules might be spelled out in the bulletin for the evening, or the person who initiates the sharing time may take some time to explain what is expected). The sharing time is the "main event," where the real work gets done, and may last from twenty to forty minutes, depending on the topic, the group, or the group's disposition on that particular day. After the energy for open sharing has wound down, participants may enact an original ritual pertinent to the theme, share communion together, or engage in a liturgical dance. A light potluck might follow, and future themes may be discussed.

Traditional Faith Communities

Those who are concerned with getting Xers to join existing spiritual communities face a challenging task. While Xers are not concerned with the survival of any particular institution, they are fascinated with tradition, which they perceive as an entirely separate phenomenon (akin to the religion/spirituality split). Tradition connects them with the past and, most importantly, with something essentially unnamable that is larger than themselves.

While they are not interested in naming this big Other (after all, that would collapse the field of metaphysical potentiality, which takes all the fun out of God in PoMo), they are very interested in how different cultures in different ages have pointed at the Mystery. Xer altars, then, are disparate collages of iconography from a motley assortment of traditions. Xers utilize these images in a freewheeling manner, making associations, connections, and connotations not necessarily intended by the image's tradition of origin.

Xers are eager to appropriate any element that speaks to them, and will soon feel a degree of ownership or connection to many traditional elements. Those in existing spiritual communities would do well to encourage this creative ownership of tradition, allowing Xers to use, morph, and own any traditional elements that speak to them, even when (and especially when) such usage seems to others to be irreverent or even blasphemous. Tolerance for this "divine play" is very important, and leaders should encourage Xers to own their traditions and do what they will with them. Such freedom will form deep connections between Xers and their traditions. While leaders and older church members may feel uncomfortable with the level of irreverence and apparent heresy, it is important to remember that Xers do not see truth as monolithic, but as multivalent, which can best be approached via a succession of experimental "lenses," many of them seemingly heretical.

The greater the degree to which Xers are given freedom to experiment, explore, and own their traditions, the greater the emotional connection that will be built. The great difficulty most Xers face when approaching traditional institutions is that existing members of the institutions insist that Xers "do it properly—like we do" and conform before they can be accepted. This attitude not only effectively excludes most young adults today from church membership rolls, but also ensures that the prophetic gifts of Xers are not utilized in the church community. While those in institutions may see Xers as spiritually impoverished, the sad truth is that they may be facilitating their own gradual spiritual impoverishment by excluding those very people who can redefine and reinvigorate their communities.

One successful strategy we have employed at our own parish is to host and support a special "service" or spirituality group for Xers. Xers are given time and meeting space as well as financial and administrative support (when it is asked for and within reason), but are allowed complete programmatic freedom. When the host community is welcoming enough, Xers will find themselves coming to other events at the host community, and hopefully elders will feel welcome dropping in on Xer gatherings. Such cross-fertilization can be beneficial for both groups, and can create a seamless opportunity for crossover involvement, mentoring, and mutual enrichment.

Gifts of the Gen-X Soul

Those communities that can make room for Xers will find in them a wealth of spiritual gifts, even if it sometimes seems that they are taking in boys raised by wolves in Borneo. Xers' history has instilled in them the very survival skills most churches and other nonprofit groups so desperately need to weather (and thrive) in the present culture. Unfortunately, Xers' perspectives are typically dismissed as irrelevant, immature, unspiritual, or even heretical. While it is true that Xers' perspectives are irreverent, their comments threatening, and their communication style often abrasive, Xers provide the prophetic edge of our day, and spiritual leaders and institutions ignore them at their own peril.

Community-Oriented and Egalitarian

Xers are far from loners, and people are far more important to them than ideals, beliefs, dogmas, or other intangibles. Their interest is not in some coming "just society" or "kingdom of heaven," but in the welfare of people in the here and now. This "realized eschatology" keeps Xers focused on justice and basic needs. More than any previous generation, they will volunteer their time and effort to help local folk in need. Xers also shatter sacred cows that elevate ideas, buildings, or institutions above the basic needs of people, and they have absolutely no patience with hierarchy or self-important posturing. Xers can bring a much-needed reality check to time-mired institutions; those directing or mentoring Xers would do well to remember their this-worldly orientation, and appeal to this strength in their spiritual practice.

Discernment and Truth-Telling

Because Xers have been lied to all of their lives by authority figures, their sensitivity for disingenuity is keen indeed, and their patience for it is negligible. Directors need to be careful to be honest with Xer directees and with themselves, because Xers will pick up on it very quickly if there is a hidden agenda, or even if the director is fooling him or herself. Communities would do well to utilize this "bullshit detector" to their advantage in their outside dealings. For those who can tolerate the prophetic impulse of this precocious generation, their ear for the truth can root out longstanding dysfunction in a community and call members to claim shared power and embrace transparency.

Openness to Mystery and Change

Since truth for Xers is found in conflicting perspectives, Xers are remarkably open to others' views and will try ideas "on for size" in a continual process of information gathering, filtering, and synthesis. Directors working with Xers should feel free to recommend disparate sources of inspiration that may seem too scattershot an approach for older generations, and those facilitating groups should encourage the use of rituals, scriptures, artwork, poetry, and music well beyond the cultural experience of those involved. Xers will welcome the novelty, have fun with the ideas, and incorporate and abandon influences fluidly.

Since there are few boundaries around the sacred in PoMo, Xers are open to the Spirit in many surprising and often seemingly profane forms, and their iconography may include such disparate elements as St. Francis and Mighty Mouse. This can make for some challenging worship experiences for elders, but it is important to remember that for Xers, Mystery has a sense of humor and often needs to be approached with one. The extreme irreverence Xers display is, in reality, a form of religious devotion that has thus far gone unrecognized by spiritual leaders. Yet this approach is a brilliant one for getting past people's protective barriers, revealing the mold on our statues, and providing a much-needed reality check. Besides, sacred cow-tipping is a sport everyone can eventually learn to enjoy, even if you are only vacationing in PoMo.

Connection to Philosophical Trends and Popular Culture

Xers are keenly aware of popular culture and find much of their spiritual expression through popular music, film, and television. While older generations dismiss such media as shallow or philosophically anemic, Xers are tuned in to its subtle (and sometimes not so subtle) prophetic content. Pop culture skewers uncritically held assumptions, challenges the status quo, and mocks authority and even itself mercilessly. Since much of this media is being produced by Xers, attention to what is being said and to the meta-messages involved will be invaluable in understanding Xer culture and mindset. For those directing Xers, the music they listen to and the movies and TV shows they enjoy are priceless archeological indicators that will reveal much about their spiritual state, philosophical wrestlings, and moral trajectory.

Those who hope to attract Xers to their spiritual communities would do well to develop a tolerance for acoustic versions of Nirvana songs at the offertory, or poetry-slam-style readings of the Canticle, or, as in the case of one Roman Catholic church in the San Francisco East Bay, aromatherapy incorporated into anointing for the healing service. Sure, it may seem inappropriate, but who are you to say what is appropriate in PoMo?

Leadership Skills and Teachability

Contrary to popular belief, Xers are not lazy slackers who don't care about what goes on around them. They care deeply about suffering and the well-being of their community. But as Richard Linklater says, "We don't want to get involved in any futile activity" (again, from *Slacker*). When the cause is just, the job fair, and the goal within reach, Xers are indefatigable workers and skilled leaders. Because their elders have told them that their opinions are not important, their contributions unneeded, and their perspectives irrelevant, Xers will often be content to keep to themselves unless invited to do otherwise. Directors can help Xers bolster their self-esteem by empowering them to assume leadership positions and to express their opinions even when they are not particularly welcome. Leaders of spiritual communities can help Xers emerge into their full potential by honoring their views, soliciting their opinions, and trusting them with positions of authority—even if the Xer him- or herself is uncertain whether he or she is ready to handle it. They will usually surprise you—and themselves—with their vision, talent, and competence.

In addition, Xers know that there is never just one perspective, one answer, one right way to approach something. Because of this knowledge, they have a built-in sense of humility that is often hard to perceive behind their defensive bluster. They are inherently teachable, and work well collaboratively with people of all generational species when an air of mutuality can be achieved.

Conclusion

Mentoring, directing, and facilitating for Generation X is no picnic—it is a dangerous journey into uncharted territory. For many it will be missionary work that entails a very different culture and language. For some it will simply be too threatening, while others will not be able to set aside their own prejudices sufficiently to be successful. But for those who can walk in Xers' shoes, can respect their indigenous culture, and can sympathize with their dilemmas, it can be very rewarding work indeed.

It is also work that desperately needs doing. As years pass, more and more Xers will enter midlife and bring their peculiar perspective to the issues we all face at that time. Furthermore, as our institutions become grayer, it will be more and more important for them to build bridges to Generation X. Bridges need to be built not just for the survival of institutions, but in order to make sure that the genuine wisdom of our religious traditions is accessible for future generations. If we do not start re-mythologizing now, the chasm between contemporary culture and traditional faith will become wider and wider until communication becomes impossible. Now the gap is narrow, and Xers are eager to help with any project that is within their grasp, important, and meaningful. With the help of understanding directors and concerned mentors, these bridges can be built. Spiritual directors, mentors, and spiritual leaders who are knowledgeable about Xers can make all the difference.

For Further Reading

Beaudoin, Tom. *Virtual Faith: The Irreverent Spiritual Quest of Generation X* (San Francisco: Jossey Bass, 1998). Using examples from pop culture, Beaudoin provides an excellent glimpse into the ironic spiritual sensibilities of Xers.

Garfield, Charles, Cindy Spring, and Sedonia Cahill. *Wisdom Circles: A Guide to Self-Discovery and Community Building in Small Groups* (New York: Hyperion, 1998). Book by Boomers easily adaptable to Xers' need for small, consensus faith communities.

Humphrey, Nathan, ed. *Gathering the Next Generation: Essays on the Formation and Ministry of Gen X Priests* (Harrisburg, Pa.: Morehouse Publishing, 2000). A collection of helpful essays on Xers in leadership positions in the Episcopal Church.

Mabry, John R. "Homecoming: Helping Xers Move from Alienation to Conversion." Available from www.apocryphile.net/jrm/articles.html. Previously published in *The Way Supplement* (2000), p. 19. Examines Xers in relation to traditional faith communities, with suggestions on how churches can effectively minister to Xers, and create a welcoming place for them in their midst.

———. "The Gnostic Generation: Understanding and Ministering to Generation X." Available from www.apocryphile.net/jrm/articles.html. Previously published in *Presence: The Journal of Spiritual Directors International* (May 1999), p. 35. Explores what makes Xers distinctive, using the Gnostic myth as a model for understanding. Contains many suggestions for effective spiritual direction with Xers.

———. "Rebels without Applause." Available from www.apocryphile.net/jrm/articles.html. Describes in detail the social forces that shaped Xers' inner world. Comprehensive and challenging.

Strauss, William, and Neil Howe. *Generations: The History of America's Future, 1584 to 2069* (New York: Quill, 1991). Phenomenal presentation of the cycles of generations in America's history and how these cycles are likely to evidence themselves in the near future.

———. *13th Gen: Abort, Retry, Ignore, Fail?* (New York: Vintage, 1993). Picking up where *Generations* left off, this is an entire book devoted to Gen-X social formation and attitudes. Indispensible.

CHAPTER TWELVE

In the Image of Godde

Feminist Spiritual Direction

Norvene Vest

This chapter explores the process of spiritual direction with feminists, a term I use to mean those persons—female or male—who are increasingly sensitive to traditional language and images that have been overwhelmingly male. For some feminists, the prevalence of male images of Godde in Christian and other religious traditions is disruptive of their prayer life and a barrier to ongoing relationship with the holy. I write as a Christian, an Episcopalian, and a Benedictine oblate, and as one who is increasingly called by the Divine Feminine into deepening relationship. For many years, this mixed situation of mine has been confusing and a source of considerable self-doubt, even as I felt certain that Godde's very self was the source of all these loyalties. It has been especially troubling that I had difficulty finding a spiritual director who could help me negotiate the particular demands and delights of this multidimensional path. This essay is a result of those years of search.

Let me say at the beginning that I and other feminists have begun to spell the word "Godde." This is the Old English way of writing the name of God. Admittedly, as spoken, this sounds the same as the three-letter spelling. But when read with the eyes, the alternate spelling forces the mind to consider, if only for a moment, the possibility that the Infinite Being that we have named Godde is not limited by maleness.

The Image of Godde

One of the basic concerns in the spiritual direction relationship is exploration of the specific images of Godde that inform the directee's experience
of the holy. Directors understand that people often have working images of
Godde that are quite different from the images they can verbalize, such as
the disparity between a concept of a loving Godde contrasted with an
expectation of divine punishment for anything short of perfection in behavior. The gentle but persistent probing of such incongruities and their causes
can support the directee's growth toward spiritual maturity and integration.

Christian theologians readily acknowledge that Godde transcends any
human concepts, including that of gender. And increasingly, contemporary
spiritual literature acknowledges that Godde may be envisioned in feminine
as well as masculine form. Even so, there is a widespread and working
assumption among ordinary Christians that Godde is really male. Imagine
the hubbub that would result in any Christian congregation you know if
the preacher referred to the Divine Being as "Goddess"! Less than a decade
ago, I was invited by my rector to offer a homily in his blue-collar congregation on "God and Gender," in which I carefully explored the theological
and scriptural basis for more inclusive use of language about Godde. I had
expected many possible responses to the sermon, but imagine my surprise
when I received not one single comment, then or later, from any person in
the congregation about my reflections. Thinking about this absence of
response, I concluded it was largely because the congregation was willing to
humor me but they knew that Godde was male, so there was nothing more
to be said about the matter.

In her careful book *She Who Is,* theologian Elizabeth Johnson points out
quite clearly that the symbol of God functions.[1] That is, how we speak
about and imagine Godde matters very much for our understanding of who
Godde is and how Godde functions in our world. Referring to Godde as
male confers added authority to men, implicitly condones the treatment of
women as "less than," and alienates women from a sense of identity and
intimacy with the divine. How we speak of Godde gives direction to our
mission and ministry, shapes our values and choices, governs our relationships, forms our prayer life. Our images or symbols of Godde shape not
only our thoughts but also our capacity for certain kinds of experience with
Godde, because at basic intuitive levels, they govern our understanding of
what is possible. Overwhelmingly male language about Godde makes it
hard for women to make a connection to our own female selves, to our own
genuine belonging in the community whose sacred values seem to be exclusively male.

Acknowledging that conceptions of femininity and masculinity vary and are understood differently in different cultural settings, we can nevertheless generalize about the set of qualities that tend to be associated with Godde's maleness in the Christian tradition. The prevalence of these qualities does not exclude other possibilities, not in Scripture, tradition, or reason. But they do function to create a certain worldview that tends to limit "acceptable" notions of who Godde is and what Godde does. By inference, we come to think that Godde's qualities include light (not dark), up (not down), journey (not home), reason (not feeling), spirit (not body), and so forth. The male Godde is associated with clear distinctions between Godde and not-Godde as well as with a sense of distance from human experience and dominance above "lesser" beings. When these tendencies are stated so baldly, we can readily see that essential Christian theology in no way requires that we identify Godde with these qualities. But we have done it for so long and so often, we have forgotten there are genuine and faithful alternatives.

The effect of this dominant viewpoint on women can be destructive interiorly and spiritually (as of course it can be on men as well). If we notice that our personal values rest in body, feeling, and home, we can feel ashamed of our "sinfulness," that is, ashamed that we are so unlike the Divine Being. We may decide firmly to set aside some of these "softer" values in order to claim the godlike powers of detachment and dominance. If we begin to think of Godde as having womanly qualities, we may fear that we are becoming heretical or dangerous. A widespread certainty of Godde's singular maleness sets up a dichotomy that does not well serve the community or its members, both by putting Godde in a box of our own making and by separating off qualities of femininity from the spiritual endeavor. Those who come to us for spiritual direction are formed by such Christian cultural assumptions in ways that are often invisible but certainly influential. Directors do not take up the task of assisting feminist spiritual growth for its own sake, but for the sake of expanding the possibilities for Godde's effective and healing presence in individuals and the world.

The Director's Role in Assisting Feminist Spiritual Growth

Some directees may come with a clear sense of desire to explore more feminine qualities of Godde; others may not have such a conscious desire, but find they are constrained by a sense of how they "ought" to be developing spiritually, based on the model of a masculine Godde. It is never the role of the director to push new ideas onto a directee, but the director is often in a teaching position, able to invite the directee to consider ways of thinking about and relating to Godde that move beyond previous limits, especially when there is a sense that the directee is blocked at present and/or that Godde may be already at work in a certain direction.

There are three ways a director can be helpful to directees seeking deeper relationship with the divine feminine. First, a director can become sensitized to the ways in which male-biased images tend to surface in spiritual talk, so that, as appropriate, those images can be questioned and broadened. Second, it can be helpful to have a sense of alternative patterns of spiritual unfolding that might be more useful for a particular directee than the more traditional approach. And finally, directors can benefit from an acquaintance with feminist biblical and theological theories currently under discussion. The balance of this chapter is devoted an overview of those three topics: 1) alternatives to male-biased spiritual assumptions; 2) alternative patterns of spiritual unfolding; and 3) some feminist contemporary biblical and theological theories.

Alternatives to Male-Biased Spiritual Assumptions

Moral Development

Conventional assessments of moral maturity can be slanted toward "masculine" qualities. It is worth taking some time to look at forms of moral judgment, because they are intimately connected to issues of spiritual development, both in terms of what we encourage in others and what we value in ourselves. While remaining aware of the limits of any generalization, nonetheless, my experience suggests that the scales of both Erik Erickson and Lawrence Kohlberg tend to favor qualities more frequently associated with male behavior patterns in our culture. Erikson suggests that "normal" development proceeds from issues of basic trust to issues of (separation and) identity, whereas issues of intimacy appear only very late in the maturation process.[2] In my observation, feminine development moves naturally toward issues of intimacy very early on, whereas the development of identity as a unique and separate person occurs only later if at all. If we expect (either of others or of ourselves) that healthy maturation includes identity definition at an early age, we may consider people (say, women) who "lag" in such developmental areas to be somehow inferior or inadequate. In a culture like ours, addicted to individualism and preoccupied with "boundaries," we might well ask whether a healthy and spiritually mature person couldn't profit by an overall emphasis on intimacy much earlier. And might this not be even more of value for those in a religious tradition that has always imagined the relation between Godde and the believer as a conjugal one?

Similar problems arise in Kohlberg's assessment that the highest stage of moral maturity is expressed in those dedicated to principle and justice, able to serve the freestanding logic of equality and reciprocity.[3] Kohlberg makes this assessment based on his respondents' answers to several hypothetical problems, of which the story of Heinz is typical. The story is told of a man named Heinz with a critically ill wife. A drug that can cure her exists, but it is so expensive that Heinz cannot afford it and the druggist refuses to lower the price. Individual respondents are evaluated in terms of moral development by their answer to the question: Shall Heinz steal the drug? In other words, the basic moral choice is envisioned as a dilemma between the values of property and life, where one is to use logic to decide.

Many of us have heard of Carol Gilligan's feminist critique of Kohlberg in her book, *In a Different Voice*.[4] Gilligan points out that girls and women tend to endeavor to deal with moral problems in terms of a web of relationships: they wonder whether the wife will get sicker if Heinz is forced to go to jail, or they want to sustain and strengthen the connection with the (human) druggist, as well as with the wife. A feminine response frequently sees the problem in terms of a need, for which there must be a means of response; yet, masculine-oriented evaluators tend to see such women's reflections as expressions of vagueness and powerlessness. Gilligan further observes that girls and women learn quickly to suppress these first instincts about the network of relationships in order to be "bilingual"—to think and talk in masculine idioms of logic and justice in order not to be discounted. Interestingly enough, Gilligan's book itself tends to be discounted by many academicians, partly because of the overall difficulty of making sharp distinctions between masculine and feminine modes of being and partly because Gilligan used a relatively small sample in her study. As a woman, my immediate response to *In a Different Voice* was a conviction of its truth because of an inner resonance with its content, a response which had nothing to do with logic, but had everything to do with trusting my instincts!

What does our image of Godde ask or invite in terms of our behavior in the world? What sort of character do we seek to develop and how do we grow in moral and spiritual maturity? These questions are intimately connected with the everyday grist of the spiritual direction conversation, and theories such as these from contemporary developmental theory have significant influence on us and on our directees.

Conflicting Spiritual and Psychological Values

A quite different approach to issues of male-biased spiritual assumptions is taken by Carol Flinders in *At the Root of This Longing*.[5] Flinders observes that in her own life she gradually became aware of continuing tensions between her serious spiritual commitment and her desire for psychological maturity as a feminist. She articulates these contrasts clearly and powerfully as four critical stress points: 1) silence versus finding voice, 2) self-negation versus strengthening the sense of self, 3) desire as enemy or as essential friend, and 4) enclosure away from the world versus supportive community. Let's look at each of these in turn.

- SILENCE VERSUS FINDING VOICE. Spiritual practice in most traditions emphasizes learning to be silent. Those serious about spiritual commitment are encouraged to learn how to still the mind, so that even thoughts are silenced. Often there is emphasis on not speaking except for essential communication. In my own Benedictine tradition, for example, St. Benedict quotes Proverbs 10:19 as admonition: "the prudent are restrained in speech." In contrast with such a focus, feminism insists that women's voices have been silenced so long that their essential perspective has been lost to us all. One of the critical tasks of emerging strength for women in our culture is for women to hear one another into their own speech, to learn to shape the terms of their own experience, and to find their own voice and speak it firmly and clearly.

- SELF-NAUGHTING VERSUS STRENGTHENING THE SENSE OF SELF. A central tenet of Christian spiritual practice is self-surrender, the denial of self-will, and indeed the complete giving away of one's own self first to Godde and then, by extension, to others. The pattern of self-surrender as a core practice of the spiritual life is deeply rooted in many religious and spiritual traditions, to the extent that any aspirant might well feel that without this central interior movement, no progress is possible in the spiritual life. But here feminism offers an equal and opposite insistence: the primary work of psychological maturity for women is to give up their dependencies upon others and to find an authentic and unique sense of self that is their own. Self-esteem is the goal, not self-surrender. Women have lived too long under the illusion that their identity exists only in what they do for others, and they are now suffering the depression and discouragement of severe disconnection from their own precious being.

- DESIRE AS ENEMY OR AS ESSENTIAL FRIEND. Spiritual practice in general and Christian tradition in particular encourage radical detachment from all desire. Desire is often seen as the enemy of peaceful and centered meditation upon the good, and initiates are directed to restrain the senses and set aside all attachment to worldly things and relationships. A great many of the "seven deadly sins" center around the danger of desire as enemy of the spiritual life—avoid too much money (greed), too little ambition (sloth), and, above all, too much pleasure in

the body (lust). Again, feminism challenges this view of desire as dangerous. Such so-called spiritual views have been largely responsible for the
hatred of the female body (or obsession with it, which amounts to the
same thing) and the disrespect of the earth that pervade contemporary
culture. For women, the sensory and affective elements of life and place
and home and beauty are often at the core of the gentle gifts of life that
sustain gratitude and praise. Attentiveness to the things we deeply desire
is a means by which we learn how Godde touches our lives directly.

- ENCLOSURE AWAY FROM THE WORLD VERSUS SUPPORTIVE COMMUNITY.
  Serious spiritual practice usually emphasizes a turning inward and away
  from the "distractions" of the world, often involving a physical removal
  from inhabited places, as well as—for women—enclosure within walls
  that separate them from contact with anyone not also a member of
  their religious community. The Christian desert monks advise: "Go
  into your cell, and your cell will teach you everything." Feminism asks,
  "What of dance, play, exuberant joy, and cherishing one another?"
  Women's strength of purpose has too long been confined, even so far as
  subtly suggesting that women must adopt narrow standards of acceptable movement throughout the day (don't walk too boldly, sit too comfortably, make too much commotion). Feminists seek to recapture the
  freedom of the world for women, the night as well as the day, the ability to walk abroad without fear of attack by madmen. Community is
  essential to the consciousness and action required in a time of needed
  change; women in particular must have one another to support their
  discoveries and action with the daily work needed for cultural health in
  this time of emerging new social paradigm.

Spiritual directors may well find their feminist directees struggling with
just such conflicting demands, and Flinders has done a service in articulat-
ing some of the crucial points of intersection of apparent conflict. Of
course, she has exaggerated the contrasts somewhat to make the essential
points. And of course, she does not leave the discussion there, but goes on
to say that what we need is a new interpretive lens to see how the various
strengths and perspectives of spirituality and feminism may actually require
each other in this day and age. Without spirituality, feminism may never
realize that at the core of women's subordination is the severance of a basic
connection with the sacred. And without feminism, spirituality may continue to be isolated from the critical needs for care in the world.[6] I com-
mend interested persons to her full discussion.

The purpose of discussing both of these books in some detail is that
they are two of the most comprehensive and challenging statements of the

ways in which male-biased spiritual assumptions can creep into our thoughts and our conversations, perhaps without our even noticing our limited perspective. Often in my experience, the hidden biases connected with such language can create the logjam behind which the directee can be held off from deeper intimacy with Godde. The director can often be of immense help by pointing out such possible biases and offering alternative ways of thinking about spiritual growth.

Alternative Patterns of Spiritual Unfolding

We turn then to an exploration of different ways of thinking about how the spiritual life might unfold, alternative patterns and images for experiencing the movement toward spiritual maturity. If the biases noted above can limit potential growth, what other ways of thinking might enhance it or offer refreshing new possibilities? Below, we will look specifically at two sources of ideas, with the awareness that many others are available, including those emerging out of directors' and directees' own experiences. A major source of vitality for alternative ways of thinking is the Holy Spirit's work within the experience and imagination of people themselves. Over the course of time, many images and metaphors arise for most of us, beginning with who and what we ourselves are.

When we begin to be conscious of noticing the ways in which the divine appears within our life settings in daily encounters and dreams and openhearted reflection on Scripture, we find a variety of possibilities, which we often discard or discount because they are different from traditional thinking. But we can learn to be open to images that arise, willing of course to test them in light of traditional teaching about Godde's essence, but open as well to Godde's ongoing inspiration. For example, one day I was sitting meditating, inviting Godde to make herself known to me in the confused darkness of my transitional thinking. And I received a flash of a glimpse of a woman in a long skirt covered by a working apron, standing before an ancient stove stirring a pot of soup. Several children were playing on the floor at her feet as she cooked, and I was one of them. I reached up my arms to be held and she scooped down and lifted me in one smooth motion, without interrupting her stirring with the other hand. I was truly embraced, while she continued her work for the world. It was a lovely and comforting image, and I felt it to be a true one for me, because it reflected the loving heart of the Godde I know by faith, and it was not an image I would likely have invented on my own. Another friend feels the potent presence of a whirling acorn at her throat, not unlike that of Julian of Norwich's hazel-nut. Yet another finds such "random" treasures as a discarded spider shell to be a source of joy and cause for praise of Godde. It is wonderfully affirming to share such an image from one's own experience with another who intuitively recognizes the presence of the divine within.

Ongoing reflection on such experiences can reveal not just single images, but alternative patterns of spiritual unfolding. Two such patterns are a feminist model of spiritual practice I have developed, and the "dance of the Spirit" from Maria Harris.

A Feminist Model of Spiritual Practice

When we begin to take our relationship with Godde seriously, we embark upon a "practice"—a particular way of ordering our lives according to certain disciplines or principles of focus. In general, Christianity has shaped the contours of appropriate practice according to criteria more appropriate to masculine than feminine sensibilities. I propose that, to begin moving toward a more feminist-friendly approach to Christian spiritual life, we consider adapting those contours in four crucial areas: 1) the dominant metaphor, 2) the goal of our effort, 3) the main barrier to wholeness, and 4) the primary spiritual task.

- THE DOMINANT METAPHOR: JOURNEY OR HOME? Traditionally, the metaphor for the spiritual life, especially in Christianity, is that of journey. The idea is that humans are wandering, away from our true home, always searching for something other and better than what we are finding. The metaphor of journey implicitly suggests that we are aliens on earth, strangers to the provision of earth itself. I wonder if a more feminist-friendly metaphor for the spiritual life might not be that of home. Might not a woman be more likely to find freedom in an image that suggests a place safe enough to conceive and then give birth to a child? What would be the effect of thinking of our basic spiritual practice as involving the rhythms of nesting, gardening, creating a place of beauty and welcome for the Holy One? Rather than being in temporary quarters, on the move, let us imagine being in a place long treasured, where we had enjoyed watching the play of light and shadow shift with the seasons and the years, taught the roses to climb around the door over decades, cherished the rhythms of aging and dying and birthing again as they appear in the cycles of all living things. The metaphor of home is not incompatible with a Godde that cherishes Jerusalem and celebrates the glorious clothing of simple grasses and mourns the fall of a single sparrow. Yet we seldom allow ourselves to dwell for long in such an image.

- THE GOAL OF OUR EFFORT: SIN VERSUS LOVE. Traditionally, the goal of Christian spiritual practice is to overcome our basic sinfulness. We are often told that the first and essential thing we must do to be saved is to know that we are sinful, repent of that sin, and get back on the right track by letting Christ change our ways. The idea is that there is a vast chasm between Godde and ourselves, and we can only begin to bridge that chasm by confessing our sins. As an alternative, what effect might there be on our spirituality if, instead of looking first at our inadequacy, we turned our whole attention to the overwhelming and passionate love of Godde for us? We exist only because of the overflowing creativity of Godde's abundant desire for us. We can notice Godde's delighted appreciation of us on every side. Perhaps the most important goal of our human movement toward Godde is to learn to enjoy and express our appreciation for the many gifts that Godde provides in our daily lives. This alternative goal need not ignore the existence of tragedy and loss in human experience, but it invites our attention to the places of delight and encourages our participation in the ongoing co-creation of abundance. Perhaps a focus on our sinfulness can narrow our spirits and limit our perspectives, so that we find ourselves hoarding and claiming our individual rights, rather than sharing the fruits of a divine generosity freely and continuously given. It is hard work to accept the possibility that we are loved more than we can ask or imagine; yet those people who do learn to focus life toward that acceptance are almost always people with immense healing energy to share.

• THE MAIN BARRIER TO WHOLENESS: PRIDE OR SELF-EFFACEMENT? The tradition offers a list of barriers, or problem areas, or sins, which prevent our full response to Godde's invitation to wholeness of life; first among them is the problem of pride. The virtue that remedies pride is humility, a word related to humus or earth, giving us a clue that the essence of pride is to think of ourselves as godlike. As we observed earlier, it is much easier for men to identify with a male-imaged Godde than for women to do so. Pride is thinking of oneself as more worthy of Godde's love than others. But for those who have been marginalized, victimized, or oppressed, those whose very essence is perceived as not-Godde, the primary problem limiting a rich spiritual life is thinking of oneself as less worthy of Godde's love. Perhaps pride is thinking of oneself the center of the world, while self-contempt is thinking of oneself as outside the margins. For women and other subdued people, the main barrier to spiritual wholeness is seldom pride, and is more usually something like self-effacement. We can believe ourselves so unworthy of Godde, so unlike what Godde seeks in relationship, that we try to erase ourselves or make ourselves somehow invisible. And this desire for invisibility is a serious barrier to receiving Godde's gaze of love. Wholeness requires that we stand open to receive the gift of Godde's indwelling life, which enables genuine transformation of self and world.

- THE PRIMARY SPIRITUAL TASK: SELF-SACRIFICE OR AUTHORITY? Traditionally, the primary task of spiritual practice is understood to be the giving up of self. We are told to lose our life, to rid ourselves of ego, to sacrifice our self. Christians are often encouraged to imitate Jesus' *kenosis,* or self-emptying, as described in St. Paul's hymn in Philippians 2:5–7: "Let the same mind be in you that was in Christ Jesus, who, though he was in the form of God, did not regard equality with God as something to be exploited, but emptied himself, taking the form of a slave, being born in human likeness."

This is an exquisite hymn, but let us notice that the writer assumed that being born in human likeness is an emptying, an acceptance of slave status. In other words, the metaphor here is that of journey, in which taking flesh and living on earth is somehow an alienation for Godde. But theologically, we could equally validly consider that Jesus' birth into human form is an act of ecstatic love on Godde's part, a sense of feeling so desirous of the beloved (humans) that Godde delights to share our form. Perhaps, having created it, Godde finds earth and its creatures so lovely, so fully an expression of Godde's own tender imagining, that Godde cannot stay away. If that is the case, then self-emptying would not be an accurate description of what Godde did and does, nor would it be an appropriate description of our primary spiritual task.

Consider another scriptural passage in Sirach 24:12–19 (Ecclesiasticus), in which Godde's Wisdom tells how she/divinity is present among us:

"I took root in an honored people, in the portion of the LORD, (Godde's) heritage.
I grew tall like a cedar in Lebanon, and like a cypress on the heights of Hermon. . . .
Like cassia and camel's thorn I gave forth perfume, and like choice myrrh I spread my fragrance. . . .
Like a terebinth I spread out my branches, and my branches are glorious and graceful.
Like the vine I bud forth delights, and my blossoms become glorious and abundant fruit.
Come to me, you who desire me, and eat your fill of my fruits."

Here we see Godde's willingness, even eagerness, to be with us in joyful activity and expansion—an enlargement rather than a diminishment. And humans, the honored people, are invited to eat—to share—this divine fullness.

We can also see Jesus' life on earth not just as self-offering, but also as a way of being in the world that is expansive and generous, perhaps best understood as his capacity to exercise authority. Authority is a confusing word in English, tending to be associated with dominance or power, the equivalent of the Greek word *dunamis*. But the word authority as applied particularly to Jesus' presence comes from another Greek word, *exousia* (*ex* = "out of" and *ousia* = "being")—meaning something that arises from the very essence of being. This is the quality of authority intended in Luke 8:24–25, where the disciples in a boat are terrified by a windstorm that Jesus stills with a word. Amazed, the disciples say to one another, "Who then is this, that he commands even the winds and the water, and they obey him?" Jesus expresses this foundational authority because he lives at one with the spirit of Godde and the rhythms of the cosmos. He has learned the secret of attunement to the holy, and thus he is able to live fully into his own being as naturally empowered by Godde.

A feminist spiritual practice might encourage living into this process of listening for and honoring the strength and power that flow from our own unique center because we are connected through that center with the divine. Knowing that Godde created each one of us especially, intending that we become fully who we are so that we can take up our rightful place in the interconnected web of life, we likewise know that Godde grieves when we refuse the wholeness meant uniquely for us. Thus, a central responsibility of the spiritual life is to imitate Jesus' authority, becoming the particular person we are meant to be. To accomplish this task, we help directees ask of their experience: "What is most healthy and nurturing for the essential core of my being?" And then we aid them in establishing personal priorities to honor the answers we found.

The Dance of the Spirit

The second helpful overall pattern of spiritual practice we will discuss here is Maria Harris's *Dance of the Spirit.*[7] Harris has immersed herself in feminine images and come up with a wonderful example of what experimenting with new frameworks can produce. She envisions the spiritual life not as a linear movement, but as a dance; a process not oriented toward a goal, but rather one of enjoyment of rhythm and shared pleasure. The dance she envisions has seven steps, moving toward the center and then back out, emphasizing the role of Godde at each step. Abbreviating her helpful guidance, we note that Harris uses the following language to describe the sequence of steps.

- AWAKENING. In this beginning movement, I awaken from something and to something, coming alive to my senses and seeing newly with wonder.
- DIS-COVERING. The second movement involves new awareness of who I am uniquely, with a corresponding sense of invitation and a willingness to say yes to life and to myself.
- CREATING. The third movement is a kind of brooding or hatching or perhaps discovering myself as a container for new life. I experience a sense that my deep connectedness with the universe is bearing fruit.
- DWELLING. This movement is a kind of stillness at the center, the essence of my dance with Godde in a place or a home for me. This is sheer presence.
- NOURISHING. From the center, I move back outward again, beginning with a movement of practicing what nurtures me, including permission to do what I want to do, receiving the support of encouraging others, and keeping a discipline of priorities.
- TRADITIONING. In this movement, the good I have known overflows from me into cherishing, teaching, modeling, and creative integration of what I have received, even as I pass it along to others.
- TRANSFORMING. This seventh movement is giving birth to renewal not just for myself, but for the world as well, listening, rejoicing and mourning, bonding. And the dance begins again with the first movement, continuing throughout life.

Harris's proposed pattern of spiritual practice is a lovely integration of feminist awarenesses. She adopts a circular movement rather than a linear or bottom-to-top one, thus avoiding both hierarchy and competitive accomplishment. She demonstrates a spiritual maturity that is not based on data, logic, or proof, but involves knowing by resonance—when an inner vibration responds to the divine stimulus. Growth is measured not as much by having right answers as by asking good questions. Strength is understood as involving relationship and mutuality rather than in being able to "go it alone." Harris encourages women and men to look inside and ask ourselves: "What do we know about the Spirit in us that we have forgotten?" And then to be gentle and accepting of whatever comes. She sets forth a nourishing model for feminist spiritual maturity.

     In asking how spiritual directors can help directees who are seeking deeper relationship with the divine feminine, we have explored sensitivity to male-biased images about the spiritual life and then suggested alternative ways of considering overall patterns of spiritual unfolding that might be more useful for feminist spiritual work. The third element now to be considered is a brief look at contemporary biblical and theological theories that support the movement toward more explicit engagement with feminine aspects of the holy.

Contemporary Biblical and Theological Theories

Today many fine Christian scholars are exploring new avenues of approach to Scripture and theology that expand the range of possible understandings about Godde and Christian discipleship, especially for women. This essay will mention only three of many examples of contemporary scholarship that can assist spiritual directors to work with feminists in such a way as to deepen their relationship with Godde and their contribution to the world.

1. A SPIRITUALLY MATURE WOMAN. In 1985, the feminist biblical scholar Elisabeth Schussler Fiorenza published a dense exegetical study called *In Memory of Her,* titled for the Gospel story she carefully explores, the anointing of Jesus by Mary.[8] The story is told in all four gospels, and in two of them, Jesus says, "wherever the good news is proclaimed in the whole world, what the woman has done will be told in remembrance of her" (Mark 14:9 and Matthew 26:13). There are several curious things about this story and the way it is told. By and large, Christians tend to remember it as the story of Mary of Magdalene, a sinner and a prostitute, bathing Jesus' feet with her tears, drying them with her hair, and anointing them with ointment. This is roughly the account in Luke 7:36–50, although the name of the woman is not mentioned, and we are told she is a sinner but not that she is a prostitute. However, the accounts in Mark and Matthew—which are the accounts that mention Jesus' promise she will be remembered—indicate that the woman anointed Jesus' *head*—not because she was a sinner, but as a sign of his impending death and in preparation for his burial. Only the Gospel of John mentions the woman's name (John 11:2 and 12:1–8), and there we are told it is Mary of Bethany. In John's gospel Mary was not seeking forgiveness, but rather was sensitively attuned to the probability of Jesus' arrest, trial, and death within the next few days, both weeping for his loss and preparing him for burial.

The shifts in this story and how it is generally told and remembered are a good example of how women's experiences of Godde can be minimized. Elsewhere in Scripture it is clear that the anointing of someone's head is an action taken to announce the naming of a king, as for example in 1 Samuel 16:3, 11–13, where David is anointed king by Samuel. Indeed, by Jesus'

time, the word for the long-anticipated king of Israel was "messiah," literally meaning "the anointed one." These records of Mary's action are the only
times in the gospels in which we are told that Jesus was anointed with oil,
that his status as Messiah was clearly seen and announced. And it is fitting
that the placement of these stories in three of the gospels (Matthew, Mark,
and John) is precisely at the beginning of Jesus' entry into Jerusalem to take
up the work of his kingship as Jesus understood it, that is, the work of his
passion and death and resurrection.

While Godde is the only one who can name and appoint kings, as we
see in Samuel's role in the book of 1 Samuel, there needs to be a human
agent to anoint. And that agent cannot be just anyone, but must have
authority, as prophet or priest. Thus, when Mary anointed Jesus as Messiah,
she was carrying out her responsibilities as prophet or priestess of Godde.
She was a woman using her spiritual power fully, rightfully, and publicly. At
the critical moment of the entry into Jerusalem, Mary saw and accepted the
paradoxical truth to which the other disciples were still blind, that Jesus
would be killed and that it was for this he was Godde's anointed Messiah.
She knew her inner authority, her exousia, and she used it. And we can
understand from his response that her action gave comfort to Jesus as he
entered his last days.

We see that the story of Jesus' anointing by Mary seems to be primarily
not the story of a sinful woman forgiven by a generous Christ, but rather the
story of a powerful and fearless woman in partnership supporting Christ in
his essential mission. What a different and exciting model this deeper understanding of the Scripture offers for a contemporary woman's spiritual work!

2. JESUS AND SOPHIA. The Bible contains a number of terms and images
that direct attention to Godde's "feminine" qualities, including *El Shaddai*
(literally, the breasted one), the *Shekinah* (the luminous presence of Godde in
the world), and especially *Hokmah*/Sophia (Lady Wisdom). Considerable
scholarship has been directed in recent years to the concept of Wisdom, or
Sophia, in part because of scriptural evidence of Jesus' own identification with
the way in which Sophia manifests the essence of Godde.

The Hebrew Scriptures contain many references to Wisdom, who is
generally personified as a feminine presence. Indeed, a whole section of
these Scriptures is called the Wisdom literature, including portions of
Psalms and Proverbs, as well as the Wisdom of Solomon and Ecclesiasticus
(also known as the Book of Sirach). The figure of Wisdom/Sophia is
ambiguous, sometimes seeming to be Godde's own self, and sometimes
seeming to be an agent of Godde, although usually it is clear that an experience of Sophia is an experience of Godde's own self. Interpreted in the

context of Hebrew monotheism, Sophia is a powerful female symbol of the one Godde.

Somewhat fewer passages directly about Sophia survived in the New Testament, largely because of the Gnostic controversy while the canon was being established. Given that reticence, it is the more striking that the New Testament shows a number of occasions when Jesus' words are remarkably similar to Old Testament words about Sophia.

Compare Jesus' words in Matthew 11:28–30: "Come to me all you who labor and are overburdened, and I will give you rest. Shoulder my yoke and learn from me," with this text from Sirach 6:23–31: "Put your feet into Sophia's fetters, and your neck into her collar . . . Come to her with all your soul . . . and at last you will find the rest she gives, and she will be changed into joy for you."

Compare Jesus' words in John 11:25: "I am the resurrection and the life. Those who believe in me, even though they die, will live," with these words of Sophia in Proverbs 8:35–6: "Whoever finds me finds life and obtains favor from the LORD; but those who miss me injure themselves; all who hate me love death."

Compare these words about Jesus from John 1:2–5: "The Word was in the beginning with God. All things came into being through him, and without him not one thing came into being. What has come into being in him was life, and the life was the light of all people," with these words about Sophia in Wisdom 7:26: "For she is a reflection of eternal light, a spotless mirror of the working of God, and an image of his goodness. Although she is but one, she can do all things, and while remaining in herself, she renews all things. . . . Compared with the light she is found to be superior, for it is succeeded by the night, but against Sophia, evil does not prevail."

Jesus' words about himself demonstrate an identification with Sophia very similar to his identification with the messiah as suffering servant derived from the Book of Isaiah. It might even be said that those two images from the Old Testament create a composite sense of Jesus' own identity as Son of Godde. Obviously, this subject is an extensive one, but for our purposes here, the point is that one significant way in which Jesus understood and imitated Godde's way of being in the world was that of Sophia, a feminine image of Godde quite different from the warrior, the victor, the judge.[9] Sophia and Jesus can both be seen as vulnerable, seeking, playful, luminous, moral, and dynamic beings, and this is a useful pattern upon which to model an unfolding feminist spiritual maturity.

3. THINKING ABOUT GODDE. For our final contemporary theory exploring feminine dimensions in Godde's very self, we return to Elizabeth Johnson's

She Who Is: The Mystery of God in Feminist Theological Discourse. In her first pages, Johnson asks, "What is the right way to speak about God?"[10] Taking into account both the rich record of tradition and the contemporary need for more inclusive ideas about Godde, Johnson articulates three primary characteristics that point toward who Godde is. They are Trinity, communion or compassion, and liveliness.

Trinity is essential to our understanding of Godde because Godde is profoundly a being in relation. Godde is not isolated, alone or self-complete, but with others in essence. That sense of "with-ness" includes a radical equality while respecting distinction, continually in a dynamic relation. A lovely word used by the early Greek theologians about Godde suggests something of this mystery of Trinity—*perichoresis.* The word is not quite translatable into English, but interestingly enough it means something like what Maria Harris suggests—a dancing in a circle as the essence of being.

The quality of communion or compassion suggests connection in mutuality with the world (as well as being inherent in Godde's self). Godde's relation to the world occurs not because of necessity, but because overflowing graciousness is essential to the being of Godde. Paradoxically, this connectedness introduces a "deficiency" in Godde in the form of interdependence, vulnerability, and risk. Godde suffers with those most in need as a foundational quality of Godde's very being.

To say that Godde is essentially lively is to suggest a creative dynamism in Godde's being that is not a static condition but one of immense wonder— a soaring, or seeking out, or going forth powerfully. Godde is more like a verb than a noun, more like energy than matter, if such contrasts can mean anything when applied to Mystery beyond knowing. Everything that exists does so by participation in the essential liveliness of Divine Being, and Godde's holy being is unquenchable. Johnson's language borders on sheer poetry when she says that Godde is "a superabundance of actuality/that transcends imagination;/. . . the unoriginate welling up/of fullness of life/in which the whole universe participates."[11]

When we place this language alongside feminist concerns, we can see how liberating such a theology can be. For example, if women deal with moral concerns in terms of a web of relationships, how encouraging to see that something of the essence of Godde is relational in Trinity. As spiritual practice explores the possibility that a holy perspective locates us in the sensory and earthy elements of "home," how delightful to know that Godde's essence penetrates the world as Godde's own body. If feminists seek to find a way to honor desire as key to spiritual unfolding, how affirming to realize that Godde's essential liveliness is a creative energy that pours forth as love. How welcome is this sense of Godde, immersed as we are in the joys and sorrows of each day, even as Godde is also always unknowable in a mystery beyond us.

These three topics have endeavored to explore some of the resources that spiritual directors can utilize to assist directees seeking a deeper relationship with the divine feminine and, by extension, seeking a more authentic honoring of their own femininity. The resources mentioned can help us work with feminists—women and men—in ways that encourage and support them in more fully becoming who Godde has created them to be. A sense of Godde's femininity alongside a sense of Godde's masculinity helps to balance our understanding of what spiritual maturity might look like. When we can become a people with a wide repertoire of possible understandings of Godde, we are better equipped to be an effective and healing presence in the world, as well as being more faithful to the ultimate mystery of the Holy.

Notes

Chapter Two: The Sufi Path of Guidance

1. Lex Hixon, *Atom from the Sun of Knowledge* (Westport, Conn.: Pir Publications, 1993), 1–5.

Chapter Three: The Guru and Spiritual Direction

1. *Yoga Sutra of Patanjali,* trans. Christopher Key Chapple and Yogi Anand Viraj (Eugene P. Kelly, Jr.) (Delhi: Sri Satguru Publications, 1990), vv. I.23–26, p. 19.
2. Baba Ram Dass, "Cookbook for a Sacred Life," *Remember Be Here Now* (San Cristobal, N. M.: Lama Foundation, 1971), p. 4.
3. Paramahansa Yogananda, *Autobiography of a Yogi* (Los Angeles: Self-Realization Fellowship, 1946), pp. 92–97.
4. Dass, "Cookbook for a Sacred Life," p. 5.
5. Ibid., p. 7.
6. In the *Bhagavad Gita,* Krishna announces: "When goodness grows weak, when evil increases, I make myself a body. In every age I come back to deliver the holy, to destroy the sin of the sinner, to establish righteousness." *The Song of God: Bhagvad Gita,* trans. Swami Prabhavananda and Christopher Isherwood (New York: New American Library, 1944), p. 50.
7. Harvey Cox, *Turning East: Why Americans Look to the Orient for Spirituality and What That Search Can Mean to the West* (New York: Simon & Schuster, 1977), pp. 95–100.
8. *Atmabodha,* attributed to Sankaracayra, trans. Swami Nikhilananda (New York: Ramakrishna-Vivekananda Center, 1970), p. 1.

9. Dass, "From Bindu to Ojas," *Remember Be Here Now,* pp. 65–66.

10. Cox, *Turning East,* 129–45.

11. Ibid., p. 100.

12. Eric Konigsberg, "The Yuppie Guru's Last Seduction," *New York Magazine,* 20 July 1998.

13. *Shree Guru Gita,* v. 13, n.d., n.p.

14. Anthony Storr, *Feet of Clay: Saints, Sinners, and Madmen: A Study of Gurus* (New York: Simon & Schuster, 1996), p. 211.

15. See Jeffrey Moussaieff Masson, *The Oceanic Experience: The Origins of Religious Sentiment in Ancient India* (Dordrecht, The Netherlands: D. Reidel Publishing Company, 1980), for his critiques of Ramakrishna and, *My Father's Guru* (Reading, Mass.: Addison-Wesley, 1993) for the intriguing story of his family's relationship with Gurdjieff.

16. Jeffrey Kripal, *Kali's Child* (Chicago: University of Chicago Press, 1995).

17. Joel Kramer and Diana Alstand, *The Guru Papers: Masks of Authoritarian Power* (Berkeley, Calif.: Frog, Ltd., 1993).

18. Georg Feuerstein, *Holy Madness: The Shock Tactics and Radical Teachings of Crazy-Wise Adepts, Holy Fools, and Rascal Gurus* (New York: Paragon, 1991), p. 259.

19. William Cenkner, *A Tradition of Teachers: Sankara and the Jagadgurus Today* (Delhi: Motilal Banarsidass, 1983), pp. 186–87.

20. Daniel Gold, *The Lord as Guru: Hindi Sants in North Indian Tradition* (New York: Oxford University Press, 1987), p. 213.

21. Ibid., pp. 44–45. For descriptions of other guru movements in India, see *Gods of Flesh, Gods of Stone: The Embodiment of Divinity in India,* ed. Joanne Punzo Waghorne and Norman Cutler with Vasudha Naryanan (Chambersburg, Pa.: Anima Books, 1985).

22. *Atmabodha,* v. 1.

Chapter Four: The Place on Which You Stand Is Holy Ground

1. All of the names of directees have been changed, as have some of the key details, in order to protect confidentiality.

2. This translation of the psalm is found in *Kol HaNeshamah, Daily Prayerbook* (Wyncote, Pa.: Reconstructionist Press, 1996).

3. Babylonian Talmud, Ta'anit 7.

4. Currently, there are opportunities to learn about or experience spiritual direction in the Reform, Reconstructionist, and Conservative Movements' seminaries; there are several new programs to train Jews in spiritual direction from a Jewish perspective—including Lev Shomea, offered at Elat Chayyim—the Jewish Spiritual Retreat Center, and the *Moreh Derekh* Program. Those interested in Lev Shomea can contact Elat Chayyim at 1-800-398-2630 or www.elatchayyim.org.

5. One of her earliest articles on this idea is found in Marcia Falk, "What About God?" *Moment Magazine* (March 1985). See also Falk's *The Book of Blessings* (HarperSan Francisco, 1996).

6. Abraham Joshua Heschel, *Man's Quest for God* (New York: Aurora Press, 1954), as quoted in Reuven Hammer, *Entering Jewish Prayer* (New York: Schocken Books, 1994), p. 17.

7. For example, "Forgive us, our Creator, for we have done wrong . . ." (the sixth blessing of the weekday Amidah), or "Behold our need, and plead our cause, and speedily redeem us . . ." (the seventh blessing). An exception to this occurs in the eighth blessing, *Refuah,* for Healing, in which the person praying can add the name or names of those for whom they are praying.

8. Berachot 16b–17a, as recorded in Hammer, *Entering Jewish Prayer,* p. 188.

9. One example is the *Birchot Hashachar,* the Morning Blessings, where the individual offers praises to God for the many ways human beings are able to function every day: "Praised are You, God. . . . who acts for all my needs," "who has made me free," etc. In addition, the psalms, woven throughout the liturgy, are sometimes written in the first person singular and thus give expression to the experience of the individual.

10. Robert M. Seltzer, *Jewish People, Jewish Thought* (New York: MacMillan,1980).

11. There have been women who have functioned in a similar capacity, particularly for women, though usually in a more informal way, such as the Meidl of Lublin, or various *rebbetzin*—wives of rebbes.

12. Besides the rebbe, there was also someone known as the *mashpiy'a,* whose job it was to spiritually prepare the hassid for the interview with the rebbe. In Zalman Meshullam Schachter-Shalomi, *Spiritual Intimacy: A Study of Counseling in Hasidism* (Northvale, N.J.: Jason Aronson, 1991), p. 73.

13. Ibid., p. 4.

14. Ibid., p. 70.

15. Ibid., p. 58.

16. A number of Jewish spiritual directors today have received training through Mercy Center in Burlingame, Calif., or the Shalem Institute in Washington, D.C. A second generation of Jewish spiritual directors is being trained by those who have been trained through these institutions, and who are making efforts to craft a Jewish model of spiritual direction.

17. This may at times present the Jewish director (particularly those who are rabbis) with a challenge, as the director may feel a responsibility to help the directee more fully embrace Jewish tradition. The director may feel compelled to admit that he or she may not always be able to be a neutral companion if the directee's spiritual journey ventures farther away from Judaism. Both the director and the directee may have to discern the effectiveness of the relationship under these circumstances. In most cases, I believe, the directee welcomes the director's commitment to Judaism, as well as the director's gentle guidance (as opposed to the overtly directive approach of the rebbe) to embrace Judaism in a more meaningful way.

18. "Master of the Universe, grant me the ability to be alone; may it be my custom to go outdoors each day among the trees and grass, among all growing things, and there may I be alone, and enter into prayer, to talk with the One to whom I belong. May I express there everything in my heart, and may all the foliage of

the field, all grasses, trees and plants, may they all awake at my coming, to send the powers of their life into the words of my prayer so that my prayer and speech are made whole through the life and spirit of all growing things, which are made as one by their transcendent Source" (Rabbi Nachman of Bratzlav).

19. Pirke Avot 1:2.

20. Pirke Avot 3:3.

21. See bibliography for this chapter.

22. An excellent resource for these writings is Norman Lamm's book, *The Religious Thought of Hasidism* (New York: Michael Scharf Publication Trust/Yeshiva University Press, 1999).

23. Spiritual direction can take different forms in the life of the Jewish community. For example, I have offered individual spiritual direction, group spiritual direction both in and outside of a synagogue setting, workshops for the entire congregation, and classes, which draw on the themes or concepts that are part of the spiritual direction experience.

Chapter Six: From a Graceful Center

1. It is important to clarify at the outset that while this article focuses on my ministry of spiritual guidance with an evangelical constituency, neither my ministry of teaching and spiritual formation nor my practice of spiritual direction has ever been focused exclusively on evangelicals. A number of the individuals and churches with whom I work would not identify themselves as evangelical nor fit any standard criteria that would identify them as such.

2. Mark Noll, *American Evangelical Christianity: An Introduction* (Malden, Mass.: Blackwell 2001), p. 13. In this context, Noll refers to the work of British historian David Bebbington for a summary of that pattern. Bebbington has identified four key ingredients that have historically characterized evangelicalism as "conversionism, biblicism, activism, crucicentrism." Very simply stated as aspects of faith and practice given emphasis within the tradition, they are: 1) need for conversion as life-changing experience of God; 2) elevation of the Bible as authority and resource for faith and practice; 3) concern for sharing the gospel message; 4) focus on the cross of Christ as the key to salvation history and personal appropriation of Christ's redemptive work.

3. Ibid., p. 13.

4. Carefully wrought statements of faith are central to the understanding and self-definition of evangelicals. Taken as a whole, they represent both the uniformity and the diversity of the tradition and its various constituencies.

5. Richard Mouw, evangelical president of Fuller Theological Seminary, was quoted to me by a friend from memory as follows: "The difference between 'simple' and 'simplistic' is that simplicity is what we come to *after* we have paid the price to confront and negotiate complexity and 'simplistic' is what we have when we avoid the struggle."

6. The crusade of Samuel Wilberforce (1759–1833) to end slavery in England resulting in the abolishment of the slave trade in June 1806, and the conversion

of John Newton (1725–1807) from slave-ship captain to evangelist, are two high-profile historical examples. The freedom of one poor family to refuse to sell a child into bondage or put themselves into debt to a money lender in order to finance a culturally imposed obligation is a potent but less visible contemporary example of Gospel freedom.

7. I pose the same kind of question in a humorous "quiz" I use to begin a class on spirituality: "Are you an evangelical Presbyterian, or a Presbyterian evangelical?"

8. My experience and intuition both suggest that this movement may provide new perspectives for dealing with some of the issues of gender and inclusion that regularly arise in spiritual direction with evangelicals.

9. The premise is inspired by the statement of Presbyterian pastor Eugene Peterson: "The assumption of spirituality is that *always* God is doing something before I know it. So the task is not to get God to do something I think needs to be done, but to become aware of what God is doing so that I can respond to it and participate and take delight in it." Quoted in Sue Monk Kidd, *When the Heart Waits* (San Francisco: Harper, 1992), p. 129.

Chapter Seven: Freedom to Souls

1. John of the Cross, *The Living Flame of Love* 3:61, quoted from *John of the Cross: The Collected Works*, rev. ed., trans. K. Kavanaugh and O. Rodriguez (Washington D.C.: ICS Publications, 1979), p. 633.

2. Teresa of Avila, *The Interior Castle* VII:4.9, quoted from Teresa of Avila, *Collected Works*, vol. 2, trans. K. Kavanaugh and O. Rodriguez (Washington, D.C.: ICS Publications, 1980), p. 447.

3. Teresa of Avila, *The Interior Castle* I:2.9, quoted from Teresa of Avila, *Collected Works*, trans. K. Kavanaugh and O. Rodriguez, vol. 2 (Washington, D.C.: ICS Publications, 1980), p. 292.

4. Cf. M. Plattig, "Die 'dunkle Nacht' als Gotteserfahrung," in *Studies in Spirituality* 4 (1994), 165–205.

5. G. Fuchs, "Rhythmen der Christwerdung: Aus dem Erfahrungsschatz christlicher Mystik," in *Katechetische Blätter* 116 (1991), 245–254; this passage is from p. 245.

6. Scripture citations are from *The Revised English Bible with the Apocrypha* (Oxford: The Bible Societies, 1989).

7. John of the Cross, *The Dark Night* I:8.3, quoted from John of the Cross, *The Collected Works*, rev. ed., trans. K. Kavanaugh and O. Rodriguez (Washington, D.C.: ICS Publications, 1979), p. 312.

8. Ibid., p. 327.

9. John of the Cross, *The Ascent of Mount Carmel* II:9.1, quoted from *John of the Cross: The Collected Works*, p. 129.

10. John of the Cross, *The Dark Night*, p. 327f.

11. John of the Cross, *The Ascent of Mount Carmel* II:29.7, p. 205.

12. John of the Cross, *The Living Flame of Love* 3:18, quoted from *John of the Cross, The Collected Works*, p. 617f.

13. Teresa of Avila, *Spiritual Testimony* 25, quoted from Teresa of Avila, *The Collected Works,* vol. 1, trans. K. Kavanaugh and O. Rodriguez (Washington, D.C.: ICS Publications, 1976), p. 332.

14. Teresa of Avila, *Spiritual Testimony* 25, p. 332.

15. Teresa of Avila, *Life* 7:20, quoted from Teresa of Avila, *The Collected Works,* vol. 1, p. 64.

16. Ibid.

17. Teresa of Avila, *The Way of Perfection* 40:4, quoted from Teresa of Avila, *The Collected Works,* vol. 2, p. 193.

18. John of the Cross, *The Living Flame of Love* 3:46, p. 627.

19. Compare Gregory the Great, *The Book of Pastoral Rule* I:1: "ars est artium regimen animarum" (PL 77.14).

20. John of the Cross, *The Living Flame of Love* 3:29; p. 621.

21. John of the Cross, *The Living Flame of Love* 3:45, p. 627.

22. Ibid., p. 633.

23. Compare U. Dobhan, *Gott-Mensch-Welt in der Sicht Teresas von Avila* (Frankfurt: Verlag Peter Lang, 1978), 52–56.

24. Teresa of Avila, *The Collected Works,* vol. 1, p. 46.

25. Teresa of Avila, *The Collected Works,* vol. 2, p. 57.

26. Ibid., p. 59.

27. *The Letters of St. Teresa,* trans. J. Dalton (London 1902), p. 147.

28. John of the Cross, *The Living Flame of Love* 3:60, p. 633.

29. I refer to the results of the study of D. R Graviss, "Portrait of the Spiritual Director in the Writings of Saint John of the Cross," *Vacare Deo* 6 (1983).

30. John of the Cross, *The Living Flame of Love* 3:30, p. 621.

31. Ibid., p. 633.

32. Ibid.

Chapter Eight: Seeking and Finding God

1. William Shannon, *Seeds of Peace: Contemplation and Non-Violence* (New York: Crossroad, 1996), p. 47.

2. See, for example, John Cassian, *Conferences,* esp. IX, X, and XIV, in *John Cassian: The Conferences,* trans. Boniface Ramsey, OP (New York Paulist Press, 1997); Saint Gertrude the Great, *The Herald of Divine Love,* ed. and trans. Margaret Winnkworth (New York: Paulist Press, 1993); and Guigo II, *The Ladder of Monks: A Letter on the Contemplative Life and Twelve Meditations,* trans. Edmund Colledge, OSA, and James Walsh, SJ, (Kalamazoo, Mich.: Cistercian Publications, 1978).

3. The one I know best is centering prayer, a method that has become widely known through Contemplative Outreach and the work of Father Thomas Keating, OCSO, as well through the work of Father Basil Pennington, OCSO, and others.

4. Michael Casey, OCSO, "Saint Benedict's Approach to Prayer," *Cistercian Studies* 15, no. 4 (1980): 327–43.

5. Thomas Merton, *Spiritual Direction and Meditation* (Collegeville, Minn.: Liturgical Press, 1986), p. 8.

Chapter Eleven: The Care and Feeding of the Gen-X Soul

1. William Strauss and Neil Howe, *Generations: The History of America's Future, 1584 to 2069* (New York: Quill, 1991).
2. Charles Garfield, Cindy Spring, and Sedonia Cahill, *Wisdom Circles: A Guide to Self-Discovery and Community Building in Small Groups* (New York: Hyperion, 1998).

Chapter Twelve: In the Image of Godde

1. Elizabeth A. Johnson, *She Who Is: The Mystery of God in Feminist Theological Discourse* (New York: Crossroad, 1993), starting on p. 4 and continuing throughout the book.
2. Erik Erikson, *Childhood and Society* (New York: Norton, 1963), esp. chap. 7, "Eight Ages of Man."
3. Lawrence Kohlberg, "The Development of Modes of Thinking and Choices in Years 10 to 16" (Ph.D. diss., University of Chicago, 1958), and later, *The Philosophy of Moral Development* (San Francisco: Harper & Row, 1981).
4. Carol Gilligan, *In a Different Voice: Psychological Theory and Women's Development* (Cambridge, Mass.: Harvard University Press, 1982), esp. chap. 2, "Images of Relationship."
5. Carol Flinders, *At the Root of This Longing: Reconciling a Spiritual Hunger and a Feminist Thirst* (San Francisco: Harper, 1998).
6. Ibid., p. 135f.
7. Maria Harris, *Dance of the Spirit: The Seven Steps of Women's Spirituality* (New York: Bantam, 1989).
8. Elisabeth Schussler Fiorenza, *In Memory of Her: A Feminist Theological Reconstruction of Christian Origins* (New York: Crossroad, 1985).
9. See, for example, Elizabeth A. Johnson, "Jesus the Wisdom of God: A Biblical Basis for Non-Androcentric Christology," *Ephemerides Theologicae Lovanienses* 16 (1985): 261–94; Elisabeth Schussler Fiorenza, *Jesus, Miriam's Child, Sophia's Prophet: Critical Issues in Feminist Christology* (New York: Continuum, 1994); and Raymond E. Brown, *The Gospel According to John I–XII* (Garden City, N.Y.: Doubleday, 1966), cxxii.
10. Johnson, *She Who Is,* p. 3.
11. Ibid., p. 240.

About the Authors

VENERABLE TEJADHAMMO BHIKKU is an Australian who was first ordained in the Theravada tradition of Buddhism in 1981 and has also studied and received teachings in Mahayana and Vajrayana Buddhism. He studied and taught at Silpakorn University in Bangkok, where he also worked in Thai jails and with the seriously ill, a commitment he continues at present in Sydney, Australia, where he is spiritual director for the Association of Engaged Buddhists and senior resident monk at Sangha Lodge in Lewisham, New South Wales. Bhante Tejadhammo regularly leads workshops offering a path of practice as a way out of suffering and unsatisfactoriness and as a means of opening the heart and mind to loving-kindness, compassion, and wisdom.

CHRISTOPHER KEY CHAPPLE, PH.D., serves as professor of theological studies at Loyola Marymount University. He obtained his undergraduate degree in religious studies and comparative literature at the State University of New York in Stony Brook and his advanced degrees in the history of religions through Fordham University's Department of Theology. He has published ten books, including *Karma and Creativity,* a co-translation of the *Yoga Sutra* by Patanjali, *Nonviolence to Animals, Earth and Self in Asian Traditions,* as well as *Reconciling Yogas.*

MARIAN COWAN, CSJ, is a Sister of St. Joseph of Carondelet. In her young life, Marian already had an Ignatian spirituality, without being able to name it. Thus it was natural for her to enter a congregation with a decidedly Ignatian flavor. In 1968, Marian made the Spiritual Exercises for the first time and has since studied Ignatian spirituality in depth, directs others through the Exercises continuously, and offers ongoing spiritual direction. She is an artist and educator, with a master's degree in spiritual theology from St. Louis University, and is a member of the editorial board of *Presence: The Journal of Spiritual Directors International.* Marian presently teaches the practicum in spiritual direction at Aquinas Institute of Theology, and teaches the Spiritual Exercises at Creighton University. With John C. Futrell, S.J., she coauthored *Companions in Grace: Directing the Spiritual Exercises of St. Ignatius of Loyola* (St. Louis, Mo.: The Institute of Jesuit Sources).

KATHERINE HOWARD, OSB, joined the Benedictine community in St. Joseph, Minnesota, in 1958, and has served that community of St. Benedict in many capacities over the years, including in the positions of academic dean and vice president for academic affairs of the College of St. Benedict, as well as subprioress and prioress of her community. She is certified by Contemplative Outreach as a teacher of centering prayer, and has been active with the Monastic Inter-religious Dialogue, a board of North American Benedictines and Cistercians fostering dialogue between Christian and Eastern monastics, including being its executive director from 1990 to 1994. Her current work includes spiritual direction and occasional retreats, teaching, writing and workshops on formation, prayer, and Benedictine spirituality.

SHAYKHA FARIHA AL-JERRAHI was born into a socially committed, eclectic Catholic family in Houston, Texas. At the age of nineteen, she began a conscious search for God. Ten years later she met her teacher, Shaykh Muzaffer Ozak of Istanbul, and received direct transmission from him in 1980. Shaykh Muzaffer also gave direct transmission to Lex Hixon (Shaykh Nur al-Jerrahi), who envisioned a radical and illumined path of the heart that he called universal Islam. After Shaykh Nur's death, Fariha took on the guidance of the Nur Ashki Jerrahi Sufi Order in New York City and throughout the United States and in Mexico City. This lineage offers the nectar of teachings of the Prophet Muhammad, peace be upon him, which guide the seeker to self-knowledge and immersion in God. Every Thursday evening, Fariha, with her husband Ali, and the dervishes invite all seekers into the circle of dhikrullah at the Masjid al-Farah in New York City. See www.ashkijerrahi.com and/or www.sufibooks.com.

THE REVEREND JOHN R. MABRY, PH.D., is the editor of *Presence: The Journal of Spiritual Directors International,* and has written and published extensively on world religions and spirituality. He also serves as associate pastor of Grace North Church in Berkeley, California, an experimental community that is congregational in governance and catholic in worship. For the past ten years John has facilitated various "wisdom circles" for Gen Xers, and also maintains a private practice in spiritual direction. His main interests at this time are historical Jesus scholarship, the Gospel of Thomas as a spiritual path, and writing and performing art-rock extravaganzas. He welcomes visits to his website at www.apocryphile.net.

JOHN H. "JACK" MOSTYN, CFC, has been a spiritual director for the past twenty-four years, during which he has helped create several training programs for spiritual directors and supervisors on both coasts of the United States. He has also served as past president of Spiritual Directors International, which he helped found eleven years ago. Presently, Jack is a member of his congregational leadership team, based in Rome, fulfilling his responsibilities in the different communities of his group around the world. Until his election to his current position, Jack was the director of personnel for the Eastern American Province of the Congregation of Christian Brothers. Jack would like to hear your thoughts on this development in spiritual direction. He can be reached at jackmostyn@aol.com.

LISA A. MYERS is an elder in the Presbyterian Church (U.S.A.) and director of spiritual guidance ministries at La Canada Presbyterian Church in California, where she provides program design, resources, training, and supervision for a group spiritual guidance program that each year involves forty to sixty persons. In addition to her practice of direction, Lisa teaches for seminaries, churches, and para-church ministries and serves as a consultant on spiritual guidance and supervision. She is a graduate of Shalem Institute's Spiritual Guidance Program and the Institute in Retreat and Spiritual Direction at the Archdiocesan Spirituality Center in Los Angeles.

MICHAEL PLATTIG, O.CARM., was born in Fuerth, Germany, in 1960 and is a Carmelite friar. He is a professor and spiritual director at the Institute for Spirituality at the University of the Capuchins in Muenster, Germany, and developed the formation program for spiritual directors at the institute. Michael has doctorates in theology from the University of Vienna and philosophy from the University of Berlin, and has published internationally on spirituality and the mystics.

THE REVEREND DR. H. PAUL SANTMIRE is the author of *Brother Earth: Nature, God and Ecology in a Time of Crisis* (1970), *The Travail of Nature: the Ambiguous Ecological Promise of Christian Theology* (1985), *South African Testament: From Personal Encounter to Theological Challenge* (1987), and *Nature Reborn: The Ecological and Cosmic Promise of Christian Theology* (2000). During his three decades of ministry, he served as chaplain and lecturer in religion and biblical studies at Wellesley College, Massachusetts, as pastor in an inner-city congregation at Hartford, Connecticut, and as the senior pastor of a large downtown metropolitan congregation in Akron, Ohio. Now retired in order to devote full time to research, writing, and lecturing, he and his wife of thirty-five years live in the Boston area.

NORVENE VEST is a spiritual director, author, and retreat leader, well known especially for her books on Benedictine spirituality for non-monks. She is an Episcopal laywoman and an oblate of St. Andrew's Abbey in Valyermo, California, along with her husband, Douglas. Norvene combines previous degrees in political science and theology with her current doctoral studies in mythology and depth psychology. She is editor of a previous collection of spiritual direction essays published by Morehouse called *Still Listening: New Horizons in Spiritual Direction,* and has written six other books on Benedictine spirituality, including a devotional commentary on the Rule of St. Benedict, *Preferring Christ.*

RABBI ZARI WEISS was ordained from the Hebrew Union College-Jewish Institute of Religion in 1991. She served as a congregational rabbi for seven years, and as a community rabbi for three years. Rabbi Weiss received her certificate in spiritual direction from Mercy Center in Burlingame, California in May 1996. She has been particularly interested in trying to bring the riches of spiritual direction to the Jewish world and has led a number of workshops on spiritual direction in synagogue settings as well as for rabbis, cantors, and rabbinic students, and has written several articles on spiritual direction from a Jewish perspective. Currently, she is an instructor in one of the first programs to train Jews in spiritual direction drawing on Jewish tradition, called *Lev Shomea* (The Listening Heart), and offers various opportunities for spiritual exploration in her new home of Seattle, Washington.